Voices from Larung Gar

Khenpo Jigme Phuntsok seated with his sister, Jetsun Ani Medron. His niece and successor Jetsun Ani Mumtso stands behind (far right). Next to her, the monks in the back row are (from right to left): Khenpos Sodargye and Tsultrim Lodro, Venerable Guangchao, and Lamas Ruba and Sodung. Singapore, 1995. Photographer unknown.

Voices from Larung Gar

*Shaping Tibetan Buddhism for the
Twenty-First Century*

Edited by Holly Gayley

SNOW LION

Snow Lion
An imprint of Shambhala Publications, Inc.
4720 Walnut Street
Boulder, Colorado 80301
www.shambhala.com

Cover photo: Pakin Songmor/Moment via Getty Images
Interior design: Gopa & Ted2, Inc.

9 8 7 6 5 4 3 2 1

First Edition
Printed in the United States of America

⊗ This edition is printed on acid-free paper that meets
the American National Standards Institute z39.48 Standard.
♻ This book is printed on 30% postconsumer recycled paper.
For more information please visit www.shambhala.com.
Snow Lion is distributed worldwide by Penguin Random
House, Inc., and its subsidiaries.

LIBRARY OF CONGRESS CATALOGING-IN-PUBLICATION DATA

Names: Gayley, Holly, translator, editor. | Larung Gar (Buddhist academy)
Title: Voices from Larung Gar: shaping Tibetan Buddhism for the
twenty-first century / edited by Holly Gayley.
Description: First edition. | Boulder, Colorado: Snow Lion Publications,
an imprint of Shambhala Publications, Inc, 2021. |
Includes bibliographical references and index.
Identifiers: LCCN 2020010359 | ISBN 9781611808940 (trade paperback)
Subjects: LCSH: Buddhism—China—Tibet Autonomous Region.
Classification: LCC BQ7549 .V65 2021 | DDC 294.3/923—dc23
LC record available at https://lccn.loc.gov/2020010359

Miraculous display, the dance of Lerab Lingpa,
emanation of Dorje Dudjom, heart son of Padma,
endowed with the splendor of erudition in scripture and logic,
Jigme Phuntsok Rinpoche, I supplicate at your feet.

May your life remain stable for oceans of *kalpas*.
May your teachings, as presented and practiced, spread in every
    direction.
May the blessings of your wisdom and intent enter my heart.
Grant your blessings so that our minds merge as one.[1]

—Karma Chopel Zangpo

CONTENTS

EDITOR'S PREFACE

THE LARGEST Buddhist institution on the Tibetan plateau is tucked away in a valley just off the main road to Serta in a nomadic area of northern Kham. Winding up from the road, after rounding a bend, the visitor suddenly beholds the Larung Valley: its hillsides are lined from top to bottom with red log cabins housing thousands of monks and nuns, two large assembly halls rise up several stories high with classrooms, and the shimmering Jutrul Temple caps the ridge. Out of the grasslands, Larung Buddhist Academy (better known as Larung Gar) appears as a rustic city of Dharma.

Founded by Khenpo Jigme Phuntsok, a towering figure in the revitalization of Buddhism in the post-Mao era, Larung Gar emerged as an encampment in the early 1980s and became established as a Buddhist academy in 1987 with the help of the Tenth Panchen Lama, Chokyi Gyaltsen. Since then, it has played an important role in reestablishing monastic scholasticism among the Nyingma and Kagyu traditions in eastern Tibet.

Larung Gar serves as an ecumenical hub for both innovation and cultural preservation. Its cleric-scholars are some of the most influential, insightful, and creative Buddhist leaders on the Tibetan plateau. They are spearheading a range of humanistic endeavors—from AIDS prevention and animal welfare to Buddhist ethical reform and the promotion of Tibetan language.

What is the vision of Larung Gar leaders for Buddhism in the twenty-first century? How are they balancing efforts to uphold their cultural heritage and to adapt to rapid modernization, addressing the social issues that Tibetans face under Chinese rule? What can we learn about how Buddhists are maintaining the best of their tradition while adapting to changing circumstances and the demands of an increasingly globalized world? The voices from Tibet translated in this book offer compelling answers.

Each chapter presents a distinct perspective on key issues facing Tibetan Buddhism in the twenty-first century. These issues include the status of women and nuns, the interface of Buddhism and science, animal welfare in tandem with environmental concerns, the transmission of tantric ritual, ethical reform in response to contemporary social issues, the rigors of monastic education, and the defense of Buddhism from secular critique.

The chapters proceed chronologically from the founding figures—the Tenth Paṇchen Lama and Khenpo Jigme Phuntsok—to the voices of second generation male and female cleric-scholars as they emerged in publication from the late 1990s to 2017. This is the first time that the speeches, essays, articles, and books excerpted and translated here appear in print in English, allowing an international readership the opportunity to learn about innovative approaches at Larung Gar and to follow the evolution of ideas across a generation of eminent Buddhist leaders in Tibet.

This book emerged out of the panel "Voices from Larung Gar," which I co-organized with Jann Ronis at the 2017 Annual Meeting of the American Academy of Religion. I would like to express my appreciation to Jann for his collaboration on the conception of this volume, to Pema Jamyang and Catherine Hardie for their advice at various stages of this project, and to Nikko Odiseos, Casey Kemp, and Anna Wolcott Johnson at Shambhala Publications for their steadfast support from beginning to end.

I would like to dedicate this volume to all those who have suffered during the coronavirus pandemic and, in particular, my father, Oliver Gayley, who succumbed to the virus as this manuscript was being finalized.

Holly Gayley
Boulder, Colorado

EDITOR'S INTRODUCTION

THE LATE, GREAT Khenpo Jigme Phuntsok (1933–2004) is internationally renowned for his command of esoteric Buddhist teachings, ecumenical approach to monastic scholasticism, and founding of Larung Buddhist Academy in Serta County, Sichuan Province, at the juncture of traditional Amdo and Kham. The khenpo was one of the foremost leaders in revitalizing Buddhism on the Tibetan plateau during the post-Mao era when liberal state policies replaced revolutionary fervor in China.[1] His formidable efforts to reestablish a rigorous monastic education system has produced a new generation of cleric-scholars who have continued at the helm of his Buddhist academy and also populated monastic colleges, or *shedras*, at Nyingma and Kagyu monasteries throughout eastern Tibetan areas. Since the khenpo's passing in 2004, several of his successors have gained acclaim throughout China and even traveled abroad, but they have yet to become widely known outside of Tibetan and Chinese communities. We hope to change this.

This anthology introduces English readers to leading voices among the second generation of cleric-scholars at Larung Buddhist Academy, better known as Larung Gar.[2] As the largest monastic institution on the Tibetan plateau, Larung Gar blends traditional and modern elements in compelling ways. On the one hand, its monastics have been successful in preserving the depth of their Buddhist inheritance, especially scholastic training, which they make available not just to monks but to nuns as well. On the other hand, some of its leaders have taken innovative approaches to Buddhist ethics, gender equality, secular discourses, and digital media in order to meet the challenges of rapidly changing social conditions and reach broader audiences. Leading monks at Larung Gar like Khenpos Sodargye and Tsultrim Lodro have shared their teachings widely with Tibetan and Han Chinese followers via teaching tours, best-selling books, websites, and social media, and leading nuns like Kusum Chodron and members of the Ārya Tāre Book Association have led unprecedented efforts to publish writings by, about, and for Buddhist women. We aim to take stock of the achievements and teachings of these and other Larung Gar leaders so as to record and amplify their voices.

In striking a balance between cultural preservation and innovation, Khenpo Jigme Phuntsok and his successors have been at the forefront of an emerging Buddhist modernism on the Tibetan plateau. They have gone well beyond merely harnessing technology to advance traditional teachings. Instead, with an interest in the progress of the Tibetan people, in step with other ethnicities or nationalities, they have vigorously promoted education and ethics in terms compatible with an unfolding neoliberal modernity.[3] For example, in his *Heart Advice to Tibetans for the Twenty-First Century* (see chapter 2), the khenpo advocates for a balance between new and old forms of knowledge as follows:

> During the past century, the way people think and the way things are made have been transformed. Whatever changes have taken place, this is the nature of existence. In the midst of these changes, we Tibetan people should maintain the worthy traditions of our ancestors so that they do not vanish, including our distinctive civilization, the beneficial aspects of our values, and local customs and habits. In addition, we should adopt new forms of knowledge of the modern period to the degree that they are beneficial in both the long and short term. Each and every Tibetan must think carefully about the ways to avoid falling behind the various nationalities of the world. . . . Now, there's no time to delay! We are on the verge of the twenty-first century.[4]

Composed in 1995, *Heart Advice* epitomizes the khenpo's concern for the progress of Tibetans in both social and economic terms, while also advocating for the preservation of Buddhist values and Tibetan civilization. His balanced message and modernist approach have been continued by his successors to the present day in their efforts at ethical reform, engagement with scientific discourse, work to preserve the Tibetan language, promotion of nonviolence, advancement of nuns' education, and continued stewardship of Larung Gar as a Buddhist academy.

To date, scholars have paid little attention to Buddhist modernism on the Tibetan plateau,[5] though significant research has been done on the widespread revitalization of Buddhism from the 1980s forward.[6] In order to address this lacuna, *Voices from Larung Gar* highlights a range of innovative approaches in the speeches and writings of leading cleric-scholars at Larung Gar.[7] The works introduced and translated in the chapters of this book articulate various elements of Buddhist modernism in the specific context of Tibetans under Chinese rule, appropriating and transforming aspects of the dominant discourse on ethnic minorities to redeem Tibetan culture and, by extension, Buddhism from the categories of "backwardness" and "superstition."[8] This does not imply, however, that traditional aspects of Tibetan Buddhism have been excluded from life at Larung Gar. Quite the contrary, the centuries-old tradition of monastic scholasticism is the centerpiece of its pursuits as a Buddhist academy, and large-scale rituals punctuate the annual calendar. Nonetheless, given its far-reaching influence on the Tibetan plateau and beyond, Larung Gar serves as a hub for both innovation and cultural preservation.

BUDDHIST MODERNISM

Among the cornerstones of Buddhist modernism is a rational and this-worldly approach compatible with secular humanism and scientific empiricism—at least in spirit. Heinz Bechert coined the term to describe the way that Buddhists in Sri Lanka countered the epistemic challenge of British colonialism and Christian missionizing by emphasizing Buddhism's rational character, its compatibility with science, importance to national identity, and continued relevance to social issues.[9] This emphasis on the rational and this-worldly, as expressed in the domains of education and ethics, likewise came to the fore in early twentieth-century modernist movements in colonial Cambodia and Burma (now Myanmar) that promoted Buddhist scholasticism; new approaches to scriptural study and preaching; the creation of Buddhist institutes, libraries, and monastery schools; and renewed attention to monastic purity and lay ethics.[10] The domains of education and ethics are most relevant to modernist approaches at Larung Gar, even as Buddhist modernism elsewhere has also entailed one or more of the following: greater lay leadership and participation in meditation practices, a humanistic vision of creating a pure land on earth, psychological interpretations of transempirical phenomena, engaged social movements, and more.[11]

In terms of education, Buddhist modernizers in China during the Republican era (1912–1949) reenvisioned Buddhist education to be a more systematic and comprehensive study of Buddhist scriptures and to include secular subjects, in part, in response to the association of religion with superstition and the forced conversion of temples into schools.[12] The specter of superstition—a category through which magical and folk practices are excluded from institutional religion and thereby denigrated, marginalized, or forbidden—is as real today in contemporary China as it was during the Republican era.[13] Tibetans on the plateau have harnessed the space that state definitions of religion and post-Mao reforms allowed in order to rebuild Buddhist institutions starting in the 1980s.[14] Given the establishment of Larung Buddhist Academy in this era, Khenpo Jigme Phuntsok and his successors have been sensitive to the language and boundaries of state discourse, even as they champion the standing of Tibetan civilization and the importance of Buddhist values. With practically driven prudence, they remain on good terms with state authorities, cooperating with the periodically enforced regulation of Larung Gar's monastic population and activities.

Although each has its distinct particularities, modernist movements tend to favor classic Buddhist texts and doctrine over ritual and magical elements, which can be more easily perceived and characterized by outsiders as superstitious. The importance of monastic scholarship is, of course, longstanding in much of Buddhist Asia, even though in Tibet it has routinely been in creative tension with the yogic tradition centered on meditation and esoteric rituals. During the nineteenth century, in a protomodernist impulse, ecumenical masters in Kham emphasized the study of Buddhist canonical works, translated centuries earlier largely from Sanskrit, as the locus of "authentic" Buddhism, thereby circumventing centuries of sectarian debate in Tibet.[15] Larung Gar leaders have followed their lead, and the monastic curriculum there is largely based on Indian classics and nineteenth-century commentaries by the polymath Mipham Rinpoche (1864–1912), among others. Both on the plateau and in the diaspora, contemporary Tibetan Buddhist teachers continue to draw on the intellectual and literary fruits of the nineteenth century, while also engaging in the wide-ranging ritual repertoire of their tantric inheritance. All the same, those who founded convert communities in North America and Europe have gone much further in demythologizing their presentation of Tibetan Buddhism than their colleagues operating within contemporary China, whose audience consists of Tibetan and Han Chinese followers.[16]

MODERNIST APPROACHES AT LARUNG GAR

Larung Gar hosts several large-scale ritual gatherings throughout the year,[17] yet as a Buddhist academy, its central mission is to preserve and propagate the monastic curriculum, focused on the five subjects of Buddhist philosophy.[18] Despite the time-honored status of this curriculum, the very nature of Larung Gar's transformation into a Buddhist academy is a product of a modernist impulse traceable to Chinese Buddhist reformers, especially Taixu (1890–1947). Taixu operated in the first half of the twentieth century during the Republican era and was a pioneer in formulating modern Buddhist education in China. As Antonio Terrone discusses in chapter 1, the Tenth Paṇchen Lama Chokyi Gyaltsen (1938–1989) was influenced by Taixu's approach and captivated by the new institution he created, the *foxueyuan* or Buddhist academy. This is significant for our understanding of the founding of Larung Gar. Due to his high-ranking position in the Communist Party, the Tenth Paṇchen Lama was able to help Khenpo Jigme Phuntsok transform the monastic community taking shape in the Larung Valley from an informal encampment to a state-recognized Buddhist academy. Unlike a traditional monastery with its sectarian affiliation, reincarnate lamas, practice path, ritual calendar, and hereditary ties to the local community, Larung Gar is an ecumenical institute focused mainly on scholasticism. In chapter 1, Terrone introduces the Paṇchen Lama's approach to revitalizing Buddhism in the wake of the Cultural Revolution (1966–1976) and translates selections from his notable "Serta Speech," delivered in 1985 at the county seat of Serta, just down the road from Larung Gar.[19]

While influenced by the Paṇchen Lama—and also inspired by ideas encountered when traveling abroad in the early 1990s—Khenpo Jigme Phuntsok had a distinctive voice and vision for Tibetan modernity in Buddhist terms. This can be seen most clearly in his seminal work of advice to the laity, a thin paperback of just over one hundred pages titled *Heart Advice to Tibetans for the Twenty-First Century*. Originally composed in 1995, it has periodically been republished, and its key themes continue to circulate in popular culture and in works by his successors. Chapter 2 contains my translation of its preamble, a rousing call to ethnic pride among Tibetans as well as a forceful articulation of their common path forward into the twenty-first century. In my introductory essay to the chapter,[20] I highlight the way that Khenpo Jigme Phuntsok integrates cultural preservation and ethical reform as pivotal to the path forward for Tibetans while positioning Buddhist values, such as compassion, as the custodian for progress for the world as a whole. Using the rubric "shades of modernism," I explore the extent to which the khenpo can be considered modernist in his advice to the laity, highlighting his reformist impulse, which has been carried forward by his successors.

At Larung Gar, Khenpo Jigme Phuntsok trained and inspired a new generation of cleric-scholars who have continued his work and spread his ideas far and wide. His successors have maintained the utmost academic rigor in Larung Gar's curriculum; improved and expanded its facilities, especially for nuns; continued performing several large-scale annual rituals; carried forward the khenpo's concern for animal welfare; and written extensive commentaries on classical topics of Buddhist philosophy as well as the khenpo's own songs, slogans, and speeches. Chapter 3 showcases two such commentaries by Khenpo Sodargye, a leading voice at Larung Gar and cleric-scholar who teaches and publishes widely in Chinese and has an extensive Han Chinese following. As introduced and translated by Pema Jamyang, the first is a commentary on the *Song of Victory* composed by Khenpo Jigme Phuntsok in 1996, which continues to be recited and studied at Larung Gar. Across just ten stanzas, it charts four key features of the Buddhist path: a virtuous character, renunciation, *bodhicitta* (characterized by love and compassion), and nondual wisdom. Khenpo Sodargye's commentary explains each of these in a thorough and accessible way in line with the systematic nature of the Buddhist commentarial tradition. His second commentary treats a supplication composed by Jamgon Mipham Rinpoche, called *Wangdu, Great Clouds of Blessings: The Prayer That Magnetizes All That Appears and All That Exists*. This is one of the translations in the anthology that illustrates the ritual side of life at Larung Gar, where *Wangdu* is recited at the start of teachings and classes. Khenpo Jigme Phuntsok has popularized this supplication within and beyond Larung Gar, emphasizing its importance to the propagation of Buddhism at large. Given its tantric references, Khenpo Sodargye's commentary is indispensable in identifying the various tantric deities invoked and the notion of magnetizing altogether. It also shows that the traditions of scholastic commentaries and tantric practice continue to thrive at Larung Gar alongside more innovative elements like engagement with secular discourses and ethical reform.

SECOND-GENERATION VOICES

What is the vision of second-generation leaders at Larung Gar for Buddhist education and ethics in the twenty-first century? The rest of the essays and translations in this anthology offer different perspectives on this question, drawing on writings and speeches by its distinguished khenpos and khenmos, male and female cleric-scholars who have attained the highest degree of Buddhist learning. These writings, published at the cusp of the twenty-first century and thereafter, address topics as diverse as the defense of Buddhism against secular critiques by urban Tibetan intellectuals; scientific support for traditional accounts of reincarnation; questions and answers on the finer points of Buddhist ontology; vegetarianism and the practice of liberating the lives of animals; gender equality; and the compilation of writings by, for, and about Buddhist women. This selection will give the reader a sense for the diverse concerns and innovative approaches by leading voices at Larung Gar in their public-facing works of advice that address, for the most part, a broad audience of Tibetan and/or Han Chinese followers. At the same time, we should note that, by nature of their high standing as scholars and practitioners, these figures are also steeped in the full range of classical Buddhist philosophy as well as esoteric practices specific to the Nyingma tradition of Tibetan Buddhism.

Although sectarian debate has long been integral to monastic scholasticism among Tibetans, a new form of persuasive writing is taking shape today that engages secular critiques of Buddhism. These critiques come from Tibetan urban intellectuals who see Buddhism as a regressive force in their culture, the very antithesis of modernity. Among the leaders at Larung Gar, Metrul Tenzin Gyatso has taken up the baton to respond to these critiques. In chapter 4, Jann Ronis introduces and translates selections from his essay, "An Analysis of the Development of Tibetan Culture When Religion Is Influential," published in 1998. The late 1990s was a time when the debate over Tibetan modernity raged in Amdo, and secular critiques by Shokdung and others among a group sometimes called the New Thinkers even made it into the province newspaper, the *Qinghai Daily*.[21] Tenzin Gyatso replies to their critiques in this and another essay discussed by Ronis, "A Rough Analysis of the New Era Essay, *A Call from Afar for Scrutiny*" (2002) by foregrounding the lack of rationality and logical consistency in essays by this group of secular intellectuals. For example, he debunks their claim that Buddhism made the early Tibetan empire (seventh to ninth century) weak by reminding readers that the empire flourished during the period when Buddhism first entered Tibet and then declined after the reign of Langdarma, who dismantled the Buddhist institutions established by his predecessors.

As another foray into new intellectual terrain, cleric-scholars at Larung Gar including Khenpo Tsultrim Lodro and Metrul Tenzin Gyatso have ventured into secular discourses to explore the interface between Buddhism and science. Readers may be familiar with the Mind & Life Dialogues between the Dalai Lama and leading scientists taking place regularly since 1987. Meanwhile on the Tibetan plateau, there are exciting developments in this domain that remain relatively unknown. In chapter 6, Michael Sheehy presents the broad context for recent interest and emerging writings on Buddhism and science by Tibetans in China and discusses an influential work by Khenpo Tsultrim Lodro that engages scientific writings in support of reincarnation. *The Mirror That Illuminates Existence: An Analysis of Past and Future Lives*, published in 2003, draws on anecdotal evidence of out-of-body and near-death experiences gathered by Western scientists, such as Raymond Moody and Ian Stevenson, and compares their accounts with descriptions of the initial stage of the dying process as depicted in *The Tibetan Book of the Dead*. Sheehy skillfully guides the reader through the khenpo's arguments and translates a selection from *The Mirror That Illuminates Existence*. Given its intended audience, including Tibetan students in Chinese universities who have embraced scientific materialism, Khenpo Tsultrim Lodro formulates a compelling case for the scientific validation of a core aspect of Buddhist belief, namely reincarnation. The articulation of "scientific Buddhism" has been a recurring feature of Buddhist modernism in many parts of Asia and in Buddhism's transmission to North America, Europe, and elsewhere.[22] In its commitment to empiricism, the Buddhism and science dialogue once again reflects a modernist emphasis on rationalism by Buddhist innovators at Larung Gar.

Even as Larung Gar leaders venture into new arenas, most of their intellectual energy remains devoted to studying and teaching on classic topics of Buddhist philosophy. Chapter 7 provides an excellent example of their scholarly acumen in a short work that attends to the finer points of Madhyamaka or Middle Way philosophy. The work, *Answers to Questions on Madhyamaka*, published in 2007, is a Tibetan style of questions and answers centered on nine questions.[23] In this format, the erudite Khenpo Tsultrim Lodro, longtime dean of Larung Buddhist Academy, poses and then resolves seeming contradictions between the two main branches of Madhyamaka philosophy inherited from India, namely Prāsaṅgika and Svātantrika. Douglas Duckworth does a masterful job introducing the work and leading the reader through the explanations that Khenpo Tsultrim Lodro offers, so the reader can feel well prepared to follow the nuances of his presentation. As Duckworth suggests, through the high quality of the scholarship produced there, Larung Gar "continues to represent and uphold a robust scholarly tradition well into the twenty-first century."

ETHICS AND ANIMAL WELFARE

Beyond intellectual and scholastic discourse, the this-worldly emphasis of Buddhist modernism can also be discerned in ethical reform and advocacy for animal welfare by cleric-scholars at Larung Gar, which have made a strong impact on Tibetan nomadic life in the areas surrounding Serta. These efforts gained widespread visibility in 2000 with Khenpo Jigme Phuntsok's appeal to Tibetan nomads not to sell their livestock for slaughter, which circulated on VCD (video compact disc) and included graphic video footage from commercial slaughterhouses. By the late 2000s, a broader ethical reform movement had grown, spearheaded by Khenpo Tsultrim Lodro and based on a novel articulation of the traditional ten Buddhist virtues.[24] The new ten virtues include not selling livestock for slaughter but also address social and environmental issues by asking Tibetans not to gamble, drink, smoke, steal, fight with weapons, hunt wildlife, sell drugs or weapons, visit prostitutes, or wear fur trim on Tibetan clothes. By 2010, whole towns and villages were taking vows en masse to uphold the new ten virtues, fundamentally altering the nomadic economy based on animal husbandry.[25] Subsequently, in 2012, Khenpo Rigzin Dargye introduced an amulet for peace, worn around the neck by those who swear an oath to stop fighting among Tibetans. The amulet for peace was a way to further reinforce nonviolent injunctions in the new ten virtues and reduce armed conflicts over grazing rights in nomadic areas.[26]

Alongside the new ten virtues, but distinct from them, is Khenpo Tsultrim Lodro's longstanding campaign for vegetarianism. Chapter 5 treats this topic within the context of a rousing call for compassion for animals and includes a translation of his 2003 speech, "Words to Increase Virtue." In introducing this work, Geoffrey Barstow shows how the khenpo combines two tacks to encourage vegetarianism and discourage slaughter. On the one hand, in this-worldly terms, he vividly depicts the suffering that livestock endure in the slaughter process after serving their owners by carrying loads or providing milk or wool. On the other hand, more traditionally, the khenpo makes reference to Buddhist teachings on karma and the repercussions for harming any creature in terms of the individual's own fate in future lifetimes. Barstow highlights the intervention Khenpo Tsultrim Lodro makes in the history of debates over vegetarianism and also calls attention to his pragmatism in providing a sliding scale of options for Tibetan nomads, whose diet, customs, and livelihood have been organized around animal husbandry for generations. If herders cannot avoid slaughtering livestock, he recommends that they minimize their suffering through the use of more compassionate methods.[27]

Another practice to do with compassion for animals has gained popularity in recent years, namely "liberating lives" (*tsethar*). A traditional practice shared by Tibetan and Chinese Buddhists, rituals to liberate fish, birds, sheep, yak, and other creatures under threat of slaughter have grown in scale and visibility in recent years. While fish and birds can be purchased and released into their natural habitats, livestock are usually tagged with a red cord (indicating their special status as liberated) and entrusted to herders to live out their lives until a natural death. The ritual features of this process, which involve blessing the creatures and making merit for the patron, distinguish it from secular forms of animal rescue. In chapter 8, Catherine Hardie explores the purport of rituals to liberate lives and responses by cleric-scholars at Larung Gar to secular critiques concerned with the environmental impact of large-scale rituals of this kind. The two works Hardie introduces and translates are "Discussing Life Liberation Again," a teaching given by Khenpo Sodargye in 2009 to correct understandings about how to properly conduct a ritual to liberate lives and "Even If You Can Only Save One Life, It Is Also Worthwhile," a 2013 essay by Khenpo Sherab Zangpo that seeks to reform shortcomings in the practice and also to respond to criticisms. In particular, these khenpos highlight the special care and attention that Larung-sponsored liberation rituals pay to habitat and ecological balance in choosing a site and staging a release of fish, birds, or other animals. As Hardie suggests, the fluency of Larung Gar leaders in current ecological terminology and environmental concerns indicates how up-to-date and responsive they are to secular discourses as well as why their speeches and writings are persuasive for urban Tibetan and Chinese audiences.

ADVANCEMENT OF BUDDHIST NUNS

In line with a reformist approach to the domains of education and ethics, one of Khenpo Jigme Phuntsok's significant legacies has been the advancement of Buddhist nuns. Over the decades, Larung Gar has been a vibrant space for nuns to live and study, and its sizeable monastic population has had at least as many if not more nuns than monks. Whereas the nuns used to have makeshift spaces for practice and study, their facilities improved with the construction of a large assembly hall with several floors of classrooms, completed in 2011. Not only did Khenpo Jigme Phuntsok make the full range of monastic education available to nuns, he also conferred the highest scholastic degree on them. Starting in the 1990s, after training for years to pass a set of rigorous exams in the core subjects of Buddhist philosophy, Tibetan nuns could become female cleric-scholars of the highest standing and receive the title of khenmo. This has authorized nuns to become teachers and authors in their own right in an unprecedented way in Tibetan areas.

The last two chapters of this anthology celebrate the accomplishments of nuns at Larung Gar and their recently published works. Their publications in recent years have entailed new kinds of literary ventures. In 2011, Khenmo Kusum Chodron founded a journal titled *Gangkar Lhamo* or *Goddess of the Snowy Range*, which features writings by Tibetan nuns and Buddhist laywomen. Chapter 9 introduces the journal and a landmark article on gender equality published in its second issue. In this chapter, Padma 'tsho discusses the khenmo's motivation for founding the journal, which had to do with the lack of publication venues for nuns, the need to encourage and improve women's writing, and an aspiration to provide a public forum for their ideas. This has allowed new voices to come to the fore with perspectives rarely articulated in Tibetan literature. One of these voices belongs to Khenmo Rigzin Chodron, whose article "The Way Forward for You and Me" offers a Buddhist view of gender equality and the future of Tibetan women. While critiquing gender bias and the lack of educational opportunities for many women, especially in nomadic areas, Khenmo Rigzin Chodron emphasizes the importance of women rising up and liberating themselves. The culmination of her argument, in Buddhist terms, has to do with the contributions that women can make to religious and secular arenas if given the chance. She concludes, "The purpose and direction of equal rights in not just for our own narrow self-interest. Nor is it only for the purpose of being equal with men in terms of opportunities and circumstances. Rather, most important is equality so we can benefit our nationality and accomplish the Dharma for sentient beings. This is equal rights in its most authentic and lasting sense." One can discern echoes of Khenpo Jigme Phuntsok in the khenmo's expression of equality in terms of the pressing need to preserve and propagate Buddhism as well as to contribute to the path forward for Tibetans as a people.

In chapter 10, Sarah Jacoby and Padma 'tsho demonstrate how the educational opportunities afforded to Buddhist nuns at Larung Gar have given rise to a novel type of anthology in Tibetan literature. This final chapter introduces the 2017 publication of the fifty-three-volume *Ḍākinīs' Great Dharma Treasury* by the Larung Ārya Tāre Book Association Editorial Office. This collection represents the culmination of six years of arduous work by a small group of Larung Gar khenmos who researched, collected, inputted, edited, and published an elegant set of hardbound books containing the lives and writings of Buddhist women in India, Tibet, and China. As detailed in chapter 10, this ambitious project was begun in 2011 by a group of seven Larung Gar nuns and gained institutional support after the first volumes were published in 2016. Sarah Jacoby and Padma 'tsho aptly note that "the concept of anthologizing Tibetan Buddhist works based on a shared female identity is a distinctively modern concept emerging out of the ethos of twenty-first-century Larung Gar." Their translation of the preface to the fifty-three-volume collection and interviews with khenmos involved in the project reveal their intent to provide much-needed role models of accomplished female masters to inspire Tibetan nuns and Buddhist women around the world. Their research and publication represent a breakthrough in the study of women in Buddhism, recovering a treasure trove of women's stories and voices. While the material they retrieved spans the centuries, their recovery project itself is decidedly modern.

CONCLUSION

What is at stake in these examples of Buddhist speeches, writings, and publications with modernist elements? On the one hand, in the voices of second-generation leaders at Larung Gar, we can recognize a strategy to harness the prestige of science and rationality in order to salvage Buddhism and, by extension, Tibetan culture from associations with backwardness and superstition. This is especially evident in their responses to critiques by Tibetan secular intellectuals and appropriations of scientific discourse to support belief in reincarnation. On the other hand, its cleric-scholars, both khenpos and khenmos, articulate the importance of Buddhist ethics and education to the future of Tibetans in the twenty-first century. This is palpable in their call to both preserve and reform Tibetan culture, advocacy for animal welfare, elucidation of the finer points of Buddhist philosophy, arguments for gender equality, and efforts to recover writings by, about, and for Buddhist women as role models. By listening to their voices and reading their works, we are better equipped to understand innovations by Buddhist leaders on the Tibetan plateau in comparative perspective, to make connections between Larung Gar's emphasis on monastic scholasticism as a Buddhist academy and its ethical and educational outreach to Tibetan and Chinese laity, and to become attuned to the different contexts in which Buddhist modernism emerges. As studies elsewhere have shown, these contexts can include, but are not limited to, shifts in the political system within predominantly Buddhist countries, colonialism or interethnic domination, the conditions of exile and diaspora, and the cultural translation of Buddhist ideas and practices beyond Asia. Adopting and adapting modern discourses has allowed Larung Gar and its monastic community to survive and thrive in the midst of rapidly changing social realities and to serve as a guidepost for Tibetans and non-Tibetans alike by articulating an alternative modernity in explicitly Buddhist terms.

Holly Gayley

Voices from Larung Gar

1. The Serta Speech

Antonio Terrone

Introduction

ONE OF THE most influential modernizers in contemporary Tibetan Buddhist history was Chokyi Gyaltsen, the Tenth Panchen Lama (1938–1989). In 1986, he founded the Tibetan High Buddhist Academy of China in Beijing, and in 1987, after two years of friendly relations with Khenpo Jigme Phuntsok, he approved the establishment of the Larung Buddhist Academy of the Five Sciences in Serta, Sichuan Province. This chapter presents this history through a reading of the Tenth Panchen Lama's speeches delivered between 1980 and 1989 and, in particular, one public talk he delivered at the county seat in Serta in August 1985, henceforth referred to as the "Serta Speech."[1]

Buddhist Academies and the Legacy of Taixu

The development of Buddhist academies by Tibetans falls within the long-term, mutually influential intellectual, political, doctrinal, and ideological interactions between Chinese and Tibetan religious hierarchs and scholars in the twentieth century. The period starting from the 1920s in Republican China epitomized a modernist streak launched by the Chinese Chan Buddhist monk and thinker Taixu (1890–1947), the father of modern Buddhism in China and inventor of the new Buddhist institutions known as *foxueyuan*, or Buddhist academies, as well as a new form of Buddhist education.[2] His influence on Chinese Buddhism since then is unmistakable and the impact of his view of modern Buddhist education was profound for Chinese as well as Tibetan Buddhist institutions.

One example is the life of Taixu's spiritual heir Zhao Puchu (1907–2000). As a lay Buddhist, he propagated a socially engaged Buddhism (Ch: *renjian fojiao*) as the head of the Buddhist Association of China in the early 1980s.[3] With the aim of revitalizing Buddhism while securing its legitimacy within the socialist ideology of the country, Zhao Puchu promoted a progressive way of thinking for Buddhism in which he envisioned a shift to production, profit-making services, humanistic education, and scholarship for the Buddhist saṅgha, both monastic and lay. Another example is the progressive yet controversial Dobi Geshe Sherab Gyatso (1884–1968) who experimented with modern Chinese education at his monastery, the Dobi Dratsang, where he organized monastic and secular classes for both monks and lay people.[4]

Through numerous Buddhist leaders, Taixu's legacy has continued to reverberate through the formation of Buddhist institutions in China until today, and it is not a coincidence that both Dobi Geshe Sherab Gyatso and the Ninth Panchen Lama Losang Thubten Chokyi Nyima (1883–1937) gave extensive teachings at Taixu's Bodhi Society in Shanghai and Hangzhou in the early to mid-1930s.[5] This is highly significant, as only within this background can we appreciate the intellectual and political forces behind the Tenth Panchen Lama's views on how to relaunch Buddhism and Buddhist education in Tibet during the 1980s after decades of suppression.

My reading of the Tenth Panchen Lama's speeches, my interviews with Tibetans, and the data available on his life suggest that he committed himself to rejuvenating the luster of Tibetan culture within a new framework of protection, rationalization, and advancement. He toured Tibetan areas extensively, met with local leaders, cadres, religious figures, students, and ordinary people, and visited schools and monasteries where he regularly addressed the importance of setting a new path for a constructive rethinking about Tibetan culture, language, and religion.

In order to contribute to the recovery of Tibetan culture, language, and religion after decades of hardships and to find ways to place Tibetan Buddhism in the new sociopolitical order of Communist China, in the 1980s, the Panchen Lama envisioned modernity for Tibet through the promotion of Buddhist morality, education, and an emphasis on rationality, all concepts modeled on or inspired by the structure and organization of the Buddhist academies that were invented and popularized by Taixu. Taixu established them in China in the 1920s, many continued to function after 1949, and their model is still followed in China today. Larung Gar is in fact a very successful example of how the Tenth Panchen Lama adapted Taixu's vision of Buddhist academies through the work of Zhao Puchu, thus influencing Khenpo Jigme Phuntsok to follow this model. Since 1987, thanks to the cooperation with the Tenth Panchen Lama, the institution became known as Larung Buddhist Academy of the Five Sciences or, in Chinese, Larong Wumin Foxueyuan.

New Sociopolitical Circumstances

The Panchen Lama, being well versed in both Tibetan and Chinese politics, became aware that modernizing Tibetan life meant adapting it to the new sociopolitical context. By the end of the Cultural Revolution in the late 1970s, traditional Tibetan life, culture, and religion were in decline as a consequence of socialist policies imposed by the central government. This decline had two aspects: a structural decline caused by years of destruction that negatively impacted Dharma teachings, Tibetan monasteries, and individual monastics; and social decline characterized by immoral behavior, coerced actions, and unethical lifestyles generally perceived as a result of the extreme policies of the Cultural Revolution. The Panchen Lama, like few other members of the Buddhist elite who remained in Tibet, focused on the improvement of the conditions of Tibetan Buddhist practitioners and institutions through finding ways to attune them with the new sociopolitical circumstances.

The developments of Buddhist modernism in Tibet, therefore, can hardly be appreciated and understood without a careful historical reading. Tibetan modern history is inevitably linked to political intersections with Chinese modernity since the late nineteenth century. But it is also the product of Tibetan thinkers and intellectuals' speeches, writings, and actions trying to make sense of new socialist ideologies, Communist Party policies, Tibetan nationalism, and religious identity. In this chapter, I argue for the primary role of Buddhist morality, religiosity, and education as catalysts for modernization and social change in Tibet after the end of the Cultural Revolution and in the wake of policies aimed at opening and reform in the early 1980s.

Chinese and Tibetan historical, biographical, and political sources related or attributed to the Panchen Lama suggest that his main preoccupation was seeking stability in the chaotic and otherwise volatile times in which he lived. This volatility was caused by the new sociopolitical order and the growing pressure of globalization and enforced cultural homogeneity that Tibetans faced during Deng Xiaoping's era. The Panchen

Lama, especially during the last decade before his demise, the period from 1979–1989, embraced a sociopolitical critique aimed at, on the one hand, assisting Tibetans in recovering from what he presented as a dangerous moral and social decline and, on the other hand, contributing to the generation of modern education in both secular and religious forms.

Reform of Buddhist monasticism and to some extent the broader Tibetan social order were fundamental to his view of a new Tibet. Harmony for the Paṇchen Lama could only be restored through the empowerment of the individual, renewed dedication to religious practice and theory, and the promotion of purification, education, and morality as central features of the modern religiopolitical imagination of the period. In his talks, the Paṇchen Lama also advanced a nuanced argument about the nature of equality and justice in human affairs. He did this by calling for a Buddhist modernity among Tibetans characterized by two main features: a religious one emphasizing purification and moral conduct; and a political one promoting education, rationalization, and social engagement as influenced in part by the socialist view and policies of his time.

Modernizing Tibetan Buddhism

The activities of the Paṇchen Lama in the 1980s in one way reflect the ideas of development and advancement that China embraced passionately after the end of the Qing dynasty in 1911 with the rise of new cultural and political movements during the decades of Republican China (1912–1949). This was a time of disillusionment with traditional Chinese culture that entailed the decline of the traditional communities and the elite role monasteries had played as leading agents in the cultural, economic, and political spheres. During this era, humanistic knowledge gained a prominent position in the modernization process including progress in science, industry, education, and the demystification or "rationalization" of religion and traditional culture. Later, as a result of the rhetoric of the Maoist period, the modernization process spurred a reflection on what the political philosophy of China, both Marxist-socialist and Confucian, saw as irrational in human life and promoted instead free choice, morality, and critical thinking.

As the highest personality in the Tibetan theocratic government's line of succession, second only to the Fourteenth Dalai Lama, who left for his exiled life in India in 1959, the Paṇchen Lama played a central role in the development of Tibet during the new era initiated by Hu Yaobang and

Deng Xiaoping. It is in this climate of liberalization and cautious reconsideration of past restrictive policies toward culture, religion, and ethnic minorities that the Paṇchen Lama was not only discharged from prison after thirteen years of detention and rehabilitated but, in order to promote harmony among Tibetans, he was also given a high position in the Communist apparatus as a vice-chairperson of the Standing Committee of the National People's Congress from 1980 to 1989, the year of his death.[6] This was an ambiguous position that won him both condemnation from many Tibetans as a Chinese collaborator and admiration from many Chinese leaders as a patriotic leader serving the motherland.[7] Nevertheless, in this capacity, he managed to operate inside Tibet relatively freely, offering support and influence to Tibetan communities, thus helping Tibetans make remarkable accomplishments in the fields of culture, education, and religion.

The last decade of the Paṇchen Lama's life (1979–1989) thus coincided with two major events: the economic and political launch of the opening and reform policy enacted by Deng Xiaoping and new philosophical and intellectual trends that, along with Marxism, influenced not only the sociopolitical but also the cultural and religious landscapes in China. Whereas before and during the Cultural Revolution, individualism, tradition, and culture were denounced, attacked, and suppressed, with the revisionist approach promoted by the new leadership to boost economic growth, self and culture became the center of philosophical discourses. New leniency emerged to cultivate and renew the legacy of religion, tradition, and culture among minority groups, which was seen to benefit Chinese civilization as a whole in the new century. In the decade after the death of Mao Zedong, the major intellectual trends focused on the exploration of the "independent existence of persons" and discussions on humanism and human nature, with emphasis on subjectivity (Ch: *zhutixing*) and the psychological structure of human intellect, affection, and volition.[8]

In his new political role—and as an influential religious leader who was a member of the Buddhist Association of China—the Paṇchen Lama shared his insights on the role of Buddhism among Tibetans both in Beijing and Tibetan areas, including how they could cultivate a more rational approach to religiosity. Moreover, he was part of debates on the role of religion in the new China and the rise of the Buddhist academies as loci for the modern and rational identity of religious intellectuals. The Paṇchen Lama traveled extensively across Tibetan areas visiting communities, monasteries, and schools, where on numerous occasions he delivered passionate speeches, offered spiritual advice, and dispensed blessings. Although yet to be richly explored by scholars, a reading of speeches by the Paṇchen Lama promises to offer a compelling view of his commitment to rehabilitating Buddhism and religious practices among Tibetans, assisting them in a gradual (albeit uneasy) reconciliation with the Chinese government, applying socialist and neoliberal discourses on modernization, and, above all, adopting new approaches toward the sociopolitical conditions of Tibetans.

The Paṇchen Lama's Serta Speech

In his speeches, the Paṇchen Lama advocates modern Buddhist interpretations, ideas, and rational discursive methods, while also pointing out with alarm a perceived departure from the authentic practice of Buddhist values such as critical thinking, rationality, and altruism. In his "Serta Speech" delivered in 1985, in terms of religiosity, the Paṇchen Lama focuses on the decay of moral values and the question of how Tibetans should behave by focusing on the classic ten Buddhist virtues, while asking Tibetans to abandon uncritical and irrational dependence on monks and to be more attentive to the degeneration of morality among monastics. When it comes to monastics, in the "Serta Speech," the Paṇchen Lama emphasizes purification and reform in order to prevent the decay of discipline and scholarship alongside a return to authentic discipline.

The Paṇchen Lama's emphasis on purification focuses mostly on developing moral conduct and the study of scriptures such as the Vinaya, which he saw as the source of monastic moral purity that would restore their exemplary behavior. Being himself a former Geluk monk, the Paṇchen Lama promoted the view that the Vinaya represented the essence of monastic discipline and moral conduct at the heart of an authentic expression of Buddhism. It is my understanding that by purification, as addressed in his "Serta Speech," the Paṇchen Lama meant both an emphasis on serious monastic discipline as well as the modernist intent, in line with a commitment to equality and social engagement, to make educational opportunities available to everyone, monastics and lay people alike, in China. The emphasis on purification for monks and personal responsibility for lay people aimed at recovering doctrinal authenticity and reestablishing the trust between the two communities (monastic and lay) damaged by decades of profound political changes, psychological trauma, cultural vandalism, and social turmoil. The "Serta Speech" demonstrates the Paṇchen Lama's concern for monastics' lack of sincerity when teaching Buddhism, superficiality in performing their offering services, and inconsistency in their recitations.

Simultaneously, the Paṇchen Lama employed the familiar platform of Buddhist ethics to address the new core values promoted by the Chinese leadership and the Marxist worldview. The classic ten virtues, as discussed in the "Serta Speech," provide guidelines not only for Buddhist morals, but also and more importantly for everybody's correct behavior, including studying hard, being clean, and acting respectfully. Correct behavior, respect for discipline, attention to personal responsibility, and development were ideas at the center of the intellectual and philosophical trends during the whole decade of the 1980s. There was no Communist Party member or government official who was not familiar with the new system of ideas and values announced in the intellectual discourse in the immediate aftermath of the Cultural Revolution. The modernization of self, motivated by concern for individuality and culture, was the main response to the forced dissolution of self that occurred through collectivization and the drastic transformations of the economic, sociopolitical, and religio-cultural character of China under Mao Zedong.[9]

The Paṇchen Lama's emphasis on modern education, purification, and a rational approach to religiosity in the "Serta Speech" illustrates his general approach: that a deeper understanding of Buddhism and its scriptures would bring monks to a correct view of their religion and culture. Additionally, his critique of popular and traditionalist practices among Tibetans such as the exaggerated reliance on monasteries, the superiority of religious education, and excessive deference to monastics was aimed at minimizing narrow-mindedness and superstition while sparking a better understanding of authentic Buddhist experience. The Paṇchen Lama considered study and education essential for improving the lives of the Tibetan people. Within that, he stressed that language—referring primarily to correct Tibetan language, Mandarin Chinese, and other foreign languages—would offer Tibetans socio-ethnic equality, prosperity, and a better life in line with their Han counterparts. The Paṇchen Lama's approaches to modernizing Buddhism drew widely on the contemporary Chinese models for Buddhist renovation promoted across China in the 1980s, which were, in turn, largely based on part of the original framework constructed and promoted by Taixu in the early decades of the twentieth century.

Conclusion

Rather than changing and transforming the practice of Buddhism and thinking of religious freedom among his Tibetan compatriots as contrasting with the values and ideologies of Communist China, the Panchen Lama proposed ways in which the values and concerns of both could meet and jointly enhance each other. In the "Serta Speech," he offers a constructive critique aimed not at deepening divides but enhancing linkages between Tibetans' right to express their religiosity and their need to adapt to a new world. Education, interpersonal harmony, purification of the monastic lifestyle, rationality, and equality are the features he suggested are the most important in modern times. With a focus on ethical behavior first and foremost for both monastics and laypeople, the Panchen Lama aimed to equip citizens with moral values for a rapidly modernizing world. I read his approach as an attempt to search for stability in otherwise volatile and chaotic times, and an intention to modernize Buddhism as a response to radical and inevitable social change.

Through his speeches, the Panchen Lama was widely influential, and his visits across Tibetan areas are still remembered to this day. In particular, the "Serta Speech" and the presence of the Tenth Panchen Lama in Serta and neighboring areas had a profound effect not only on a vast portion of the local population. It also and more significantly affected local cultural and political life at the institutional level, including the reopening and relaunching of religious institutions, the rejuvenation of Tibetan language, and the reaffirmation of the Tibetan identity. These latter points can be appreciated in the Tenth Panchen Lama's staunch support and participation in the promotion of local Tibetan traditional dances and performances, customs, and festivals, as well as belief in interethnic unity and cooperation. The promotion of Khenpo Jigme Phuntsok's Larung Gar as a Buddhist academy and his direct involvement in its popularity as a new center for the scholastic and experiential study of Buddhism open to both Tibetan and Chinese devotees, monastic as well as lay, male as well as female, had an indelible and lasting impact on its contemporary organizational structure and its approach to Buddhist training and education. By virtue of the Tenth Panchen Lama and his vision of "modern Buddhism" modeled on Chinese Buddhist reforms and religious policies (in alignment with the Communist Party), Larung Gar became a model of the new Buddhist institution in the new Tibet. Therefore, although the Tenth Panchen Lama is not exactly one of the voices *from* Larung Gar in that he did not reside there, he was definitely one of the important voices *for* Larung Gar.

In his unique position as a politician, leader, and the highest Buddhist hierarch in Tibet, in the last decade of his life, the Panchen Lama was a key figure in harnessing the potential of Buddhism to heal and regenerate the psychological damage inflicted by previous decades of hardships and the overwhelming challenges caused by sociopolitical change in Mao's China. Out of pragmatism and fresh appeals to ancient principles long neglected, he employed tools already at his disposal within the Buddhist tradition—particularly rationality, education, equality, self-control, and altruism—in order to promote a modern form of approach to Buddhism, one that built directly upon Buddhist tradition while adapting it to the rapidly changing world around him.

Excerpts from the "Serta Speech"

The Tenth Panchen Lama, Chokyi Gyaltsen (1985)

Virtues and Moral Reform

According to the Buddhist teachings, the Buddha Śākyamuni himself said, "Do not perform any sins, perform excellent virtues, and tame your mind completely!" You should try to eliminate your sins as much as possible and realize as many virtuous deeds as possible. Tame your own existing pernicious natures such as attachment, hatred, delusion, pride, and envy. In the context of the body, killing human beings and animals—all taking of lives— is to be avoided. Additionally, we can talk about taking what is not given: stealing, depriving others of their property, and robbing. Sexual misconduct, such as having sexual intercourse with the spouse of another person while turning away from one's own spouse, must also be abandoned.

In the context of speech, telling lies is to be abandoned. Telling lies must be abandoned if lying leads to deceiving others. Divisive speech generates disharmony among those who are amicable, and therefore this way of acting is harmful. Divisive speech must be abandoned. Talking by way of employing harsh speech, generating unpleasant feelings toward others, generating harsh speech at others, discrediting others, and generating unhappy thoughts and anger, since they involve harsh words, all must be abandoned. Moreover, foolish chatter is unnecessary; it is at odds with the Dharma, and we must abandon all those unnecessary silly and ambivalent conversations that conflict with respectable behavior. Some convey all this to others by virtue of intentionally expressing greed and vanity. How can they believe that their actions are without any effect? Greed and harm damage others completely, and holding on to thoughts that are harmful toward others gives rise to malice. As for wrong views, there is no way to deny that there are past and future lives, and there is no way to deny karmic causality. Accruing virtuous deeds produces positive results, while accruing unvirtuous deeds produces frustrating results. Thus, it is extremely important to uphold the discipline of the ten virtues, abandoning the production of all unacceptable wrong views. So, similarly, please bear this in mind in order to strive for a good human existence.[10]

IRRATIONAL DEPENDENCE ON MONKS

During the Cultural Revolution, the Buddhist teachings were threatened. Nowadays, however, there is a further dissemination of the Buddhist teachings. At this time, acts [by monastics] should be pure. When nothing is done well and with responsibility, such as pretending to recite scriptures offered as a mass offering or pretending to teach Dharma in a fraudulent way, this is just deceiving people, and it is absolutely wrong.[11]

If people think lamas are good, monks will say they are lamas even if they are not. If they are not erudite, they will say they are. Even as they wear the yellow robes, their already red faces blush further and turn to their herdsmen's way of thinking. Herdsmen are naive. Thinking, "This one must be a lama! We must give him plenty of offerings and donate a lot of supplies," they make offerings randomly. Acting this way is extremely damaging to the advancement of our Dharma.[12]

MONASTIC PURIFICATION

Buddha Śākyamuni established precepts based on the Vinaya. He offered precepts to novice monks. He offered *bhikṣuṇī* precepts to nuns. However, does anyone know what the monks' precepts are? What are the precepts for novices? It is not acceptable not to know all of them in their totality.

Monks should uphold purity in monasteries. Being pure monks who know the dharma is a perfect virtue appropriate for every monk. How many monks are virtuous nowadays? Also, not knowing the dharma is equal to impurity. Members of the saṅgha who live this way in the monastery have no purpose whatsoever. Every progress, even the smallest one, should be taken as an encouragement. This is what the Buddha said. It would be appropriate for each of you to cherish this truly in your heart and stay at monasteries wearing monastic robes and clothes. But, in the community currently, these types of actions, although necessary, are completely missing.[13]

EDUCATION

We Tibetans, thanks to the responsibility of the Party, have achieved equality in terms of political rights. But, as for wealth and culture, since we lag behind, equality will be absolutely impossible. This is really not right, and it is a mistake, because it demonstrates a lack of concern for culture. You should all study hard and learn language well. Study the ancient Tibetan language well. Master the Tibetan language. Then, beside a good Tibetan basis, study Chinese well. Then turn to foreign languages. We all wish that by studying languages in this way, many experts will arise, and we hope that they will succeed in the progress and promotion of our national language.[14]

RELIGION AND POLITICS

My opinion about religion and politics is that from the political side we should respect the Communist Party and safeguard the country of the People's Republic of China at all times, while opposing those separatists of the motherland. From the religious side, we should have faith and trust in the guru and the Three Jewels, maintain pure refuge, avoid nonvirtuous deeds, welcome the [karmic] consequences of virtuous deeds, and put all our strength into daily recitations and spiritual practice. By exerting ourselves in performing virtuous deeds and acting with cognizance of the great opportunities of this life, we can work well to achieve all religious and secular goals.[15]

2. Heart Advice for the Twenty-First Century

Holly Gayley

Introduction

In his seminal work of advice, *Heart Advice to Tibetans for the Twenty-First Century* (composed in 1995),[1] the renowned Khenpo Jigme Phuntsok articulates a path forward for Tibetans as a nationality.[2] His vision of progress entails preserving Tibetan culture and its civilizational heritage while adopting new forms of knowledge and improving the standard of living for Tibetans in the arenas of economics, technology, and infrastructure. This vision of progress, which the khenpo encapsulates at one point as the "synthesis of the ancient and modern," represents a Buddhist approach to the challenges signaled by the turn of the millennium, a key moment which for him, on the one hand, risks the decline and disappearance of Tibetan culture and, on the other hand, holds out the possibility of Tibetans making a grand contribution on the world stage.

Among the most revered Buddhist teachers in recent decades, Khenpo Jigme Phuntsok played a major role in the revitalization of Buddhism in Tibetan areas of the PRC beginning in the 1980s. He is best known for founding an ecumenical academy in Serta, certified in 1987 as Larung Buddhist Academy of the Five Sciences but more commonly referred to as Larung Gar.[3] His revival of monastic scholasticism stands as one of the crowning achievements of his legacy, yet the khenpo also helped to shape an emerging Buddhist modernism at Larung Gar through his dual emphasis on Buddhist ethics and cultural preservation in works of advice to the laity. In this chapter, I introduce *Heart Advice to Tibetans for the Twenty-First Century* (hereafter *Heart Advice*) and offer a translation of its opening section.

While influenced by other lamas of his day,[4] Khenpo Jigme Phuntsok brings a distinct vision and voice to his articulation of the path forward for Tibetans in this work, providing an early example of how Buddhist leaders have participated in an ongoing contest over what "modernity" means in Tibetan areas of the PRC.[5] Rather than capitulate to a secular or state version of modernity,[6] the khenpo redefines the very language of progress to promote an alternative Tibetan form of modernity in explicitly Buddhist terms.

Unified Approach to the Path Forward

In *Heart Advice*, Khenpo Jigme Phuntsok calls for a united outlook as the basis for progress and articulates a "path forward" for Tibetans as a people.[7] This is an appeal to collective action in which the khenpo asks the population as a whole—male and female, young and old, lay and cleric— to consider the greater good of the Tibetan people. Specifically, he asks experienced elders and intelligent youth to band together with Buddhist lamas to guide the general populace in this endeavor. Instead of detailing a plan of action, however, Khenpo Jigme Phuntsok is more concerned with establishing the ideological underpinnings for progress as rooted in Tibetan history and a Buddhist episteme or worldview. To do so, he prescribes a set of values centered on preserving Tibetan culture and upholding Buddhist ethics, which both defines Tibetans as a people and also serves as the foundation for the path forward into the twenty-first century. In the process, the khenpo links culture and ethics in his construction of Tibetan identity and in his vision for a unified approach to the future.

To articulate a unified outlook, Khenpo Jigme Phuntsok first delineates a common ground of what it means to be Tibetan. Being a teacher in the Nyingma tradition of Tibetan Buddhism,[8] it is not surprising that he turns to the imperial period of the seventh to ninth centuries for a shared sense of Tibetan identity: as a time of political unity and military expansion, as an origin point of Tibetan civilization with the introduction of Buddhism, and as a source of common ancestry (symbolically conceived). In the opening pages of *Heart Advice*, Khenpo Jigme Phuntsok harkens to the imperial period when "commonplace and distinctive systems of knowledge" were first propagated by "our ancestor" Songtsen Gampo. In the khenpo's usage, "knowledge" here refers to the erudite, textual, and transregional dimension of Tibetan culture,[9] which he traces to the time of the emperors Songtsen Gampo and Trisong Detsen, after which the rest of Tibetan history is glossed over as various periods of flourishing and decline. In this way, he emphasizes the shared history and cultural inheritance of Tibetans, eliding periods of political fragmentation, regional and doctrinal differences, and other religions.

For him, the imperial period provides a rallying point and source of pride and inspiration for Tibetans. Khenpo Jigme Phuntsok states, "It is not hyperbole for us to praise our own nationality; we should know that our people have a truly magnificent history." One can only imagine that, in promoting ethnic pride in this way, he endeavors to reverse the label of backwardness assigned to Tibetans and other minorities in state-sponsored media and publications.[10] Indeed, the khenpo's emphasis on Tibet's long history as a civilization dating back to the seventh century may be an attempt to subvert the tendency among minorities in China to develop a stigmatized identity.[11] In other words, he queries the Han civilizing project vis-à-vis ethnic minorities by asserting that Tibetans have long been civilized.

Following the same logic, Khenpo Jigme Phuntsok asserts the moral worthiness of Tibetans, harkening to a longstanding nobility of character. Tibetans are depicted by him as "a righteous people—brave and heroic warriors imbued with kindness, honesty, and a noble demeanor." Extending this into a Buddhist framework, the principle of compassion is depicted as integral to the fabric of Tibetan culture. For example, when discussing the socialization of children, the khenpo recounts the adage that Tibetan infants learn how to say *ama* (mother) and *maṇi* (shorthand for OM MAṆI PADME HŪṂ, the mantra of the bodhisattva of compassion Avalokiteśvara) at roughly the same age.[12] Additionally, Tibetans are characterized as compassionate, honest, and courageous based on the perceptions of outsiders, that is, how Tibetans are known throughout the world. By asserting the ethical character of Tibetans based on their reputation outside of China (to which he would have been exposed during his travels abroad in 1990 and 1993), Khenpo Jigme Phuntsok pits Western fantasies of Tibet against the "internal orientalism" of Han representations.[13]

However, a common history and ancestry is not enough to constitute Tibetan identity in his view. Rather, the principal markers of "Tibetanness" are cultural and ethical and, therefore, can be lost due to assimilation. The issue of cultural survival is explicitly raised by the khenpo when he calls for the preservation of Tibetan language, customs, and civilization likening esteem for these to the life force of a people, without which they are no longer a discrete nationality. In his estimation, it is up to Tibetans as a people whether or not they embrace their heritage and make a concerted effort to maintain the factors he defines as quintessentially Tibetan.[14] To remain indifferent to these and merely imitate the customs of another nationality is presented as the road to extinction: Tibetan culture would vanish and Tibetans would turn into another nationality, presumably (though unstated) Han. For him, the loss of Tibetan language and rejection of the Tibetan character among urban Tibetan youth is a "grave situation" and "source of extreme disappointment." The khenpo expresses his dismay as follows: "If Tibetans do not even wear our own dress and also do not use our own language, at that point, we will have cast aside the name *Tibetan*."[15] It is his emphasis on cultural and ethical criteria in defining "Tibetanness" that sets his formulation apart from state definitions of ethnicity.[16]

Values for the Twenty-First Century

By constructing Tibetan identity in cultural and ethical terms, Khenpo Jigme Phuntsok articulates a vision of progress based on values inherited from the past, which are an extension of the "worthy traditions of our ancestors." He delineates these as the beneficial aspects of Tibetan values, its distinctive form of civilization, and local customs and habits. The first of these, namely values, occupies the bulk of the text in a section called "values for our Tibetan people in the twenty-first century." It details a set of four values, framed as both an inheritance of the past and a unified outlook to be cultivated for the future. The latter two, civilization and local customs, are treated in the concluding pages of the *Heart Advice* in a section on "brief recommendations for points of action."

The emphasis placed on values in *Heart Advice* suggests that the khenpo is more concerned with the ideological basis for progress than the specifics of its implementation. This can be seen in the internal outline given in the text as follows:

Introduction (1)
A. Values for Our Tibetan People in the Twenty-First Century (5)
    1. To always endeavor to have a good heart (5)
    2. To be genuinely honest without pretext (9)
    3. To greatly cherish one's people and the knowledge of one's
       people (10)
    4. To have conviction in the sublime Dharma (12)

Notice that the bulk of the text (pages 5–90) focuses on values or more literally "modes of thinking."[17] We could consider these to be guiding principles that orient action and allegiance. For example, a good heart (A1) and honesty (A2) are orientations that guide ethical action, whereas cherishing Tibetan forms of knowledge (A3) and conviction in Buddhism (A4) are orientations toward sources of authority and cultural practices inherited from the past. What is at stake in this enumeration of values is the worldview that underlies and informs progress, and particular emphasis is given to conviction in a Buddhist episteme. Indeed, the khenpo spends more than half of the text offering scientific evidence for reincarnation, presenting arguments for karmic cause and effect, and emphasizing the rational character of faith in Buddhism.[18]

Not until the final section of *Heart Advice* (page 90 onward) does he suggest a series of actions that derive from these values. Only here do we see the full scope of the khenpo's vision, related not only to advocating cultural preservation and adherence to ethical principles, but also to promoting secular education and economic development. This exemplifies the way he advocates maintaining the "worthy traditions of our ancestors" in conjunction with adopting "new forms of knowledge of the modern period." In the final pages, he provides a wide range of recommendations expressing this approach: urging parents to send their children to school, endorsing monasteries as the stewards of traditional domains of knowledge, surveying issues related to the study and promotion of Tibetan language, advocating the compassionate treatment of animals, encouraging Tibetans to wear traditional dress, and proposing avenues for economic development. As may be apparent from the variety of subjects the khenpo covers in just over a dozen pages, his recommendations read more like a to-do list than a coherent plan of action.

Despite his interest in promoting new forms of knowledge, Khenpo Jigme Phuntsok's message when it comes to values is to hold fast to tradition and not waver. This can be seen most clearly in his slogan, "Don't lose self-determination. Don't agitate the minds of others."[19] The slogan is well-known in the nomadic regions surrounding Serta, and in the mid-2000s, it could be spotted hanging on the wall of a pool hall or teahouse, painted on the outside of a school, and even referenced in the music video of a Tibetan pop song.[20] The first half of the slogan, which is of most interest to us here, has two senses for Tibetans at large: to uphold one's moral character and to preserve Tibetan culture. According to a commentary by Khenpo Rigzin Dargye, it entails "not abandoning a good heart and demeanor as well as ceaselessly endeavoring to uphold, preserve, and propagate the civilization of one's own people, held in high regard."[21] Here again, Tibetans are essentialized as a "pious people who hold the Three Jewels as the source of constant refuge . . . who like to engage in noble conduct, and who naturally have a good heart, kindness, and compassion."[22] The call is to not lose these qualities. Similarly, by advocating adherence to values inherited from the past in *Heart Advice*, Khenpo Jigme Phuntsok is asking Tibetans not to abandon their heritage and moral character in the process of modernizing.

Buddhist Ethics as the Custodian of Progress

In *Heart Advice*, the khenpo also advocates for the special role of Buddhist ethics as the custodian of progress. By emphasizing their ongoing relevance to contemporary social problems, he salvages ancient values as the necessary complement to modern technology and science. In what could aptly be termed a modernist approach, he widens the sphere of Buddhist ethics from governing an individual economy of merit (as the means toward a favorable rebirth) to serving as the cornerstone for social welfare, expressed with respect to local communities, nations, and human civilization as a whole. A good heart—synonymous here with the ethical principles of love and compassion—is identified as the basis of both individual well-being and social harmony in ever-widening circles: in one's family, community, and nation, and finally on a global level, where nothing short of world peace and prosperity would result. However idealized, this vision is modernist in its emphasis on the this-worldly social dimensions of

Buddhist ethics. Unlike the more typical language of compassion toward all beings in the six realms of Buddhist cosmology, the khenpo emphasizes the collective fate of humanity and more specifically of Tibetans as a people.[23]

Indeed, the Buddhist ethical mainstays of love and compassion are cast as vital to the fate of the world. According to *Heart Advice*, with the advance of technology and the advent of modern weapons, the world has reached a dangerous threshold where one errant general could destroy the planet. This scenario allows the khenpo to globalize the issue of cultural survival by highlighting the precarious position of human civilization as a whole in the current era. Specifically, he refers to the destructive power of modern weapons unleashed in World War II and the first Gulf War in order to forge a link between the source of suffering according to Buddhist doctrine, which is desire for one's own gain at the expense of others, and the cause of social calamities, which is aggression leading to the loss of life on a massive scale in modern warfare. Khenpo Jigme Phuntsok goes on to assert that the absence of love and compassion—when countries or ethnic groups have little regard for each other—is at the root of all oppression and tyranny. By emphasizing the importance of love and compassion to humanity at large and having essentialized the Tibetan character as moral, he employs a dual strategy of heralding the specialness of the Tibetan people and taking an inclusive, global perspective, preserving Tibetan culture in and for the world.[24]

For him, Buddhist ethics are important for social welfare in other ways as well. Without them, Khenpo Jigme Phuntsok asserts that improving material standards of living can lead to a more agitated and crude state of mind, ever inflamed by desire and aggression. In his view, a good heart leads to happiness despite a destitute standard of living, and the inverse is also true. He asserts that to seek one's own wealth and comfort based on the poverty and destitution of others leads to suffering despite a high standard of living. In terms reminiscent of Bhutan's pursuit of Gross National Happiness, he suggests that progress requires a balance between material prosperity and ethical values in order to produce psychological well-being. In an interview, Khenpo Tsultrim Lodro elaborated on this point by distinguishing between material life and mental life, noting the apparent disjuncture between them in contemporary lifestyles, which offer more comforts along with more stresses.[25] In *Heart Advice*, Buddhist ethics are a necessary complement to improved material standards as a means to ensure the psychological well-being of the individual alongside the safety and welfare of society.

If taken at face value, many of the khenpo's assertions seem idealistic, to say the least. But, when analyzed in the context of competing epistemes, *Heart Advice* can be seen as a compelling response to Maoist rhetoric and the more recent encroachment of global market capitalism. What is at stake is allegiance to a worldview that in turn regulates social behavior and corresponds to different sources of authority. From this perspective, what the khenpo is advocating is not simply one or another Buddhist tenet but adherence to an entire episteme, or what counts as true in one's worldview. By suggesting ways in which Buddhist principles bolster progress and accord with scientific research, Khenpo Jigme Phuntsok contests the stigma of backwardness and superstition with which religion has at times been associated in twentieth-century China.[26] Instead, he positions Buddhist ethics as an important complement to economic development and as the custodian of progress ensuring that the benefits of technology are harnessed for the greater good. In this way, he redeems the categories of religion and tradition from being signifiers of backwardness and advances Buddhist ethics as essential to the path forward not just for Tibetans but for the whole world.

Shades of Modernism

To conclude, let us consider to what extent the message of *Heart Advice* can be considered modernist. Bruce Lawrence has distinguished between modernity (the trappings of the modern world, such as mass media and technology) and modernism (the values and mindset deriving from it, particularly individualism and, I would add, scientism and humanism).[27] One of the valuable points that he makes with this distinction is that the use of mass media and other technology to disseminate religious messages does not, in and of itself, guarantee that the message is modernist. In light of Lawrence's distinction, one might be tempted to conclude that Khenpo Jigme Phuntsok is not a modernist, since the very thing that he advocates in *Heart Advice* is to make good use of the trappings of the modern world—to harness technology toward economic development and improved standards of living for Tibetans—but to do so while maintaining a Buddhist episteme. However, to conclude thus would not adequately account for the revisionist element of his approach.

If we consider labels of "traditional" and "modern" to be discursive representations rather than transparent descriptions of social realities,[28] we can see that the khenpo is operating at the level of discourse to articulate an alternative modernity. In other words, he attempts to reconfigure categories, such as progress, and thereby reposition Tibetans vis-à-vis other ethnicities or nationalities of the world. By valorizing a "synthesis of the ancient and modern," he implicitly rejects the bifurcation of traditional and modern into mutually exclusive categories, a dichotomy that would condemn Tibetans to an impossible choice: to attempt to recreate an idealized pre-1950 Tibet or to assimilate into a wholly Chinese version of modernity. In his terms, the first option would not be a "path forward" and the second would mean the extinction of Tibetan culture and Tibetans as a discrete ethnicity or nationality. Instead, it would be more apt to think about "shades of modernism" in recognition of a gray zone in which Buddhist leaders are attempting a synthesis that transcends this dichotomy.

Khenpo Jigme Phuntsok is surely to some degree a modernist.[29] Though he does not accept a model of outright assimilation, neither does he promote a regressive isolationism. For him, education is a vital means for preserving Tibetan culture and moving forward into the twenty-first century. And, it should involve not only the study of Tibetan language and literature—without which for him "the path forward for Tibetans is finished"— but also learning other languages, so that a connection can be forged with outsiders and as a means to develop intellectually and economically. Moreover, in the conclusion to *Heart Advice*, he promotes the study of science and technology to enable Tibetans to become more involved in commerce, manufacturing, construction, and so forth. In these ways, although the khenpo sees materialism as insufficient to guarantee social welfare, he also does not seek to turn back the clock toward an idyllic, pastoral subsistence economy. Instead, in pragmatic terms, he insists that education provides the opportunity for a higher standard of living, so that Tibetans do not fall behind in comparison with other nationalities.

Beyond this, in *Heart Advice*, Khenpo Jigme Phuntsok emphasizes the rational and ethical dimensions of Buddhism, which are central components of Buddhist modernism. Evidence for this can be found in his arguments for Buddhist ethics as the basis for social welfare, in his attempts to show the compatibility of Buddhism with scientific research, and in his emphasis on the rational character of Buddhist faith. Needless to say, his recommendations for the path forward concentrate on the this-worldly fate of Tibetans as a people rather than soteriological or eschatological concerns. Indeed, the urgency of the khenpo's concern with the preservation of Tibetan culture and adherence to Buddhist principles derives from what he sees as a critical historical juncture for Tibetans and humanity at large.

However, Khenpo Jigme Phuntsok does not go as far in his social vision or empiricism as his Southeast Asian counterparts, like Ariyaratne in Sri Lanka or Buddhadāsa Bhikkhu in Thailand, for whom, respectively, social work provides a path to liberation and ritual is rejected as irrational.[30] Indeed, when discussing the role of clerics as stewards of traditional knowledge, he insists that the work of monks and nuns is primarily to study and only after that to engage in worldly issues to benefit society. And while Larung Gar is progressive in its setup as an ecumenical Buddhist academy, let us not forget that as a treasure revealer, Khenpo Jigme Phuntsok is steeped in the visionary and ritual dimensions of Tibetan Buddhism. Furthermore, although he puts Buddhism in conversation with science, he does so principally to confirm rather than question its tenets. Thus, in the terms introduced by Lauran Hartley, we might be tempted to say that he is a "conservative modernist," who is "unwilling to toss much—if any—of the old."[31]

Yet even this characterization falls short of capturing the way that Khenpo Jigme Phuntsok reenvisions Buddhist principles and institutions in the process of asserting an alternative Tibetan form of modernity. Recall that he recasts Buddhist ethics in social terms, bringing them into conversation with the state discourse on nationalities and global concerns over weapons of mass destruction. Moreover, by assigning clerics to the role of stewards of traditional knowledge, the khenpo refocuses monasticism on scholastic pursuits over adherence to ritual. Although he harkens back to the ancient roots of Tibetan civilization, he does not treat tradition as if it were a static entity to be reproduced wholesale. Rather, he constructs a version of the past that is useable for the future, simultaneously defining what is worthy and distinctive about Tibetan culture and underscoring the importance of preserving it for the twenty-first century. Thus, it might be more apt to consider his approach to be reformist and constructive rather than conservative per se, and the same is true for his successors, as other chapters in this anthology show. Khenpo Jigme Phuntsok embodies a modernism that seeks continuity with the past, while nevertheless advocating reform, embracing scientific knowledge, and promoting economic development.

Though less radical that some Buddhist modernists elsewhere in Asia, Khenpo Jigme Phuntsok's reformist and modernist legacy may prove to be far-reaching. Suffice it to say that he has spawned somewhat of a modernist movement among second-generation cleric-scholars at Larung Gar with publications by Metrul Tenzin Gyatso on mind-science and by Khenpo Tsultrim Lodro defending rebirth with scientific research (see relevant samples of their writings in chapters 4 and 6).[32] In these examples, among others, we can see that Khenpo Jigme Phuntsok has created a significant cultural space within the PRC for Tibetan modernity to be negotiated in explicitly Buddhist terms.

Acknowledgments

The introduction to this translation from *Heart Advice* is an abridged and revised version of a chapter originally published in *Mapping the Modern in Tibet* (2011) titled "The Ethics of Cultural Survival: A Buddhist Vision of Progress in Mkhan po 'Jigs phun's *Heart Advice to Tibetans for the Twenty-First Century*." I first presented on this material at the Eleventh Seminar of the International Association of Tibetan Studies (IATS), hosted by the University of Bonn in Königswinter (2006). My thanks to the publisher Dieter Schuh, the IATS convener Peter Schwieger, and the volume editor Gray Tuttle for allowing me to adapt the chapter for publication here.

Preamble to Heart Advice to Tibetans
for the Twenty-First Century

KHENPO JIGME PHUNTSOK (1995)

At the very pinnacle of the world, the Land of Snows was foretold by the omniscient one, our teacher the Buddha, the incomparable friend to all beings, and became the field of conversion for noble Avalokiteśvara.[33] For many thousands of years, this place was known to history as the Buddhist kingdom of Tibet with its righteous people—brave and heroic warriors imbued with kindness, honesty, and a noble demeanor.[34]

During the time of our ancestor Songtsen Gampo, many commonplace and distinctive systems of knowledge were developed. In the reign of Trisong Detsen, the empire held sway from the banks of the Ganges River in the west to the Chinese city of Chang'an (present-day Xian) in the east. There is no need to be bashful about the extent of Tibetan territory, power, and wealth.

Later, when Lord Atiśa, the crown ornament of all Indian *paṇḍitas*, arrived in Tibet, he blessed the land with the aspiration that Tibet remain a Buddhist kingdom in line with a prophecy made by Orgyan Padmākara, the second buddha: "When the dharma no longer flourishes in India, it will spread throughout Tibet." That came to pass based on the kindness of Dharma kings and the efforts of the masses across the vast expanse of Tibet.

This is testimony to our history, which gives us both pride and inspiration. In this regard, it is not hyperbole for us to praise our own nationality; we should know that our people have a truly magnificent history. Then gradually, due to fluctuations over time, various periods of flourishing and decline occurred in Tibet. At present, in this new era, we can tell whether or not we are on par with the most advanced peoples. Now, there's no time to delay! We are on the verge of the twenty-first century.

During the past century, the way people think and the way things are made have been transformed. Whatever changes have taken place, this is the nature of existence. In the midst of these changes, we Tibetan people should maintain the worthy traditions of our ancestors so that they do not vanish, including our distinctive civilization, the beneficial aspects of our values, and local customs and habits.

In addition, we should adopt new forms of knowledge of the modern period to the degree that they are beneficial in both the long and short term. Each and every Tibetan must think carefully about the ways to avoid falling behind the various nationalities of the world. For example, even the most humble home, like an anthill, is protected from collapse when all the members of a household are united in purpose: "If we don't do such and such, then in the future our home will deteriorate in one or another way."

We as a people with a magnificent history can benefit the entire world with our distinctive civilization. Otherwise, if we don't think like this—and make do with just food and shelter—then we are more dim-witted than cattle. What a sad state of affairs!

In terms of action, above all, Tibetans should try to work together and each contribute according to his or her own capacities—virtuous and experienced elders with an orientation toward the greater good of Tibetans as a people, young intellectuals able to discern what is worthwhile in a synthesis of the ancient and modern, and lamas and tulkus who have extensive knowledge of secular and religious affairs and are able to influence others on the path to virtue. The vast majority of the population should follow their lead. With a unified approach, let us endeavor on the path forward into the future. This is very important!

Cultivate a Good Heart

For the future, in the twenty-first century, what should our approach be as Tibetans? First and foremost, everyone—young and old, male and female—should continuously cultivate a good heart. As it is said:

> If your heart is good, the ground and path are also good.
> If your heart is base, the ground and path are also base.
> Everything depends on the purity of your intent.
> So always endeavor toward a good heart.[35]

In this regard, a good heart or intent refers to concern for other beings, including all types of people and animals down to insects.[36] If you see any living creature suffer, you should think, "How wonderful if I could alleviate their suffering even for a moment."

For example, under the hot sun we hope for the slightest cool breeze, and in the cold we hope for just a bit of sunlight. Likewise, if a spark falls on our skin or a thorn pricks us, we don't like it. If someone speaks harshly to us, we don't want to hear it. In the same way, we should set aside wanton thoughts of harming or killing others, not only all types of people but even insects.

Further, with sensitivity, we should be pleased when the destitute find a little money, when animals are freed from slaughter, or even when someone loses something and later finds it. This is what is called love and compassion. We should regard not only our own Tibetan people but all living beings universally in this way. At the same time, we should have special affection for our own people, who share the same flesh and bone as relatives.[37] In particular, within that, we should cherish the unique characteristics of our nationality. An attitude like this is invaluable.

Whoever has such love and compassion, without agitation in their hearts, is always joyful. Wherever they go, they bring benefit to others, experience harmony among friends, and garner praise from everyone. All their aspirations are spontaneously fulfilled. Also, in the next life, the fully matured result of love and compassion is enjoying the higher realms as a god or human. As it says in *The Way of the Bodhisattva*, "The result of a clear intent is abiding in Brahmā's realm or such."[38] Since the result follows from the cause, for anyone who benefits others with love and compassion, this will be true not only for this life but in all subsequent lives as well.

Moreover, if all the members of a household have a good heart, then no matter how destitute, they will spend their days with a sense of well-being, since "the source of all well-being is a joyful mind." The same is true if all the members of a community have this attitude or all the citizens of a nation. And, if everyone in the world were goodhearted then, without a doubt, peace and joy would come to the entire world.

If we look back at recent history, the damage and losses that have occurred around the world in general and within specific countries all have been the result of a detrimental mindset that wishes benefit for one's own at the expense of others. At the beginning of this century, during World Wars I and II, there were countless causalities. When America dropped the atomic bomb on Japan, hundreds of thousands of lives were lost in a single instant. More recently in the Gulf War, terrifying modern weapons were used. How many hard-won valuables and priceless lives were lost?

Furthermore, the source of all oppression and tyranny between nations and peoples who have little regard for each other comes down to simply this: the absence of love and compassion. Specifically, if we reflect on the present course of the world, terrifying modern weapons that never existed before have been manufactured and fill the earth from top to bottom. At this juncture of time, if we sever the cord of love and compassion, all hope for human life, prosperity, and civilization on earth as a whole is lost.

If you are unable to give rise to the good intention to benefit others a hundred times, at the very least, while enjoying this human life, do not harm others. If you don't want to suffer physically or mentally, then abandon malice that seeks to harm or kill another in order to obtain a little happiness for yourself.

Needless to say, our minds are like young stallions in need of training. A mind that is naturally oriented to benefit others from the start, without need of transformation, is rare indeed. If you want to lead a meaningful human life, then from now onward there is no choice but to train the mind. If you have good intentions, based on that alone, you will enjoy all the good things in life, both temporal and spiritual. This is vital.

BE GENUINE AND HONEST

Second, one should be genuine and honest. Within human society, from birth until death, it's important to be genuine at heart and honest in demeanor, whether toward individuals or other ethnicities. Make no mistake, acting in a straightforward manner without deception is a source of well-being for self and other. So, whatever you do, act without pretense or cunning, examining your motivation. For the most part, people seem to do whatever they want. But, it's worthwhile not to do that so you won't have anything to regret later. Otherwise, if you deceive others for your own gain, it will be difficult to sustain with no one else finding out. In the end, you don't achieve your heart's desire and instead encounter misfortune.

Generally speaking, Tibetans are actually quite genuine and honest. Our Tibetan brothers and sisters scattered around the world have had the opportunity to live alongside people from various places for a long time. Based on that, Tibetans are often praised for being compassionate, helpful, honest, brave, and courteous. With such an excellent legacy from our ancestors, it's crucial not to allow our worthy traditions to decline.

VALUE TIBETAN CULTURE

Third, we should greatly cherish our own nationality and its special characteristics. This is true for any ethnic group around the world. Whether or not the heritage, culture, and customs of a group survive depends mainly on whether or not the people themselves value, respect, and cherish their own heritage. If we ourselves do not act as stewards of our own culture, it will be quite difficult for anyone else to help preserve it. At the point in which we, lacking any regard for the unique characteristics of our own nationality, become simply an imitation of others, our civilization for the most part will begin to disappear from the face of the earth. There are already visible signs of this.

Throughout the world, are there any people who do not have affection for their own nationality and its special characteristics? If so, they are foolish, naive, and nonsensical like monkeys. Recently, the Upaiku language was lost.[39] On the planet, there was only one man, more than eighty years old, who still knew how to speak and write the language. Beyond that, even with a research institute, there is no way to save the Pālu'u language.[40] When something like this happens, it is a great loss, whatever the nationality.

For any people, once their language, customs, and civilization vanish, they have actually turned into another nationality. Thus, everyone should greatly cherish the unique characteristics of their own nationality. These are like the life force of a people. What could be more significant?

Therefore, we Tibetans of the three provinces—from the highest lamas, leaders, and young intellectuals down to students in elementary school— should have a unified outlook [in order to preserve] the civilization that we inherited from our ancestors. Nowadays, we can be confident about the traditional Tibetan domains of knowledge alongside the zenith of worldly scientific knowledge within advanced countries. When evaluated by colleagues around the world, both are deemed to be elevated and rational in character.

For the benefit of future Tibetans, as our path forward into the future, please don't remain indifferent to preserving, propagating, and spreading the distinctive customs of our ancestors. With the best intentions and genuine engagement, we can ensure that our people's way of life and culture will flourish in perpetuity. Even if we've tried everything and that's not enough, never give up!

Maintain Faith in Buddhism

Fourth, we should maintain faith in the sublime Dharma. First and foremost, this entails belief in past and future lives. The sublime Dharma of the Buddha came into existence in Tibet during the reign of the Tibetan king,

Lhato Thori. It was established during Songten Gampo's time and further spread and flourished during the time of Trisong Detsen. The mentality of Tibetans as a whole people is profoundly bound up with the Dharma. It is the core and substance of all Tibetan civilization.

The Dharma has influenced every aspect of our civilization. With its focus on benefitting others, our way of thinking has many virtuous aspects, such as contemplating love and compassion for all beings including animals and being conscientious when considering a suitable course of action. For Buddhists, this is the kindness of the Dharma. Further, the *Four Hundred Verse Treatise* by Āryadeva defines the Dharma in this way:

> In sum, Dharma is nonharming,
> as spoken by the tathāgata,
> and the true nature transcends sorrow;
> these two alone are it.[41]

Accordingly, nonharming is avoiding all actions of body, speech, or mind that injure others. On top of that, there is performing deeds to greatly benefit others. These are the teachings of the earlier ordinary vehicle (Hīnayāna) and the later extraordinary vehicle (Mahāyāna). Whatever individual, society, or nation is able to put these two aspects of Dharma into practice will pass from joy to joy in this life and the next; there is no doubt.

When people practice nonharming toward others, they prevent negative deeds by themselves and have no need whatsoever for external laws. On the other hand, when it comes to fearsome and violent criminals, it doesn't matter whether or not there's a law in place, they'll be lawless. And, if the whole world acted that way, there would be no path forward whatsoever for humanity.

Regarding a good heart, you cannot find it for sale in the marketplace, not even for a thousand coins of gold. No matter how much stature and wealth you have, you cannot come by it through extortion. No matter what kind of trickery you apply, you also cannot steal it from the wise. Why is that the case? The reason is that it needs to be cultivated in one's own mindstream. It doesn't arise from elsewhere, not even in the slightest. Since its highest expression is taught in the sublime Dharma, one should rely on that alone— nothing else.

These days, throughout the whole world, science and technology are flourishing. For that reason, externally with respect to things, material life is progressing rapidly. Due to the invention of airplanes and rockets, it's now possible to travel to the moon. There are also large factories with machines and robots that I have seen for myself. Since the creation of computers, various implements are being produced that no one could have imagined in their dreams.

A variety of machine-manufactured weapons to conquer enemies and defend allies are being deployed. It's beyond comprehension. Alongside that, in an instant, the whole world as we know it could be destroyed, reduced to dust through the right quantity and combination of noxious substances that don't decay.[42] With weapons filling the earth from top to bottom, this is an age of intense concern for the survival of every type of creature, who are [as vulnerable] as butter lamps in the wind.

Internally, with respect to mind, as material life improves, feelings of desire and hatred have become more crude, wild, and prevalent. This is really the case. In previous times, the harm that a single king or general could do was only to destroy one or two regions, not more than that. Now the president, representatives, or generals of warring nations could completely destroy the whole world. For that reason, the path forward for all living creatures depends on whether or not we have the intent to not harm others as well as to only perform their benefit. Here and now, apart from these two, what other way is there?

Furthermore, those so-called developing nationalities need to advance with respect to both external prosperity *and* internal values. For our well-being, we should not wish for the suffering of others and impoverish them for our own enrichment. There is no benefit whatsoever to giving rise to negative feelings of malice, deceit, and greed. If the greater society is filled with debased activities [based on such feelings], then whatever the outer wealth and standard of living will only lead to various kinds of suffering.[43]

Who is the creator of all our happiness and suffering? Both mind and body. However, among these two, it is the mind that guides action. If we seek perpetual well-being and joy, then from now onward, it will not be skillful to disturb the minds of people in general and specific nationalities in particular.[44] In that way, from the very beginning, it is explained in the Buddhist scriptures that we must certainly take rebirth within *saṃsāra* in one of the six realms.[45] Whether or not we understand this is therefore very important for the path forward into the future—if it is to be beneficial or harmful—for humanity at large.[46]

3. A Spontaneous Song of Victory

PEMA JAMYANG

INTRODUCTION

IN THE LAND of Snow under the clear blue sky stands one of the largest Buddhist institutions in the world, Larung Buddhist Academy. It is in this sacred place founded by Khenpo Jigme Phuntsok, referred to honorifically by Tibetans as His Holiness Jigme Phuntsok Rinpoche, that Khenpo Sodargye started his Dharma activities and has been giving systematic Dharma teachings to students from all over the world for more than thirty years. Khenpo Sodargye served as the translator for Han Chinese students in 1987 when Jigme Phuntsok Rinpoche visited Mount Wutai in central China. Shortly thereafter, the Han Chinese saṅgha formed at Larung Gar, and Khenpo Sodargye has been its esteemed teacher.

Over the years, the khenpo's teachings mainly focused on those treatises that Jigme Phuntsok Rinpoche had taught, such as treatises on the five major sūtra categories and also numerous esoteric tantric texts. Most of these texts were composed or commented on by Longchenpa and Jamgon Mipham, but they also include well-known treatises of the Sakya, Geluk, Kagyu, and Jonang schools.[1] In addition, the khenpo has delivered oral commentaries on songs by Jigme Phuntsok Rinpoche and prayers that he emphasized. Two such commentaries are translated in this chapter, elucidating the *Song of Victory: The Wondrous Sound of the Celestial Drum* by Jigme Phuntsok Rinpoche and *Wangdu, Great Clouds of Blessing* by Jamgon Mipham.[2] More specifically, Khenpo Sodargye has guided most of his Han students into Buddhism through two substantial texts, Śāntideva's *The Way of the Bodhisattva* (201 lectures in total) and Patrul Rinpoche's *Words of My Perfect Teacher* (144 lectures in total). In recent years, he has also spent considerable time explaining Buddhist scriptures such as the *Lotus Sūtra*, the *Vimalakīrti Sūtra*, and other fundamental texts for the Pure Land and Zen schools.

In recent years, Khenpo Sodargye has spent his time half at Larung Gar and half on tours to give talks in universities and other venues. In addition, every year he spends several months on translation. In this restless and chaotic modern age, Khenpo Sodargye does a good deal of online teaching, sharing his pure and profound wisdom by means of modern technology. His teachings, in person and online, include not only the most traditional Buddhist philosophies, but also contain the most sublime pith instructions of Vajrayāna. Never satisfied with only the traditional way of spreading the Dharma, he always pays attention to the world at large and to how people feel within their hearts and then discovers a suitable way of sharing the Dharma that can be easily accessible to modern people.

The Scope of Khenpo's Teachings

To thoroughly train his students in Buddhist studies, Khenpo Sodargye emphasizes a systematic approach of listening, contemplating, and meditating on the Dharma. Nowadays, hundreds of thousands of monastic disciples and lay followers around the world study traditional Buddhist scriptures with a modern approach under the guidance of Khenpo Sodargye. Through on-site, livestream, and video teachings, most students start with Patrul Rinpoche's *Words of My Perfect Teacher* and Śāntideva's *The Way of the Bodhisattva* and then go deeper with the whole collection of Five Great Treatises,[3] as well as many other related texts.

For those who have completed the preliminary practices for Dzogchen or Great Perfection teachings, Khenpo Sodargye gives them the profound Vajrayāna teachings and practices such as the *Guhyagarbha Tantra, Yeshe Lama, Trilogy of Finding Comfort and Ease, Trilogy of Natural Freedom, The Dzogchen Practice of Peaceful Mañjuśrī*, and more.[4] The khenpo believes it is fundamentally important for a Vajrayāna master to lay a solid theoretical foundation of Vajrayāna for his disciples; otherwise, Vajrayāna could easily become empty rituals and lose its profundity. As he said,

> In order to become a fit vessel for Vajrayāna, one must thoroughly understand how Mahāyāna and Vajrayāna are seamlessly integrated through the systematic learning of relevant theories. This is the basis for Vajrayāna practices, or else one could encoun-

ter many obstacles and even generate wrong views toward the Dharma.

Being aware that the cultivation of a good personality is indispensable in order to make oneself a capable vessel to receive and practice these Mahāyāna and Vajrayāna teachings, in recent years the khenpo has also given teachings on quite a few Chinese traditional scriptures, such as *Standards for Being a Good Pupil and Child* (*Di Zi Gui*), *The Classic of Filial Piety* (*Xiaojing*), and *The Analects of Confucius* (*Lun Yu*). Khenpo Sodargye believes that the traditional Chinese scriptures, particularly the wisdom of Confucius, provide a proper education to improve oneself into a person with noble qualities.

Beyond these traditional teachings, in 1999, Khenpo Sodargye wrote a book about Buddhism and science, where he elucidated many consistencies between these two fields.[5] The khenpo believes that in this modern age, Buddhist education must keep up with science. That does not mean that Buddhism needs to be verified by science, but, rather, it is easier for modern people to develop an initial understanding of Buddhism in secular terms compatible with science. If Buddhist education does not keep up with science, sooner or later, as an ancient religion, it will become outdated and disappear in this world.

For this reason, since 2010, the khenpo started a lecture tour in different universities in China and abroad. Originally, he aspired to give talks at one hundred universities. Very quickly, he achieved this goal; yet, he continues with this project and has also extended his public talks into the business community as well as prisons. Public talks in various settings have become one of the most productive ways for him to share Buddhist philosophy and practices with a general audience.

Starting in the late 1990s, people outside of Larung Gar could listen to the khenpo's teaching through MP3 audio recordings as well as on video, initially VCDs (video CDs) and more recently DVDs. It was in 2010 that the khenpo started livestreaming his formal teachings at Larung Gar. Every week from Monday to Friday, and sometimes also Saturday, the khenpo gives teachings at Larung Gar, and all these teachings are livestreamed to an online audience of up to tens of thousands. The spring of 2018 was the first time that the khenpo's live teachings on the *Vimalakīrti Sūtra* became available through simultaneous translation into English and Japanese. Over two years, Khenpo Sodargye finished the entire teaching with sixty-six lectures in August 2019, and following that, he started giving teachings on the

Śūraṅgama Sūtra, Uttaratantra Śāstra, as well as *The Analects of Confucius* in the same way.

For his websites and social media accounts in Chinese and English, there are special teams working on them, and the khenpo is regularly involved in the release of new material. For example, for every video or article based on a university lecture, he would take a look before uploading it online. He maintains his Weibo account himself, without getting any team members involved, while his Facebook page is maintained by his translation team, though we would frequently ask his advice on specific posts.

Brief Introduction to the Song of Victory

The *Song of Victory*[6] was an extemporaneous *vajra dohā*[7] recited by Jigme Phuntsok Rinpoche on September 21, 1996, when he had just recovered from a serious illness and returned to Larung Gar. Among many extemporaneous poems directly flowing from his enlightened wisdom, this is one of the most important. In this short song, Jigme Phuntsok Rinpoche summarizes the entire path of enlightenment into four main aspects, which are a virtuous personality, renunciation, *bodhicitta* (awakened heart), and nondual wisdom. Unlike Lama Tsongkhapa's *Three Principal Aspects of the Path*, where nondual wisdom is explained in the Mahāyāna context, Jigme Phuntsok Rinpoche here describes nondual wisdom from the perspective of Dzogchen, or the Great Perfection, the highest level of realization in Vajrayāna according to the Nyingma tradition.

Jigme Phuntsok Rinpoche requested that anyone who took refuge in or relied upon him should memorize the *Song of Victory* and grasp its profound meaning. As a tradition at Larung Gar, the *Song of Victory* is taught or chanted at least once at the beginning of each semester before a Dharma text is formally taught so that any obstacles that may occur during the process can be dispelled.

Khenpo Sodargye crafted the final translation of this text on March 6, 1997 and extensively explained this text to his Chinese disciples twice. The first time was in 1996, right after it was composed, and the second time in 2009, before he gave an extensive teaching on Patrul Rinpoche's *Words of My Perfect Teacher* to his monastic disciples and lay followers. Thereafter, the khenpo would frequently give the transmission of this text on different occasions. The current commentary on this text was based on those two oral teachings in Chinese, and the translation into English below was completed several years ago by his translation group, consisting of monastic disciples and lay followers.

Brief Introduction to Wangdu

Wangdu, Great Clouds of Blessings: The Prayer That Magnetizes All That Appears and All That Exists [8] is a highly valued practice at Larung Gar; it is a "pure vision" teaching, which arose in the wisdom mind of Jamgon Mipham. As a tradition, every teaching and every tutorial at Larung Gar begins with the recitation of this prayer three times. Jigme Phuntsok Rinpoche once said, "If I and my future lineage holders want to benefit sentient beings for all future lives, recitation of this prayer is the most effective means." Also, before he passed away, he said, "In the future, if my disciples recite *Wangdu* often, the heart transmissions of the guru will continue."

According to many great masters, the success of the Dharma activities of Jigme Phuntsok Rinpoche can be attributed to the practice of *Wangdu*, which makes Larung Gar one of the most influential Dharma centers in the world today. In order to create favorable conditions for his students to benefit sentient beings, Jigme Phuntsok Rinpoche made offerings to commission the monastic community at Larung Gar to recite *Wangdu* three times every day. Later, this was increased to five times a day. After he passed away, his niece Jetsun Ani Mumtso continues to make offerings to the monastic community for its daily recitation. Together, they have accumulated millions and millions of *Wangdu*.

In June 2012, when Khenpo Sodargye visited Mount Wutai and did a retreat there, he aspired to chant *Wangdu* ten thousand times and also promised to give a teaching on it in a thorough way. Then, during the annual Dharma Assembly of the Awareness Holders in February 2013 at Larung Gar, he gave an extensive teaching on this prayer with the hope that many Dharma practitioners could understand its profound meaning. Since then, Khenpo Sodargye has repeatedly encouraged Buddhist followers to recite *Wangdu* ten thousand times a year for the benefit of their own Dharma practice and as an aspiration to contribute to the flourishing of the Dharma. As he said during the teaching, "His Holiness Jigme Phuntsok Rinpoche had completely mastered the enlightened activity of magnetizing. I dare not say I want to achieve the same level of mastery as His Holiness, but as his disciple, I should at least follow the steps of the activities he created and endeavor with all my efforts to continue his traditions."

The commentary translated below is based on the khenpo's oral teaching in 2013; it was translated into English several years ago by his translation group.

About the Translation

Since the original sources for our translations are the khenpo's oral teachings, we needed to reorganize the materials to make them into a more coherent written format. This is true of the two commentaries translated in this chapter, which include outlines to help organize and relate the commentary to the root verses, which are, respectively, songs by Khenpo Jigme Phuntsok and Jamgon Mipham. The khenpo's teachings are extensive and systematic, yet also have a sense of humor. In our translation, we try to stay close to all of his key points, but sometimes we are afraid that many of his jokes are unfortunately missed.

Acknowledgments

Thanks to Ruth Wang for her initial translation of the *Song of Victory* and Yinqing Quan for her initial translation of *Wangdu* from Chinese transcripts into English, which allowed me to finalize the two translations and further reorganize them into well-structured texts. Thanks to Michael Glass for his careful and considerate editing to make the two translations more fluent and impressive. Thanks to other colleagues for their kind proofreading to make sure the final translations correctly rendered the original meaning of Khenpo Sodargye's teachings. Finally, thanks to Holly Gayley for her corrections of special Buddhist terms and for compiling everything to make it possible for these commentaries to be published.

Song of Victory: The Wonderful Sound of the Celestial Drum

Khenpo Jigme Phuntsok (1996)

HOMAGE

The embodiment of the wisdom of all the buddhas, who are the
    protectors of all sentient beings,
Venerable Mañjughoṣa, who appears as a young boy—
may you abide forever in my heart on the stamens of an eight-petaled
    lotus.
Bless me such that my words will benefit all sentient beings.

ENCOURAGEMENT TO PRACTICE VAJRAYĀNA

The Merit of Practicing Unsurpassed Vajrayāna

The Great Perfection, profound and luminous—
just hearing its verses allows one to break the roots of saṃsāra.
And, through the six-month practice of its essence to achieve
    liberation,
may you all engrave this in your hearts.

The Conditions for Practicing Vajrayāna

Those who with great fortune encounter such supreme teachings
must have been accumulating merit in previous lives through
    numerous eons
and possess the same conditions for achieving enlightenment
    as Buddha Samantabhadra.
Dharma friends, may you all be joyful.

ENCOURAGEMENT TO AROUSE THE MIND OF BODHICITTA

The Reasons for Arousing Bodhicitta

For the sake of all sentient beings submerged in the fearful ocean
  of saṃsāra,
in order to help them attain the eternal happiness of buddhahood,
you should shoulder the responsibility of benefiting others
and discard the poisonous food of attachment to yourselves.

The Merit of Arousing Bodhicitta

This blocks the gate to the lower realms,
allows you to attain the happiness of the higher realms,
and eventually leads you to ultimate liberation from saṃsāra.
You should practice this essential teaching without being distracted at all.

ENCOURAGEMENT TO AROUSE THE MIND OF RENUNCIATION

The Merit of Observing Precepts

For all kinds of grand events in saṃsāra,
do not have any thought of desire.
Do observe the pure precepts, the magnificent adornment of the world
to which human and gods make supreme offerings.

The Fault of Breaking Precepts

Since all temporary and ultimate happiness
results from observing the pure precepts
and breaking precepts leads one to take rebirth in lower realms,
you must make the right choices and not fall into confusion.

Encouragement to Develop a Virtuous Personality

The Reasons for Developing a Virtuous Personality

Always comply with your friends in word and deed.
Be a person of integrity filled with kindheartedness.
In order to benefit yourselves in the long term,
the pith instruction is to benefit others at the present moment.

The Merit of Maintaining a Virtuous Personality

These are the pure standards for being a good person,
the skillful means of all buddhas of the past, present, and future,
and the essence of the four dharmas of attraction.[9]
Each of you, my disciples, should never forget them!

Dedication

I dedicate this virtue to all sentient beings.
May they transcend the abyss of saṃsāra.
May all my heart disciples be joyful
and take rebirth in the western pure land of ultimate bliss.

In the seventeenth cycle of the Tibetan calendar and the year of the fire rat [1996], the teacher and the disciples had overcome all the external, internal, and secret hindrances. On this auspicious day, Ngawang Lodro Tsungme[10] celebrated the victory and sang extemporaneously among the almost five thousand monastics. SĀDHU!

Commentary on the Song of Victory

Khenpo Sodargye (1996 and 2009)

Importance of the Text

The Dharma activities of His Holiness Jigme Phuntsok Rinpoche's life can be divided into six main phases. Each phase is marked by an important pith instruction text. These six texts are *Advice Like the First Light of Dawn, Drops of My Heartfelt Advice, Nectar Drops of Advice, Song of Victory, Teachings of the Four Vehicles,* and *Teachings on Magnetizing All That Appears and Exists.* As well as these texts, there are also the teachings given just before His Holiness entered nirvāṇa.

These texts are not like ordinary articles drawn from a few years of academic research, but rather they are the essence of His Holiness's wisdom gained through a lifetime of study, reflection, and practice. His attained realization, his biography, and his considerable merit have proven him to be a great saint and an enlightened master in each of his lifetimes spanning from the time of Buddha Śākyamuni to that of Guru Padmasambhava. Not only has he accumulated abundant good karma in his previous lives, but during his present life, he has spent more than sixty years focused on the study, reflection, and practice of the Buddha's teachings, which he began around five years of age and continued into his late sixties. His Holiness has devoted his entire life to all sentient beings and Buddhism, and his words and teachings, distilled from such a deep well of wisdom, are indeed very precious.

The *Song of Victory* was an extemporaneous vajra dohā sung by His Holiness in front of almost five thousand ordained saṅgha on an auspicious victory-celebrating day, September 21, 1996, when His Holiness and his disciples had dispelled all the external, internal, and secret hindrances.

Those with wisdom will fully understand how transcendent the *Song of Victory* is after they study it. In the past, when His Holiness gave us teachings, we did not recognize their great worth to begin with. However, after constant contemplation of the Dharma and as time went by, along with exposure to various religious doctrines, we realized that His Holiness is indeed the most extraordinary of human beings.

The fact of the matter is that even though the Buddha taught eighty-four-thousand teachings, few would be able to master them all in one lifetime. However, now that His Holiness has summarized these teachings into this wonderful pith instruction based on his practice and realization, we should treasure it and try to comprehend its profound meaning.

Theoretically speaking, Dharma practitioners should study both sūtras and tantras extensively, such as the five great Mahāyāna treatises.[11] But, life is short, and it is hard to know how much longer one will live. Many changes can happen in a few brief moments, and nothing is certain. Therefore, the study of a short text containing great pith instructions is of enormous value to all practitioners; otherwise, they may not be adequately prepared when the time comes to leave this world.

His Holiness requested all his lineage disciples to teach or chant the *Song of Victory* once before they teach or study a Dharma text so that any obstacles that may occur during the process can be dispelled. Likewise, if someone aspires to follow the Dharma, chanting this text once beforehand will make their aspiration come true and protect them from encountering any obstacles. Additionally, any obstacles that may be encountered while studying or practicing the Dharma can be transformed into favorable conditions just by reading this text or by taking it with you everywhere. Therefore, His Holiness requested again and again that anyone who took refuge in or relied upon him should memorize the *Song of Victory* and grasp its profound meaning.

BACKGROUND OF THE TEXT

In September 1995, His Holiness Jigme Phuntsok Rinpoche planned to visit Taiwan and then to leave for Nepal to stay in Padmasambhava's cave for an Amitāyus Buddha retreat. But, after he arrived in Chengdu, there were some problems related to the processing of his passport application. He also suffered a deterioration in his physical health, and the hospital in Chengdu was unable to diagnose the cause of his illness. Consequently, he stayed in Chengdu for more than five months remaining in a state of samādhi, and, except during mealtimes, he did not utter a word.

Then one night, His Holiness had a dream in which Venerable Atiśa, Venerable Dromtonpa,[12] Jamgon Mipham, and Lama Lodro[13] all appeared to him. Venerable Atiśa silently cast his kind and loving gaze at His Holiness. Venerable Dromtonpa said, "We have come here because Venerable Atiśa is very concerned about you. These huge surging waves of the ocean will terminate on March 10. Do you understand the implications?" By this he meant that His Holiness would, at that time, fully recover from his illness. Venerable Atiśa and Venerable Dromtonpa then disappeared.

Jamgon Mipham remained seated majestically and prayed forcefully to Padmasambhava in an extremely wrathful way in order to dispel all external, internal, and secret hindrances and to vanquish various kinds of evils manifested from confusion and differentiation. After that, he transformed himself into a flash of light and disappeared.

Lama Lodro gave some merciful advice: "You should reside in the luminous state of Great Perfection, the great union of appearance and emptiness. Out of this profound concentration, you should benefit sentient beings with bodhicitta, exchanging others' suffering with your own happiness. Then, all unfavorable conditions will disappear into emptiness." He gave some other teachings and then also dissolved into luminosity.

After this dream, His Holiness began to recover slowly and, as predicted by Venerable Dromtonpa, he had completely recovered his health by March 10. On returning to Larung Gar, all his disciples gave His Holiness a most ceremonial welcome. He sang the *Song of Victory* extemporaneously among the fourfold assembly of all the disciples. Everybody's happiness at that moment was indescribable. His Holiness also named the college of Han disciples Victoriously Māra-Subduing Land, indicating the great victory.

THE MEANING OF THE TITLE

In the title, the word "victory" means that practitioners are able to dispel all external, internal, and secret obstacles and achieve the complete victory through the blessings of the guru and the Three Jewels. "Song" refers to a dohā, a song composed extemporaneously by an enlightened being with a certain level of realization. "The celestial drum" is a huge drum in the thirty-third heaven, the appearance of which is due to the great merit of celestial beings.

This "song of victory" is described by the metaphor "the wonderful sound of the celestial drum" because this drum has a natural sound that means, "all you celestial beings, do not fear." When celestial beings were battling the asuras, with the help of the wonderful sound of the celestial drum, they were able to defeat the asuras and win the battle. Hence, the title draws this analogy between the *Song of Victory* and the *Wonderful Sound of the*

Celestial Drum. This short text contains the essence of all the Sūtrayāna and Tantrayāna teachings, as well as the very profound pith instructions of His Holiness's lifetime of practice.

FOUR MAIN ASPECTS OF THE PATH

In the *Three Principal Aspects of the Path*, Lama Tsongkhapa discusses three main aspects, which are renunciation, bodhicitta, and nondual wisdom. However, in this short text, His Holiness summarizes the entire path of enlightenment into four main aspects, including the additional aspect of a virtuous personality. Also, nondual wisdom can be explained within both the Mahāyāna and the Vajrayāna paths. In the *Song of Victory*, nondual wisdom is described from the perspective of the Great Perfection, or Dzogchen, the highest level of realization in Vajrayāna practice, based on the view of emptiness in Mahāyāna teachings.

The realization of the Great Perfection is the most desirable enlightenment worthy of seeking by spiritual practitioners. What is the prerequisite for such enlightenment? It is bodhicitta. Without bodhicitta, as Śāntideva says in *The Way of the Bodhisattva*, there is no way to achieve full enlightenment no matter how much supreme merit one possesses. Then, how can bodhicitta arise in one's mind? For this to occur, one needs to first possess a mind of renunciation, which is in turn derived from a virtuous personality. Therefore, the sequence of practice should be: a virtuous personality to be a good person, a mind of renunciation to abandon all worldly attachment, an aspiration of bodhicitta to guide all living beings to achieve buddhahood, and, eventually, the practice of Dzogchen to achieve full enlightenment within a single lifetime. These are the four main aspects of the path that are summarized in this *Song of Victory*.

HOMAGE: SINCERE DEVOTION TO MAÑJUŚRĪ

The embodiment of the wisdom of all the buddhas, who are
    the protectors of all sentient beings,
Venerable Mañjughoṣa, who appears as a young boy—
may you abide forever in my heart on the stamens of an
    eight-petaled lotus.
Bless me such that my words will benefit all sentient beings.

In this verse, His Holiness Jigme Phuntsok Rinpoche is saying that the bud-dhas of all the worlds in the ten directions are the protectors of all sentient beings and that the aggregate wisdom of all the buddhas of the ten directions is embodied in Mañjuśrī, who appears as a young boy to benefit all sentient beings. So, we pray that Mañjuśrī will fill our eight-petaled lotus-hearts with his uniquely blessed bright sunlight and will remain perpetually in the stamens of our lotus hearts. And, we pray that, with the power from Mañjuśrī's compassion, our words can universally benefit all sentient beings in this world.

Here, an analogy is drawn between the eight-petaled lotus and the heart, which has many external, internal, and secret meanings in Vajrayāna and will not be discussed in detail here.

This is an homage to Mañjuśrī. His Holiness Jigme Phuntsok Rinpoche regarded Mañjuśrī as his main deity, and after meeting Mañjuśrī in person at Mount Wutai,[14] whenever he was going to compose a treatise, he would always first pay homage to Mañjuśrī. This demonstrates his extraordinary faith in Mañjuśrī.

His Holiness has always had a close affinity with Mañjuśrī since his child-hood. According to his biography, he recited the Mañjuśrī mantra OM A RA PA TSA NA DHĪḤ aloud as an infant immediately after he was born. At the age of six, he discovered a copy of the Speech Lion of Mañjuśrī hidden in a pile of rocks and noticed a verse at the end that said there was a man in India aged ninety-nine years old who after just one day of practice attained enlightenment when Mañjuśrī appeared before him.

His Holiness thought, "If someone that old could meet Mañjuśrī after just one day's practice, I should be able to practice and attain enlightenment without any problems because I am beginning at such a tender young age." He was thrilled and practiced with full concentration for a few days. Con-sequently, he experienced many signs of attainment and naturally mastered all the scriptures and commentaries in the sūtras and tantras.

His Holiness often emphasized that dharma practitioners should chant Mañjuśrī's mantra frequently and pray to Mañjuśrī often, because the power of the blessings from Mañjuśrī are quite special compared to those from other buddhas. As ordinary beings, we cannot determine whether Buddha Śākyamuni's blessing or Bodhisattva Mañjuśrī's blessing are more powerful, but it is quite possible to make a reasonable judgment according to relevant sūtras, since this has been explained in the related sūtras.

On the surface, Mañjuśrī appears as just a bodhisattva, but based on what is mentioned in the sūtras, he actually attained buddhahood a long time ago. He is the embodiment of the aggregate wisdom of buddhas and bodhisattvas from all the worlds of the ten directions and is regarded as the father of all buddhas. He guided infinite sentient beings to achieve buddhahood by motivating them to arouse bodhicitta. Hence, the power of his blessing is inconceivably amazing.

Everyone can benefit from the blessings of Mañjuśrī. The key lies in whether or not one has authentic faith in him. Once, when I visited Mount Wutai, I was constantly filled with the hope that I would see Mañjuśrī in person, and in the end, although I did not see Mañjuśrī, I was quite sure that I did receive some blessings, which enabled me to memorize and fully recite certain Dharma texts after reading them only a few times. So, I would say that different people may have different levels of faith, but as long as they are blessed by Mañjuśrī, all the scriptures and commentaries in Sūtrayāna and Tantrayāna will come to manifest in their minds. If one constantly prays to Mañjuśrī, wisdom will be bestowed upon this person lifetime after lifetime. And, meanwhile, blessings from all the buddhas can be transferred and integrated in the continuum of his or her mind.

A Great Story of Mañjuśrī

Once, when the Buddha was teaching the Dharma at Vulture Peak in the city below the mountain, there was a prostitute named Suvarṇottamaprabhāśrī.[15] She was very beautiful and enticingly attractive. But, more amazingly, her entire body glowed with a golden aura. Thus, the emperor, ministers, and all sorts of men became extremely enchanted by her. Although she was just a prostitute from a lowly caste, a huge crowd always surrounded her.

One day, she accompanied the son of a business owner on a shopping trip to the market. They were planning to have some fun at the amusement park. Along the way, Mañjuśrī transformed himself into a handsome young man, for he knew the circumstances were ready to enlighten Suvarṇottamaprabhāśrī. His entire body glowed with an extraordinarily dazzling light. Suvarṇottamaprabhāśrī noticed that the light radiating from the youth far surpassed her own golden rays and as she stood in the glow of his light, her own light was fading away. She became greedy for his clothing and immediately dumped the son of the business owner, climbed out of the vehicle they were traveling in, and attempted to seduce the young man with her beauty.

At that moment, Mañjuśrī empowered Vaiśravaṇa to say to Suvarṇottama-prabhāśrī, "You must not be envious of the young man, as he is the Bodhi-sattva Mañjuśrī, who is the aggregate of all the buddhas' wisdom. He can fulfill all your wishes. What do you need?" Suvarṇottamaprabhāśrī said, "I do not need anything except for his beautiful clothing." Mañjuśrī then replied, "If you can enter the door of bodhi, I will give my clothing to you." As she did not understand what that entailed, Mañjuśrī then started to give her detailed instructions.

At Vulture Peak, Śākyamuni Buddha voiced his praise, saying "Well done!" during the course of Mañjuśrī's teaching, which was so profound that it jolted the cosmos of a billion universes. Mañjuśrī's retinue asked the Buddha why he had said this. The Buddha replied, "Bodhisattva Mañjuśrī is preaching the Buddhadharma with compassion and wisdom in order to enlighten a prostitute. You may go there if you would like to listen." Many of the Buddha's disciples went over to hear Mañjuśrī's teaching. Some gained the purity of the Dharma eye and saw the truth clearly and purely. Some gained the full apprehension of the truth of no-birth; some achieved non-regressive fruition. Tens of thousands of sentient beings benefited from lis-tening to the teachings of Mañjuśrī.

Suvarṇottamaprabhāśrī also developed a firm understanding of the theory that nothing possesses a real existence. She really wanted to follow Mañjuśrī and to live her life as a Buddhist nun. But, Mañjuśrī told her that the path of renunciation did not necessarily mean shaving one's head but, rather, involved practicing Buddhadharma diligently and giving up one's self-interest for the benefit of others. Mañjuśrī also advised her to return to the vehicle of the business owner's son and leave with him.

When Suvarṇottamaprabhāśrī and the son of the business owner re-turned to the amusement park, they came face-to-face with imperma-nence as she died in his embrace. At first, he was greatly saddened. But as her body started to gradually decay, with blood and pus effusing from her eyes, ears, nostrils, and mouth, and a foul smell emanating from her body, the businessman's son became extremely frightened and ran all the way to Vulture Peak to seek protection from Śākyamuni Buddha. Śākya-muni Buddha imparted the Buddhadharma to him, and he attained full apprehension of the truth of no-birth. The Buddha then predicted: "Due to the empowerment of Bodhisattva Mañjuśrī in inspiring her motiva-tion, Suvarṇottamaprabhāśrī will attain buddhahood in the future and will be named Ratnaprabha.[16] And, the son of the business owner will become a bodhisattva acting on her behalf and will be named Bodhisattva Guṇaratnaprabha."[17]

The son of the business owner was puzzled: "Why will the disciple of Bodhisattva Mañjuśrī Suvarṇottamaprabhāśrī attain Buddhahood, but I, a disciple of the Buddha, will only become a bodhisattva?" He could not understand this. The Buddha said, "The merits of Bodhisattva Mañjuśrī are inconceivable. I also made my initial vow to develop bodhicitta in front of Mañjuśrī, as did the immeasurable number of buddhas in the past, so have the immeasurable number of buddhas of the present, and so will it be for the immeasurable number of buddhas in the future."[18]

The Right Motivation of Receiving the Teaching

His Holiness Jigme Phuntsok Rinpoche composed this text neither for the sake of recovering from his grave illness nor for the desire to become wealthy or to attain happiness for himself. Rather, he prayed for Mañjuśrī's blessing in order to benefit all living beings, temporarily or ultimately, through his words and his teachings. Likewise, we also need to examine our motives when receiving his teaching. Some people muddle along without any sense of purpose. They see others go for the teaching, so they follow them without any specific purpose. As a matter of fact, the purpose of receiving Dharma teachings should be to benefit the numerous sentient beings, not just for the benefit of oneself. Each practitioner should adjust his or her motivation accordingly.

Encouragement to Practice Vajrayāna

The Merit of Practicing Unsurpassed Vajrayāna

The Great Perfection, profound and luminous—
just hearing its verses allows one to break the roots of saṃsāra.
And, through the six-month practice of its essence to achieve
   liberation,
may you all engrave this in your hearts.

The Incredible Merit of Dzogchen
The unsurpassed Great Perfection, or Dzogchen, which proclaims the luminous essence of *tathāgatagarbha* (buddha-nature), is difficult for ordinary

people to fully understand, and so it is often criticized by those with little wisdom. However, one can cut off the root causes of saṃsāra simply by listening to its verses, and those with great capacities are able to attain liberation if they practice its essence diligently for six months. Therefore, we should all seek to have this Great Perfection deeply engraved in our hearts.

The Great Perfection is the essence of all sūtras and tantras, and its merits are beyond all description. People can attain liberation by merely hearing its words, touching its texts, attaching them to their body, or understanding their meaning. According to Āryadeva's *Four Hundred Stanzas on the Middle Way*, people with doubts about emptiness are still able to break free from the cyclic existence of the three realms. This is even more true for those who have learned the unsurpassed Vajrayāna.

If someone with extraordinary faith and strong conviction practices Dzogchen by following the sequence of preliminary, main, and concluding practice, that person may attain liberation in six months. It is stated in the *Vajrapañjara Tantra*, "If one has been practicing for six months with unshaken faith and conviction, one will be able to attain the fruit of Vajradhara." It is also mentioned in the *Tantric Solemn Oath*, "With determined faith and conviction, one will attain the fruit of Vajradhara in six months." This is also stated in the *Chetsun Nyingthig* and the *Longchen Nyingthig*.

Hence, the Great Perfection is truly transcendent. Jamgon Mipham said in his teachings, "In this degenerate age, sentient beings are burdened with deep and heavy afflictions, which cannot be easily mitigated by other dharma methods. But, one can completely cast off all the afflictions with the unsurpassed Great Perfection."

Here, His Holiness told us that since the Great Perfection is so extraordinary, we must not abandon or defame it. If one really cannot arouse faith in it, it is okay to leave it alone or to bring up one's doubts in front of authentic teachers. However, one must not have preconceived negative ideas about Vajrayāna without a proper reason.

An Amazing Example of a Dzogchen Practitioner

I have personally witnessed quite a few Dzogchen practitioners who achieved the realization of Dzogchen and had auspicious appearances before death. And, I was particularly impressed with a Han bhikṣuṇī named Ming Hui. Below is her story.

Ming Hui had enormous faith in the Vajrayāna. Originally, she was being treated for an illness in the Han area. Later, she learned that His Holiness

Jigme Phuntsok Rinpoche was going to teach Dzogchen at Larung Gar. She recognized the impermanence of life, and not knowing how much longer she had to live, she decided to go back to Larung Gar to receive the teaching. His Holiness lectured on Longchenpa's *Finding Comfort and Ease in the Nature of Mind* for about one hundred days, and she studied very diligently during that period.

On September 1, 1993, after the teaching ended, she returned to the Han area to receive further treatment from the doctor. On March 1, 1994, her caretaker and Dharma friend, the bhikṣuṇī Zhen Ru called me from Jinfeng Monastery, where they were living, and said that Ming Hui had died and at the moment of her passing, she held a dignified sitting position and prayed to her lineage guru and Amitābha. When her body began to shrink, a number of auspicious signs appeared. It was exactly six months after her completion of the teachings to the day of her death, not one day more or less. This was indeed a very rare occurrence.

Ming Hui did not always appear to be the most intellectually gifted, but her faith was indeed very strong. The prerequisites for those with great capacities to practice the Great Perfection are primarily their faith and conviction. Those with the strongest faith in their gurus, in the Three Jewels, and especially in Vajrayāna, who will not abandon their faith even at their deathbeds, will indeed achieve great accomplishments. Hence, His Holiness said, "It is very difficult to encounter the Great Perfection during this degenerate age, for it is such an extraordinary path." We must keep these words firmly in our hearts.

The Preliminary Practice of Dzogchen

Many Vajrayāna followers nowadays believe one must rely on the original purity or luminosity in order to effectively discover the true nature of one's mind. Indeed, as an ordinary practitioner, one must start with the preliminary practice and can then become empowered to take on the main practice. Venerable Longchenpa, Jamgon Mipham, and His Holiness Jigme Phuntsok Rinpoche have all set out rigorous requirements for the practice of Dzogchen. It is crucial to abide by this sequence of practice; otherwise, one would struggle to achieve proper realization. As such, it is like trying to paint beautiful motifs on the walls of a building when its foundation has not yet been stabilized. The risk is that, after a while, the whole building would collapse. Therefore, we should only start painting on the walls after the foundation has been made secure and safe.

The Conditions for Practicing Vajrayāna

Those who, with great fortune, encounter such supreme teachings
must have been accumulating merit in previous lives through
  numerous eons
and possess the same conditions for achieving enlightenment as
  Buddha Samantabhadra.
Dharma friends, may you all be joyful.

The Same Conditions with Buddha Samantabhadra

Here, "supreme teaching" refers to the great teaching of Dzogchen, and "those with great fortune" refers to those who have received the initiation for or listened to the teaching of the Great Perfection or those who have a similar auspicious connection with Dzogchen. His Holiness says, "For those who have had the opportunity to encounter the Great Perfection, it is a result of accumulated merits over many lives. To be able to encounter such a great teaching is like sharing a similar karmic circumstance with Buddha Samantabhadra, a position that is worthy of joy and delight."

All of us have had the good fortune in this life to have met our gurus, to receive their teachings on Vajrayāna, and to have received empowerments and pith instructions. Such wondrous encounters with Vajrayāna are the result of the good karma accumulated through numerous previous lives. Venerable Longchenpa made two inferences in *The Treasury of the Supreme Vehicle*. First, since we have encountered the unsurpassed Vajrayāna in this life, we must have made offerings and attended to an infinite number of buddhas and have been their followers or disciples in our past lives. Second, since we have encountered the unsurpassed Vajrayāna, we will definitely attain realization in this present life, during the *bardo*, or in a future life.

So, according to the inferences of Buddhist logic, if one has heard and studied Vajrayāna, this person must possess a transcendental affinity with Vajrayāna. We are, in fact, sharing a similar circumstance with Buddha Samantabhadra which has allowed us to encounter Dzogchen in this present life. It is because of this transcendental tantric Dharma that Samantabhadra attained the state of self-liberation in one split second. It is an accumulation of our good karma in numerous previous lives to encounter this supreme teaching.

As it is said in *Prajñāpāramitā Sūtra*, a person who is lost and wandering in the forest would have the sense that he was close to a village once he saw a cattleman. By seeing a cattleman, he would know he could leave behind his fear of being lost. Similarly, once we have encountered a vajra guru who guides us on the Vajrayāna path, like a fish that has been hooked and will surely be pulled to the shore, we will soon be liberated.

Do Not Break the Vows of Vajrayāna

However, if one slanders Vajrayāna or betrays the guru and his teachings, the consequences will be very serious. The Vajrayāna vows are very rigorous, and if one breaks the vows, this person will indeed accumulate negative karma that can lead him or her to the lower realms. This applies not only for Vajrayāna vows, but also for the bodhisattva vows, and even the precepts for lay Buddhists, which are also very stringent. If one takes refuge in the Three Jewels today and criticizes the Three Jewels tomorrow, one will definitely sink into the three lower realms. Therefore, His Holiness said in his other teachings that as long as one does not break the vows in this present life, one will become accomplished in the next life even if one does not practice diligently. Vajrayāna practitioners must be determined to keep the vows in this very life.

ENCOURAGEMENT TO AROUSE THE MIND OF BODHICITTA

The Reasons for Arousing Bodhicitta

For the sake of all sentient beings submerged in the fearful ocean
     of saṃsāra,
in order to help them attain the eternal happiness of buddhahood,
you should shoulder the responsibility of benefiting others
and discard the poisonous food of attachment to yourselves.

Why Should We Take the Responsibility of Altruism?

We must shoulder the immense responsibility of benefiting others by discarding the unhelpful and dangerous attachment to our own egos in order to help sentient beings steeped in the cyclical horror of saṃsāra to achieve the ultimate happiness of buddhahood.

In general, living beings can be classified into two categories. First, the enlightened beings are those who have already obtained either temporary or ultimate peace and happiness. These are *arhats, pratyekabuddhas,* bodhisattvas, and buddhas who have achieved perfect merit and wisdom. The other category includes deluded or ignorant beings who have never tasted such peace and happiness gained through enlightenment and have been driven by karma to wallow in saṃsāra and be exposed to dangerous circumstances.

Saṃsāra means wandering about or moving on without interruption. There are six realms of beings in saṃsāra: gods, asuras, human beings, animals, hungry ghosts, and hell beings. All these beings wander about in the six realms. Some would be lifted into the three higher realms where the suffering is not as fierce. But some could be instantly dragged into the abyss of three lower realms by their own negative karma. As said in Candrakīrti's *Introduction to the Middle Way,*

> Beings think "I" at first and cling to self.
> They think of "mine" and are attached to things.
> They, thus, turn helplessly as buckets on a waterwheel,
> and to compassion for such beings, I bow down![19]

Based on the authentic teachings and the personal perceptions of the enlightened buddhas and bodhisattvas, we have learned clearly that all deluded beings have previously been our parents and now are suffering. So carefully have they cared for and tended to us that we are closely connected to each other. Even though they do not recognize us now, anyone with any conscience would never leave them behind to pursue his or her own peace and happiness but would also seek to give them as much peace and happiness as possible, that is, to liberate them forever from the dreadful ocean of saṃsāra and attain supreme enlightenment.

Therefore, we need to assume responsibility to help them gain temporal happiness by providing them with good food and clothing, while at the same time guiding them to achieve the ultimate happiness through the realization of arhats, bodhisattvas, and buddhas. We must, as much as possible, rid ourselves of the poison that is selfishness to avoid serious retributions. It is stated in Śāntideva's *The Way of the Bodhisattva,*

> If to serve myself I harm another,
> I'll suffer later in the realms of hell.
> But if for others' sake I harm myself,
> Then every excellence will be my heritage.[20]

Discard the Poison-Like Attachment to Oneself
When Ra Lotsāwa[21] was meditating on his deity in a quiet place, he realized that he had wanted to be in this kind of solitary retreat all of his life. But, one day his deity told him, "You might as well go out to benefit living beings. The merits of even a brief moment of doing so will be much greater than diligently meditating on your deity in quiet isolation for billions of eons." Hence, the merits of being altruistic and helping others are far greater than self-absorbed penance even for endless years.

Again, Śāntideva's *The Way of the Bodhisattva* says,

> All the joy the world contains
> Has come through wishing happiness for others.
> All the misery the world contains
> Has come through wanting pleasure for oneself.[22]

Therefore, we must not allow our bodhicitta to drift away in the course of our practice. Patrul Rinpoche said, "If you practice the unsurpassed Great Perfection without the basis of bodhicitta, it will become the practice of Hīnayāna or a *tīrthika*."

That was why His Holiness Jigme Phuntsok Rinpoche said that selfishness is like a poison, an excellent metaphor that we should often contemplate. People with a strong sense of selfishness will fail eventually, regardless of where they are situated. Most of our arguments, afflictions, and quarrels are the products of selfishness, which would not appear if we became selfless. Thus, we should strive toward this goal to become real bodhisattvas.

In fact, we need not pay much attention to what people say, but instead should just do whatever is possible to benefit others when we are still alive and able. Whether people are aware of what we are doing or not, it is quite alright either way. I believe that some of the things that we have done may not ever be known by other people in our lifetime, but all the buddhas and bodhisattvas, as well as our gurus, will clearly know. The law of causality will always prevail. Therefore, it is of no value to help others for the sake of our own reputation and fame. Rather than being contaminated by all kinds of worldly concern, we should solely resolve to try our best to benefit others.

The Merit of Arousing Bodhicitta

This blocks the gate to the lower realms,
allows you to attain the happiness of the higher realms,
and eventually leads you to ultimate liberation from saṃsāra.
You should practice this essential teaching without being
    distracted at all.

The Merit of Bodhicitta

The merits of arousing bodhicitta include: blocking the gate to the lower realms, allowing us to obtain relative temporal peace and happiness in the higher realms of human beings and gods, and enabling us to ultimately attain liberation from saṃsāra. With the understanding of this fact, every Dharma practitioner should focus on the practice of this essential teaching.

The merits of bodhicitta, either the bodhicitta of aspiration or the bodhicitta of action, are immeasurable and boundless. This has been addressed in great detail in *Compendium of Trainings, The Way of the Bodhisattva*, and many other Mahāyāna sūtras. Simply put, the merits of bodhicitta can be manifested in two ways. First, if one arouses genuine bodhicitta, all negative karma can be eliminated in one's mindstream; as a result, the doors to the lower realms are blocked. Śāntideva says:

> Just as by the fires at the end of time,
> Great sins are utterly consumed by bodhicitta.
> Thus, its benefits are boundless,
> As the Wise and Loving Lord explained to Sudhana.[23]

The "great sins" refer to heavily negative karma that is difficult to purify, such as those accumulated through the five crimes with immediate retribution[24] or by criticizing the Dharma. But, they can all be eliminated the moment bodhicitta arises in one's mind, like the fire at the end of time burning out the entire world. If one's negative karma is cleansed, there will be no chance of falling into the lower realms.

Hence, His Holiness said that a person with bodhicitta cannot possibly fall into lower realms. We must try our best to generate bodhicitta before we die and must make sure our bodhicitta is not impaired after it arises. In this way, we will avoid rebirth in the lower realms.

Second, with bodhicitta, one's virtuous roots will become stronger and stronger. Consequently, one can gain rebirth as a human being or god to enjoy all the temporal peace and happiness of the higher realms. Furthermore, one can perfect all the merits of the five paths and ten bhūmis and attain the ultimate and unsurpassable fruit of buddhahood.

Therefore, the benefits of bodhicitta are indeed immense for living beings. Śāntideva also said,

> The pain-dispelling draft,
> This cause of joy for those who wander through the world—
> This precious attitude, this jewel of mind,
> How shall we calculate its merit?[25]

Conclusion Made by Buddhas

It is the conclusion made by buddhas through long-term contemplations with their unsurpassable wisdom in numerous eons. They are just like scientists who devote themselves to research for a long period of time so that they can invent something they believe will be of great benefit to all humankind. Similarly, the Buddha discovered that bodhicitta would bring the most benefit to all living beings. After repeated observations over a long period of time, it was found that innumerable living beings can readily attain the supreme fruit of buddhahood by arousing bodhicitta in their minds. Therefore, Śāntideva said,

> The mighty buddhas, pondering for many ages,
> Have seen that this and only this will save
> The boundless multitudes,
> And bring them easily to supreme joy.[26]

Hence, His Holiness encourages all his disciples to cultivate bodhicitta and practice this essential teaching without distraction. We must not allow our minds to be tempted by the eight worldly concerns and lose our direction. We must earnestly practice the pith instruction of bodhicitta, for it is the most important and precious approach among all the practices.

ENCOURAGEMENT TO AROUSE THE MIND OF RENUNCIATION

The Merit of Observing Precepts

For all kinds of grand events in saṃsāra,
do not have any thought of desire.
Do observe the pure precepts, the magnificent adornment
of the world,
to which human and gods make supreme offerings.

Real Mind of Renunciation

In order to achieve ultimate liberation from saṃsāra, we must not have even the slightest thought of desire toward the glitz and wealth of this ordinary world. Instead, we should conscientiously observe the pure precepts, to which humans and gods make their transcendent offerings.

For those who hope to break away from reincarnation and attain liberation, the attainment of fame, power, high social status, and sensual enjoyment should be totally meaningless and not stir up any desire within them. If they sincerely view luxurious cars and mansions as if they were just objects in a dream, illusions, or bubbles, and truly feel that the three realms are nothing but a house on fire without any momentary bliss, they have aroused a real mind of renunciation.

However, in the beginning, many people are just like Nanda (the Buddha's half-brother) and have difficulties in completely abandoning yearnings and attachment toward worldly life. But, if we persist in studying Buddhist teachings, we will eventually become aware of the insecurity of saṃsāra and further arouse renunciation in ourselves.

So, how to arouse a real mind of renunciation? There is no better approach than contemplating the four thoughts that turn the mind away from saṃsāra: the preciousness of being born a human being, the impermanence of life, the defects of saṃsāra, and the infallibility of the law of cause and effect. After we have completed these four common preliminary practices, true renunciation will most certainly arise in our mindstreams. At that time, we will constantly long for liberation from saṃsāra, just like a prisoner desperately wanting to be freed from his prison. Lama Tsongkhapa says in his *Three Principal Aspects of the Path*,

Freedom and endowments are difficult to find
and life has no time to spare.
By gaining familiarity with this,
attraction to the appearances of this life is reversed.

By thinking over and over again
that actions and their effects are infallible,
and repeatedly contemplating the miseries of cyclic existence,
attraction to the appearances of future lives is reversed.

When, by having trained in that way,
there is no arising, even for a second,
of attraction to the pleasures of cyclic existence,
and all day and night the intention seeking liberation arises—
then, the thought of renunciation has been generated.[27]

The Magnificent Adornment in the World
Having aroused renunciation, we must receive and uphold the pure precepts, which are the most magnificent adornment in the world and to which
humans and gods make offerings. The precepts are the foundation of all
virtuous qualities. This is declared in the *Sūtra of Individual Liberation*,
that "it is a bridge for going to good destinies." It is not very appropriate for
monastic Buddhists to adorn themselves with jewelry such as earrings and
bracelets. But, a practitioner endowed with untainted precepts, which is the
most dignified adornment, is worthy of prostration, worship, and offerings
from humans and gods.

All sentient beings have different capacities to receive their own levels of
precepts. Those with a stronger mind of renunciation can receive ordination
and observe the novice, bhikṣu, or bhikṣuṇī precepts. But, if circumstances
do not allow one to leave home and join a monastic community, one should
at least observe one of the five precepts for lay practitioners or take the refuge vows guided by a mind of renunciation. It is almost impossible for a
practitioner to accumulate any merit if none of these precepts are carefully
observed. In *Letter to a Friend*, Nāgārjuna states,

Keep your vows unbroken, undegraded,
Uncorrupted, and quite free of stain.

Just as the earth is the base for all that's still or moves,
On discipline, it's said, is founded all that's good.[28]

The earth is the basis of everything on this planet. Similarly, all merit is born on the basis of precepts. If one does not receive or uphold any precept, it will be difficult for that person to be reborn even as a human or a celestial being, not to mention attain liberation. That is why in the *Thirty-Seven Practices of a Bodhisattva*, Thokme Zangpo says,

If, lacking discipline, one cannot accomplish one's own good,
It is laughable to think of accomplishing the good of others.
Therefore, to observe discipline
Without saṃsāric motives is the practice of a bodhisattva.[29]

The Fault of Breaking Precepts

Since all temporary and ultimate happiness
results from observing the pure precepts
and breaking precepts leads one to take rebirth in lower realms,
you must make the right choices and not fall into confusion.

The temporary benefits of taking rebirth in the realms of humans and gods and the ultimate happiness of enlightenment and liberation all result from observing the pure precepts. If one breaks the vows and does not repent completely, one will definitely fall into one of the three lower realms. Therefore, it is imperative that a practitioner chooses correctly in his or her own conduct in order to avoid falling into confusion.

It is stated in the *Sūtra of Individual Liberation* that the only destination for those who break precepts is the three lower realms of the hell beings, hungry ghosts, and animals. Accordingly, the *Condensed Prajñāpāramitā Sūtra* also says, "Those who break their precepts cannot even help themselves, let alone benefit others."

Observing the pure precepts has become more and more difficult in this degenerate age. In particular, it is becoming more difficult for monastics to follow uncontaminated precepts in this highly commercialized information age. Televisions, laptops, and cell phones provide constant sensory stimulation and continual temptation. As a result, many people do not have true renunciation in their minds, and very few can stay in remote and solitary places and focus solely on the practice of Dharma, as did practitioners in ancient times.

Therefore, if one has a certain level of renunciation and a sincere desire to achieve enlightenment, it is quite necessary to take the threefold refuge vow and observe the five precepts. If a person has broken any of these vows, he or she should receive them again from a qualified teacher.

The reason for this is that, in the same way that flowers, grass, and trees can only grow from soil, all merit grows and prospers on the basis of precepts. In one of his texts, *The Main Path to Enlightenment*, Lama Tsongkhapa specifically refers to a teaching in the sūtras that says in the degenerate age, the merit of holding even one day's precepts would outdistance the merit of making offerings to buddhas and bodhisattvas in thousands of millions of eons. Therefore, we must not be confused and miss our aim in this degenerate age. We should be extremely careful in our choices to accept the causes and conditions that will help protect our precepts and to discard the unfavorable conditions that will lead us to break our vows. This should be the goal we all strive toward!

ENCOURAGEMENT TO DEVELOP A VIRTUOUS PERSONALITY

Reasons for Developing a Virtuous Personality

Always comply with your friends in word and deed.
Be a person of integrity filled with kindheartedness.
In order to benefit yourselves in the long term,
the pith instruction is to benefit others at the present moment.

The Importance of a Virtuous Personality

A virtuous personality entails that we must always be respectful with our family members and friends in what we say and do, to be kind and act with integrity, and to benefit others in the present moment if we wish to benefit ourselves in the long run.

Dharma practice requires a virtuous personality. This is the essential teaching summarized by His Holiness through many years of his teachings. His Holiness required that anyone who studies at Larung Gar must follow three rules: to cultivate a virtuous personality, to uphold the pure precepts, and to listen, reflect, and meditate on the Dharma teachings.

Regardless of whether one studies the Mahāyāna or Vajrayāna teachings, it is imperative that one has a virtuous personality; otherwise, making any progress in one's Dharma practice becomes impossible. Jamgon Mipham says in *Words on the Mundane and Transmundane Codes*,

> Worldly rules are the foundation of Buddhadharma.
> If one does not act nobly in the world,
> one will never grasp the supreme principle of Buddhadharma,
> not to mention achieve enlightenment.

What Is a Virtuous Personality?

In this verse, His Holiness identified the following standards for a virtuous personality and expected us to remember them well.

Always comply with your friends in word and deed.

We must always get along peacefully with our family members and friends regardless of their age and status. From a worldly perspective, a person with good characteristics is respectful to those of higher status, compassionate to the less privileged, and gets along harmoniously with those who are their equals.

There is a metaphor in Tibetan areas: "When one hundred yaks climb uphill, the *gaba* (the inferior type of yak) runs downhill." This is a very vivid illustration. A man who has a negative personality is always clashing with others in his behavior. People all feel relieved when someone like this leaves the group. It is like having a pterygium removed from one's eye; its departure is reason for celebration.

As the Buddha says, "I will comply with worldly people." If the Buddha behaves in this way, we ordinary human beings must surely do the same. Of course, compliance does not mean being without principles. Compliance does not mean that one should comply with other's greed or hatred. We comply with deeds that are rational and in accordance with the Dharma, and in this way, we get along harmoniously with everyone.

Be a person of integrity . . .

Whatever we say and do, we must be fair-minded, honest, and impartial. We must be free of self-attachment and aversion to others. Additionally, we must never place ourselves in a dominant position nor judge things unfairly. We must abide by the truth and be impartial. Hence, it is imperative to be a person of integrity. Then, no matter how we have been misunderstood or defamed, we will never really be harmed. Our kind and honest nature will shine like pure gold and not be tarnished by hindrances or darkness.

. . . with kindheartedness.

If someone appears to have integrity and seems to be willing to comply with other people, but is vicious in mind, then this person's moral quality is questionable. The mind is the root of everything. Lama Tsongkhapa said,

> If the intention is good, the levels and paths are good.
> If the intention is bad, the levels and paths are bad.
> Since everything depends on intentions,
> always make sure they are positive.[30]

If one is kindhearted, everything will be bright; but if one does not set his or her heart right, one will only be moving toward darkness.

These three principles of being a decent person are of great importance. His Holiness further pointed out that if we would like to benefit ourselves in the long run, being of benefit to other people in the moment is fundamental. As ordinary human beings, it is impractical never to think of our own well-being, but if we harm those around us in the process of pursuing our own goals, we will not advance. It may appear to be a kind of selfishness to help others for the sake of our own benefit. It is indeed better to not have such thoughts. If you really cannot arouse a truly altruistic mind, you should at least try to be kind to other people for your own advantage and survival.

His Holiness once said jokingly, "After having lived for this many years, I have noticed that many people have very little worldly wisdom. Most of them are only selfishly trying to benefit themselves, even though this is not necessarily a good strategy. For example, a young person may love someone and try everything possible to possess the other party, including restricting his or her freedom. The result is often counterproductive. Others may take a different approach by wholeheartedly supporting and helping the person they love. By doing so, they are more likely to be accepted by the objects of their affection. When we study Buddhadharma, if we do not realize how important a virtuous personality is, and do not try to cultivate good characteristics, we will not be able to reach any state of realization in our practice."

The Merit of Maintaining a Virtuous Personality

These are the pure standards for being a good person,
the skillful means of all buddhas of the past, present, and future,
and the essence of the four dharmas of attraction.
Each of you, my disciples, should never forget them!

From a secular and purely ethical perspective, possessing a virtuous personality is seen as synonymous with being a good person. From the perspective of seeking enlightenment, it is the most effective means of achieving buddhahood for all buddhas of the past, present, and future. It is also the essence of the four dharmas of attraction that bodhisattvas follow. All Buddhists should keep this in mind and never forget.

Virtuous personalities are "pure standards for being a good person," the basic principles that govern the life of a decent human being. During Buddhism's prime period in Tibetan history, Emperor Songtsen Gampo set up sixteen guidelines for being a good person,[31] which included developing devotion for the Three Jewels, seeking out and practicing the sacred Dharma, repaying the kindness of one's parents, being honest, having little jealousy, and so on.

A virtuous personality is not only essential in a worldly life, but more importantly, it is a guide to an enlightened life. In fact, it is the path of the most skillful means to attain buddhahood for all buddhas of the past, present, and future. Regardless of which buddha we are referring to, he or she must have been a good person prior to enlightenment.

Even if we put aside the accomplishments of their realization and enlightenment, we can easily tell that truly enlightened masters are extremely attractive in terms of their personal charisma. For myself, I have followed and relied upon many great spiritual teachers in my life, and the appeal of their words and deeds exceeds ordinary people's imagination. These great teachers, as a result of their virtuous personalities, have reached a unique state beyond the secular world.

Virtuous personalities are also "the essence of the four dharmas of attraction," which include: giving what others like in order to lead them to love and receive the truth; speaking gentle words with the same purpose; giving benefit to others with the same purpose; and cooperating with and adapting oneself to others to lead them into the truth. These are the four major methods of bodhisattvas to benefit sentient beings, and they are all built upon a virtuous personality. With a virtuous personality, one is willing to give, to speak pleasing words, to benefit others, and to cooperate with and adapt oneself to others in order to lead them to enlightenment.

The Heart Advice of His Holiness

Because of the reasons given above, His Holiness offered this heart advice: "Those of my students who have faith in me must always remember to be a virtuous person now and in the future. If you cannot be a good person, all your other cultivations are like trees without roots and will never grow and flourish."

In the past, the esteemed Kadampa masters would first observe the personality of students before admitting them as disciples. If students were not decent people, the masters would not accept them as disciples nor pass on the Dharma lineage to them. On the other hand, if a student was a good person but may have been less learned, the masters would still expect him or her to be a good student. Therefore, a virtuous personality, rather than intelligence, is the critical element here. A good person is not necessarily one with an attractive appearance, a beautiful voice, and elegant manners; he or she must be kindhearted.

It is not unusual for people to have differences in opinions on minor issues. Even some bhikṣus and bhikṣuṇīs in the saṅgha around the Buddha experienced these kinds of problems. But, overall, no matter which school is followed, either from a Mahāyāna or Vajrayāna background, a saṅgha needs to remain a congenial community and to have a harmonious and cohesive atmosphere. This is also a manifestation of a virtuous personality.

In summary, His Holiness Jigme Phuntsok Rinpoche addressed four major pith instructions in this text, which are nondual wisdom in the context of Mahāyāna and Vajrayāna teachings, bodhicitta, renunciation, and virtuous personality. These four pith instructions are the essence of all eighty-four thousand Dharma teachings being summarized through his theoretical study and personal realization. Each of us must keep them firmly in mind.

DEDICATION

I dedicate this virtue to all sentient beings.
May they transcend the abyss of saṃsāra.
May all my heart disciples be joyful
and take rebirth in the western pure land of ultimate bliss.

The merit and virtuous roots resulting from the composition of this song have been transferred to all sentient beings to help them transcend the horrifying abyss of the six realms of saṃsāra. The essence of the eighty-four thousand Dharma methods has been summed up in the four pith instructions addressed above. May great bliss arise in the hearts and minds of those with faith in His Holiness Jigme Phuntsok Rinpoche and in Buddhism. May all sentient beings, with auspicious affinity, be reborn in the western pure land, attain ultimate peace and happiness, and benefit innumerable sentient beings in the future.

COLOPHON

In the seventeenth cycle of the Tibetan calendar and the year of the fire rat [1996], the teacher and the disciples had overcome all the external, internal, and secret hindrances. On this auspicious day, Ngawang Lodro Tsungme celebrated the victory and sang extemporaneously among the almost five thousand monastics. SĀDHU!

There are sixty years in a full cycle of the Tibetan calendar. The chronological record of Tibetan history began in 1027 CE. The year His Holiness composed the *Song of Victory* was in the seventeenth cycle of the Tibetan calendar in the year of the fire rat on September 21, 1996. As mentioned earlier, this was when His Holiness returned to the monastery after overcoming all external, internal, and tantric hindrances, and had a joyous reunion with all of his disciples. The monastery arranged a Vajra Entertainment Dharma Assembly for this special occasion, during which the entire narrative of His Holiness's illness and recovery was performed, including some dohās originally sung by Venerable Dromtonpa and Jamgon Mipham as a blessing to His Holiness.

Ngawang Lodro Tsungme is His Holiness's Dharma name. He sang the *Song of Victory* extemporaneously surrounded by almost five thousand monastics. SĀDHU! SĀDHU!

Wangdu, Great Clouds of Blessings: The Prayer That Magnetizes All That Appears and All That Exists

Jamgon Mipham Rinpoche (1879)

The Maṇḍala to Which One Prays

Symbolized by the Mantra

oṃ āh hūṃ hrīḥ

The Maṇḍala Itself

The Qualities of All the Magnetizing Deities

In the magnetizing palace where great bliss is ablaze
are the bodies of discerning wisdom—the union of bliss and emptiness.
Blissful is your lotus nature, yet free from all attachment—
the splendor of the vajra sun's great brilliance.

The Magnetizing Deities

Dharmakāya buddha of Boundless Light and Vajradharma,
sovereign of the world, Avalokiteśvara—embodiment of great
  compassion,
the Lotus King who reigns over all of saṃsāra and nirvāṇa,
overpowering Heruka—formidable subjugator of all that appears and
  exists,
Ḍākinī Secret Wisdom and Vajravārāhī,
Mahādeva, king of desire, supreme bliss, reservoir of great passion,
Kurukullā—enchantress of all living beings without exception.

How to Pray
Visualize the Qualities of the Vajra Body

Dancing in effortless bliss and emptiness with supreme and
  ordinary mudrās,

an assembly of vajra warrior *ḍākas* and *ḍākinīs* attract and
magnetize.
Remaining always within the state of great equality of appearance
and emptiness,
the dance of your vajra bodies shakes the three realms of existence.

Visualize the Qualities of the Vajra Speech

The sounds of laughter of your unimpeded speech reaches the three
worlds.
You radiate red light rays that spread throughout saṃsāra and nirvāṇa.
Luminous essence of existence and cessation, you tremble and gather.

Visualize the Qualities of the Vajra Mind

With your enlightened mind of great vajra passion,
you bestow the supreme and common *siddhis*.
With your vajra iron hooks and lassoes,
you bind all that appears and exists in supreme bliss.

Pray for the Accomplishments

Dancers in the play of a boundless web of illusions,
who fill space and overflow, like a vast outpouring of sesame seeds,
to the countless Three Roots, deities of magnetizing activity,
devoutly, I pray for your blessings to come down.
Grant me all of my heart's desires—the supreme and common siddhis!

This was composed on the first day of the seventh month of the Earth Hare year (1879)
by one named Dhīḥ. Anyone who prays in this way will, without any doubt, accomplish
all magnetizing activities exactly according to their wishes. This prayer may be written
on red flags and flown in the air or used in prayer wheels powered by heat or wind.
MAṄGALAM!

Commentary on Wangdu, Great Clouds of Blessing

Khenpo Sodargye (2013)

Background of Teachings on this Prayer

At Larung Gar in February 2013 (over the new year according to the Tibetan calendar), I gave the oral teaching on *Wangdu, Great Clouds of Blessings: The Prayer that Magnetizes All That Appears and All That Exists* during the annual Dharma Assembly of the Awareness Holders. There were two reasons for giving this teaching. The first is that when I visited Mount Wutai in June 2012, I aspired to chant this prayer ten thousand times and also promised to give a teaching on it. The second reason is that, because of its powerful blessings, many dharma practitioners had been chanting this prayer for many years, but some of them had still not fully grasped its meaning. Although this prayer is short and consists of a mere seven stanzas, its content is most excellent and profound. So, I felt it necessary to explain the depth of its meaning in a thorough way.

Wangdu is a practice of Vajrayāna Buddhism. Usually, the prerequisite for receiving such a teaching is an empowerment. But, because it is a prayer and does not contain explicit Vajrayāna practice instructions and, furthermore, because many Tibetans, Han Chinese, and others overseas are already chanting this prayer, I think there is no harm to be had from listening to (or reading) this teaching. For this reason, I authorize those who have not received an empowerment, if you promise to recite the short Vajrasattva mantra ten thousand times, you are permitted to receive this teaching.

The Great Benefits of this Prayer

Even though *Wangdu* is not identified as a *terma*, it is generally understood to have come from Jamgon Mipham Rinpoche's wisdom mind, from the great bodhisattva Mañjuśrī. *Wangdu* is an extraordinary prayer that brings within one's power all phenomena in the entire universe, and, more potently, it bestows the ability to tame one's mind. Therefore, it can be said to have two main effects: an outer and an inner one. By relying on the prayer, one gains, in the outer sense, the ability to benefit all living beings, while its inner effect offers one the ability to control discursive thoughts and thereby attain full control of the body and the mind.

As a person who has already generated bodhicitta, you should devote your best efforts to the welfare of all sentient beings. This is not always easy, however, and in fact, if one is relying completely on one's own abilities, it can be quite difficult. One must, on the one hand, remain personally diligent, while, on the other hand, one must pray for the blessing of the personal deities, ḍākinīs, and Dharma protectors.

In terms of the outer effect of prayers, sometimes the influence of deities is more important than our own efforts. Of course, atheists might not agree with this, as they believe that the origin of success depends upon one's own diligence and nothing more. While it is true that one's own efforts are important, one also needs beneficial outer circumstances. It is only when inner and outer conditions harmonize that success will follow.

Some people think that propagating the Dharma and benefiting sentient beings is such a large project that the individual efforts of an ordinary person make little or no difference. However, this is also an incorrect way of thinking. Although our activities to benefit sentient beings might not have a great impact in this life, if we persist in reciting *Wangdu*, we can create an auspicious karmic connection for the benefit of sentient beings in our next life.

In terms of inner effects, through recitation of this prayer, we gain full control over the body and the mind. In essence, all afflictions of sentient beings come from the fact that they are not the masters of their own body and mind. The inability to control discursive thoughts is what causes the mind of all beings in saṃsāra to become constantly perturbed by every changing situation, which causes immeasurable suffering. If we recite this prayer often, we will gain command of our own mind and eventually realize its nature. Then, not only will mental afflictions cease to exist, but we will be able to master all external phenomena as well.

IMPORTANCE OF THIS PRACTICE AT LARUNG GAR

Because of these incredible effects, *Wangdu* is a highly valued Dharma practice at Larung Gar. Every teaching and every tutorial begins with the recitation of this prayer three times. His Holiness Jigme Phuntsok Rinpoche once said, "If I and my future lineage holders want to benefit sentient beings for all future lives, recitation of this prayer is the most effective means." In order to create favorable conditions for his students to benefit sentient beings, His Holiness made offerings to commission the saṅgha at Larung Gar to recite *Wangdu* three times every day. This was later increased to five times a day. After His Holiness passed away, Jetsun Ani Mumtso also made offerings to the saṅgha to continue the daily recitation.

The practice of *Wangdu* can also remove obstacles and enables one to influence ordinary adverse circumstances and transform them into positive ones. At Larung Gar, people often ask the saṅgha to chant *Wangdu* in order to do something smoothly and successfully. For example, when there is a water shortage at Larung, a driver from Serta will volunteer to transport water to us. In order for him to be successful without encountering obstacles, the saṅgha will be asked to all recite *Wangdu* together.

This prayer is not only popular at Larung Gar. Even outside the institute, one can often see old, white-haired, and toothless Tibetans, unfamiliar with even the most basic *sādhana* (tantric liturgy) reciting *Wangdu* fluently with great vigor. Also, we can obviously see that, although we never made any effort to promulgate the prayer, *Wangdu* has grown spontaneously and is now recited by many domestic and overseas practitioners. This must surely be a sign of successful magnetizing!

The Title

Wangdu is short for *Great Clouds of Blessings: The Prayer That Magnetizes All That Appears and All That Exists*. Here "all that appears" refers to the outer world that appears, and "all that exists" refers to all living beings who exist within the outer world. Briefly speaking, there are three things we need to know regarding this prayer. First, the purpose of this prayer is to accomplish the activity of magnetizing. Second, we should chant this prayer if we want to accomplish the activity of magnetizing. And third, the prayer is directed to the ocean-like countless magnetizing beings of the Three Roots, who are represented by the nine deities of magnetizing.

The Four Tantric Activities

In Vajrayāna Buddhism, there are four types of activities: pacifying, enriching, magnetizing, and subjugating. A prerequisite to accomplishing these activities is having achieved a certain level of realization in one's own Vajra-yāna practice.

Pacifying

This activity eliminates disease, hindrances, and negative karma of oneself and others. For example, Vajrasattva practice is a pacifying activity. Through Vajrasattva's purification practice, one can eradicate all of one's negative karma that has accumulated since beginningless time.

Enriching

The activity of enriching brings fame, wealth, social status, wisdom, and so on. There are many practices of enriching. Those who want to increase their intelligence can practice Mañjuśrī, those who want to increase their compassion can practice Avalokiteśvara, and those who want increased wealth can practice Jambhala.

Magnetizing

Through magnetizing, one first gains complete control of one's own body and mind and then gains the power to magnetize and conciliate all other humans and nonhumans. Some people are met with difficulties wherever they go. They are in conflict with their parents, nonhumans seek to inflict harm upon them, or even the dog they pass on the street barks at them. In fact, all our external disharmony is fundamentally caused by a loss of control over our own body and mind. If we can practice magnetizing activity well, we can gain control over our body and mind and consequently will be able to have greater influence over all external conditions.

Subjugating

When people have perfected the power of their great compassion and are free of the last thread of selfishness, they can forcefully transfer the consciousness of certain barbarous beings to the pure land through the practices of wrathful deities such as Hayagrīva, Vajrakīla, and so forth. On the surface, it may appear as if subjugating is killing, but the two actions are radically different. Killing is a heinous deed that harms sentient beings, while subjugating is an expedient means of benefiting them. If one does not understand Vajrayāna Buddhism or if one is prejudiced against it, one might find it difficult to accept these tantric activities. From this perspective, it would be a normal reaction. Just as the sunshine cannot reach a north-facing cave, a person without faith can never understand the teaching or receive the blessings of the Vajrayāna.

The Power of Magnetizing Activities

For those who want to spread the Dharma to benefit sentient beings, it is very important to accomplish magnetizing activity. Otherwise, no matter how determined your efforts, people will dismiss you. If you have perfected the activities of magnetizing, your efforts are combined with the power of the deities of magnetizing, which can give an added impetus to your activities, even if you are just an ordinary person. With the help of magnetizing activities, you do not need to engage in extraordinary efforts with your Dharma activities, nor does it require that you petition people around you to take refuge in the Three Jewels or to take the bodhisattva vow. In fact, all of these can be accomplished without any difficulties.

His Holiness Jigme Phuntsok Rinpoche is the perfect example of someone who obtained this power and revived the Dharma after the Cultural Revolution in China. In that dark period, His Holiness single-handedly accomplished something that many others had failed to achieve. He resurrected the banner of Dharma in this world by calling upon the power of magnetizing.

I, myself, feel a strong personal affinity toward the activity of magnetizing as well. In 1985, when I was newly arrived in Larung Gar, the first Dharma assembly I took part in was the Dharma Assembly of the Awareness Holders, then called the Dharma Assembly of the Nine Deities.

There is an unusual reason why the name of the Dharma assembly was changed. In 1995, many monks and nuns gathered in Larung Gar to attend the Dharma assembly. At that time, His Holiness Jigme Phuntsok Rinpoche stated, "This Dharma assembly is not only being attended by human beings; many awareness holders from different buddha realms have come to join us as well. There are gathered here a total of one hundred thousand human and nonhuman awareness holders. For this reason, this Dharma gathering should be called the Dharma Assembly of the One Hundred Thousand Awareness Holders." Ever since that time, the Dharma Assembly of the Nine Deities has been called the Dharma Assembly of the Awareness Holders.

As a matter of fact, whatever our practice, the right conditions for interdependent arising are very important. Observing these conditions from many different perspectives, one will find that Larung Valley is a place where the activity of magnetizing is easily achieved. A *terton* once made this prophecy for His Holiness Jigme Phuntsok Rinpoche:

> In the valley of magnetizing activity, a lotus blossoms
> and the golden eagle of Loro[32] soars in the sky.
> His call resonates loud and clear in ten directions.
> All birds gather under his wings.

"In the valley of magnetizing activity, a lotus blossoms" indicates Larung, a valley whose mountain ridges form the shape of a lotus. "Golden eagle" is a symbolic reference to His Holiness, who was born in the year of the bird. "All birds" refers to the disciples of His Holiness. This prophecy is very clearly about Larung Valley being a suitable place to practice magnetizing.

Actually, the practice of magnetizing is more significant to people living out in the world compared to its significance for practitioners living in seclusion. Living in the world, one is inevitably confronted with problems of relationships, money, social status, and so forth, and so there is great suffering and unhappiness in people's hearts. The activity of magnetizing will have positive effects in dealing with these daily issues. His Holiness once said: "In addition to benefiting sentient beings, those who have accomplished the activities of magnetizing will improve their own lives as well."

Sometimes, I jokingly say to my students, "When you find yourself in financial difficulties and you have to borrow money every day, even if you have reached the point where others avoid you out of fear of having to lend you money, this would be a good time to start practicing magnetizing. Once you have accomplished the activity of magnetizing, you will never find yourself in this kind of situation again."

So, generally speaking, if one can practice magnetizing and receive the blessings of the deities, ḍākinīs, and Dharma protectors of magnetizing activities, one will find that both the body and mind gradually come under control and one's problems change for the better.

The subtitle of this prayer is "Great Clouds of Blessings." This refers to the blessings of the Three Roots of magnetizing which will descend like the great rains of summer and bring an uninterrupted flow of siddhi (accomplishment) to whomever earnestly recites it.

Those who consistently recite *Wangdu* will not only receive blessings from the Three Roots, but will also form a bond with His Holiness Jigme

Phuntsok Rinpoche, who personally promised that even after his passing, he would not abandon those disciples who had formed a karmic bond with him. Those who recite *Wangdu*, even if they have never seen or heard His Holiness personally, will be counted among his disciples and be received into his sphere of influence.

The blessing of His Holiness is indeed incredible. For my personal experience, I thought back to my decision to come to Larung Gar and realized that it must have been the result of His Holiness's blessing. I hadn't even graduated from school yet, but for an unexplainable reason, I felt the irresistible impulse to come to Larung and learn Buddhism. It was as if I had been pulled by an unstoppable force.

The fact that the Dharma has reached such levels of prosperity at Larung Gar is also the result of His Holiness Jigme Phuntsok Rinpoche's great blessing. Some people from other monasteries have attempted to spread the Dharma out of a sense of compassion, but their activities have seldom been fully effective. This is not the case at Larung Gar. There, it is common knowledge that His Holiness is the reincarnation of Dorje Dudjom, a great *siddha* who accomplished the activity of magnetizing. While His Holiness was still alive and even after his departure from this world, Larung Gar has continued to be a holy site of the prosperous Dharma.

I used to think that once His Holiness passed away, I would no longer wish to live at Larung, that without His Holiness, Larung would be like a land of ruins. I thought that even if some people remained, their number would be few. Indeed, thanks to the benevolent influence of His Holiness, so many Buddhists remain gathered together at Larung Gar, and Larung Gar continues to play such an important role in Buddhism today. This is not an exaggeration. As Mipham Rinpoche said, "Never use untruthful language even if the subject of your praise is your root guru." For those who live in worldly society, speaking the truth is a crucial quality, and it is even more so for those who are committed to Buddhist practice.

Throughout his life, His Holiness always had the highest regard for *Wangdu*. Regardless of which holy site he visited, he would recite this prayer at least three times. I also chant this prayer when on pilgrimage or anytime I see a statue of a victorious buddha. If I don't have the time to recite a longer prayer of aspiration, I will chant this prayer a minimum of three times. In the same way, I'd like to encourage everyone to understand the importance of *Wangdu* and to keep it as an important prayer to practice throughout their entire lives.

THE MEANING OF THE MANTRA

The Maṇḍala to Which One Prays: Symbolized by the Mantra
OṂ ĀH HŪṂ HRĪḤ

OṂ ĀH HŪṂ is the all-encompassing mantra of the buddhas of the three times. OṂ represents the vajra body of the buddhas of the three times, ĀH represents their vajra speech, and HŪṂ represents their vajra mind. Therefore, by reciting OṂ ĀH HŪṂ, you receive the blessings of all buddhas.

HRĪḤ is the core seed syllable of the Three Root magnetizing deities of the Lotus family and represents the natural radiance of the wisdom of discernment. Because this prayer is dedicated to the deities of the Lotus family, which consist primarily of nine principal deities, we must recite HRĪḤ.

Mantras are the unparalleled, creative means by which buddhas and bodhisattvas benefit sentient beings. Whichever Buddhist mantra that you recite, you are immediately brought into resonance with its associated deity. While it is true in the ultimate sense that the primordial nature of buddhas and bodhisattvas transcends concept and form, in relative terms, when sentient beings recite mantras with devotion, buddhas and bodhisattvas will descend and appear to them. Similarly, when a child cries for its mother, the mother quickly comes to its aid. And so, when we recite OṂ ĀH HŪṂ HRĪḤ with diligence and devotion, we receive the blessings of all buddhas and bodhisattvas, and more specifically, we receive the blessings of the nine principal deities of the Lotus family and their extensive retinues.

The Nine Deities of Magnetizing Activity

There are many different ways of visualizing the nine deities of magnetizing activity. Mipham Rinpoche's *Wangdu* represents one of these. The sādhana that is recited during the Dharma Assembly of the Awareness Holders, *Profound Practice of the Illusory Lasso of Avalokiteśvara's Nine Principle Deities*, a terma revealed by Lerab Lingpa, is another one. In these two practices, the descriptions of the nine deities are slightly different.

His Holiness Jigme Phuntsok Rinpoche once asked an artist to draw the nine deities according to the description in *Wangdu*. In the drawing, the *dharmakāya* buddha of Boundless Light, Amitābha, is located at the top in the center. Amitābha is equivalent to Samantabhadra with the exception that Samantabhadra is generally identified by his blue color, whereas

Amitābha is red. Positioned directly below Amitābha is the *saṃbhogakāya* buddha, Vajradharma, the equivalent of Vajradhara. Below Vajradharma is the nirmāṇakāya Padma Gyalpo, a manifestation of Padmasambhava. At the top left is red Avalokiteśvara, below that is Guhyajñāna, and at the bottom left is Kurukullā. On the top right of Vajradharma is Hayagrīva, below that is Vajravārāhī, and then Mahādeva is on the bottom right.

If Vajrayāna practitioners place this picture on their shrine, over time, they will certainly receive blessings from these deities. However, this only applies to practitioners of sincere devotion to Vajrayāna Buddhism. Those without much understanding of Vajrayāna might develop bad feelings toward these deities. Although there are no images of deities in sexual union, there are figures wearing only bone ornaments.

It is important to keep in mind that if one prays to the nine magnetizing deities with joy, it is easier to resonate with them. The instructions to practitioners for the sādhana practiced in the Dharma Assembly of the Awareness Holders states, "Commence your practice with a pure and joyful mind." Naturally, even when in a bad mood, chanting *Wangdu* and receiving the blessings of the nine deities might lift your spirits. Some people start with a sad countenance, but after chanting *Wangdu* a few times, they show no more signs of negative emotion, and their enunciation becomes loud and clear and even their prayer wheel spins faster. This is a sign of receiving the blessings of the deities through chanting this prayer.

THE MAṆḌALA ITSELF

Qualities of All the Magnetizing Deities

In the magnetizing palace where great bliss is ablaze
are the bodies of discerning wisdom—the union of bliss and emptiness.
Blissful is your lotus nature, yet free from all attachment—
the splendor of the vajra sun's great brilliance.

This stanza summarizes the qualities of the magnetizing deities. The descriptions are applicable to each deity introduced in the later verses.

The Support of the Magnetizing Deities

"The magnetizing palace where great bliss is ablaze" refers to the dwelling place or the support for the magnetizing deities. "Great bliss" is not bliss in the ordinary sense, but the immaculate wisdom that transcends all conceptual thoughts. In appearance, these deities reside in a magnetizing palace, blazing with the fire of blissful wisdom.

Residences of buddhas can be classified into three categories—the dharmakāya palace, the saṃbhogakāya palace, and the nirmāṇakāya palace—corresponding to the three *kāyas* of their manifestation. The dharmakāya palace is in fact the primordial wisdom, which is beyond expression, transcending all duality, direction, language, and thought. The saṃbhogakāya palace is the boundless palace in the saṃbhogakāya buddhafield. In the *Guhyagarbha Tantra*, it is said that this boundless palace has five kinds of majestic qualities and is invisible to the ordinary human eye. It is exclusively visible to enlightened beings that have reached the first *bhūmi* or beyond. The nirmāṇakāya palace is a palace in the apparent pure realms. Its virtues are visible to ordinary human beings whose mindstreams are not so contaminated. The boundless palace of Amitābha's pure land is an example of a nirmāṇakāya palace.

The Basic Form of the Magnetizing Deities
"Bodies of discerning wisdom—the union of bliss and emptiness" refers to the basic form of the magnetizing deities. Regarding "the union of bliss and emptiness," from the perspective of the perceiver, it is unchanging great bliss, and from the perspective of the perceived, it is profound emptiness. The magnetizing deities have completely realized the nonduality of the perceiver and the perceived, abide in the perfect union of bliss and emptiness, and irreversibly transform lust and desire into the wisdom of discernment.

The wisdom of discernment is one of the five buddha wisdoms. By relying on the wisdom of discernment, the magnetizing deities are able to perceive all phenomena with perfect and precise discernment. The magnetizing deities possess the qualities of five buddha wisdoms, but this prayer specifically approaches them from the perspective of the wisdom of discernment.

The Family of the Magnetizing Deities
"Blissful is your lotus nature, yet free from all attachment" tells us to which buddha family the magnetizing deities belong. In the *dharmadhātu*, each buddha belongs to a particular buddha family. The buddhas of the east belong to the Vajra family; the buddhas of the south belong to the Ratna family; the buddhas of the west belong to the Lotus family; the buddhas of the north belong to the Karma family; and the buddhas of the center belong

to the Tathāgata family. The magnetizing deities belong to the Lotus family of the west.

The general characteristics of the Lotus family are that they are red in color, and they reside in the west, or more specifically, in Sukhāvatī. It is for this reason that His Holiness used to say: "For those of us who aspire for rebirth in Sukhāvatī, whether from the perspective of practices of the ground, path, or fruition, the practice of *Wangdu* is very suitable."

Why is this buddha family called the Lotus family? It is named after the symbol of the lotus that represents it. Like the lotus flower that grows from muddy water and yet whose blossom is untainted and pristine, the buddha figures of the Lotus family appear to be overflowing with desire yet are free from the constraints of desire, manifesting the pure wisdom of great bliss. This is why the lotus is the metaphorical name of the deities of this buddha family.

Because the symbolic color of the Lotus family is red, the Dharma implements used to practice magnetizing should preferably be red. It will be best to chant *Wangdu* using a red *mālā* (rosary). Once, there was a lama in Pelyul who pursued a variety of different practices. He designated a different mālā for each practice and carried a dozen mālās with him at all times. Because of his advanced age, his eyesight had become quite poor. So, before he could begin a practice, he had to search through his pockets for quite a while to determine which one was the right mālā. On the surface, this may appear to be grasping, but it actually shows how important Dharma practice was to him.

If we can pray often to the magnetizing deities, we can free ourselves from the constraints of desire. People are driven by burning desires during these times of degeneration. When faced with temptation, most people are not able to control their bodies or their minds. Some even transgress or abandon their vows. To address this problem, His Holiness said, "As a practitioner who wants to maintain his precepts untainted throughout future lives, you should recite *Wangdu* or pray to Kurukullā with diligence. If you can do so, you will be transforming your impure thoughts into immaculate wisdom, which is like transforming iron into gold."

The Activities of the Magnetizing Deities
"The splendor of the vajra sun's great brilliance" refers to the magnetizing deities' activities. *Vajra* is a term used to describe their indestructible quality. "The vajra sun's great brilliance" is a metaphor for the indestructible wisdom

of the magnetizing deities. What are these activities? With the sunlike brilliance of their indestructible wisdom, they can dispel wrong views, negative thoughts, and all the darkness of ignorance that hinders sentient beings from attaining enlightenment.

The minds of people are deeply afflicted by the darkness of ignorance. Many do not have the power to tame their own mental afflictions, nor do they possess the ability to benefit sentient beings through the Dharma. If these people can devoutly pray to the magnetizing deities, by virtue of the blessing that they receive, the darkness of ignorance in their mindstream can be swiftly dispelled and their Dharma practice, along with their other Dharma propagating activities, can progress smoothly.

There are different ways of understanding Mipham Rinpoche's vajra words. Some think that this line refers to the dharmakāya buddha of Boundless Light. I personally think that this verse is a summary of all the qualities of the magnetizing deities. Their residence is the boundless magnetizing palace, their basic form is the wisdom of discernment, their buddha family is the Lotus family, and their activity is dispelling obstacles to enlightenment.

The Magnetizing Deities

Dharmakāya buddha of Boundless Light and Vajradharma,
sovereign of the world, Avalokiteśvara—embodiment of great
  compassion,
the Lotus King who reigns over all of saṃsāra and nirvāṇa,
overpowering Heruka—formidable subjugator of all that appears
  and exists,
Ḍākinī Secret Wisdom and Vajravārāhī,
Mahādeva, king of desire, supreme bliss, reservoir of great
  passion,
Kurukullā—enchantress of all creatures without exception.

Dharmakāya Amitābha

Dharmakāya means the union of emptiness and wisdom, which is beyond all form and concept while possessing all kinds of merit. The deities of the Lotus family manifest in three kāyas. Buddha Amitābha is the dharmakāya representation. His body is red in color; he is completely naked without any adornment. He appears like the primordial buddha, Samantabhadra, except that he is red instead of blue.

In Vajrayāna, naked representations of buddha figures symbolize the intrinsic nature of all phenomena. In this saṃsāric world, normally a person depicted without clothes is considered shameful. However, in this case, as the nature of all phenomena is devoid of intrinsic existence and the nature of mind is bare naked, from this standpoint, no adornment is necessary.

According to *The Tantra of Liberation through Contact*, "The unchanging light body of the primordial tathāgata is naked, unadorned, red and yellow in color, and abides in the meditation posture." Clearly, Amitābha is unadorned, his body is of reddish yellow color, his hands form the *mudrā* (gesture) of meditation, and he is seated in the vajra posture.

The fact that the first deity in *Wangdu* is Buddha Amitābha gives rise to a special favorable condition for rebirth in the pure land. His Holiness Jigme Phuntsok Rinpoche once said, "All of you should aspire for rebirth in Sukhāvatī upon death. Reciting *Wangdu* creates a karmic cause that will lead to rebirth in the pure land." Therefore, those who practice Pure Land Buddhism should also recite *Wangdu* often.

Among the nine principal magnetizing deities apart from Amitābha, a few of the ḍākinīs appear naked as well. From this perspective, Vajrayāna is indeed the practice of those with sharp natural capacities. If a person still holds onto the notion of shame, buddhas and bodhisattvas merely assume graceful and majestic forms. But if a person has realized the bare-naked nature of the mind, where all conceptual thoughts and attachments have ceased to exist, then buddhas and bodhisattvas appear in another form. Therefore, if a person thinks that Vajrayāna's naked representations of buddhas are inappropriate, it is a sign that they are not yet ready for Vajrayāna practice. Therefore, in order to protect the practices of such people, the images of naked buddhas or buddhas in sexual union, along with certain practices, are disclosed with caution.

Buddhas and bodhisattvas approach us in boundless ways. In addition to imparting Dharma to us by means of language, they also use unique ways to demonstrate the true nature of all phenomena. Regarding the images of buddhas in sexual union, from an ordinary perspective it does appear that the buddha father and mother are embracing each other. However, such an embrace is symbolic of the union of emptiness and appearance, emptiness and luminosity, and emptiness and bliss.

Sexual union can also be explained as the mind and phenomena dissolving into nonduality. An average person may have difficulty grasping the meaning of emptiness as taught in the second turning of the Dharma wheel and the concept of tathāgatagarbha luminosity taught in the third turning of the Dharma wheel. This same person may not see how one is not different from the other. Therefore, the imagery of buddhas in sexual union serves as a visual aid to demonstrate this notion. Upon seeing a buddha embracing a consort, a person with sharp natural capacities might instantaneously realize the innate wisdom that emptiness and luminosity are inseparable and be able to transform all negative emotions into the great wisdom of the union of emptiness and bliss.

Nowadays, due to its increasing popularity, many people study Vajrayāna Buddhism, but very few people really understand it. Most people are simply curious. When they see a naked buddha representation or a buddha with a consort, they immediately take a snapshot with their smartphone. They believe that what they are seeing is an artistic image of the human body, and even graver misunderstandings about Vajrayāna can sprout from such uninformed conclusions. A person who understands the Vajrayāna teachings, especially a person who has experience with its advanced practices, knows that such imagery does not represent ordinary lust and that Vajrayāna Buddhism would never advocate attachment of this nature.

Vajradharma

According to the esoteric Buddhism of the Tang dynasty, Vajradharma is a bodhisattva of the Lotus family. He is a member of the retinue of the Buddha Amitābha. In certain sādhanas of Tibetan Buddhism, Vajradharma and Amitābha are also two different entities. But in this text, Vajradharma and Amitābha are not different. Vajradharma is the saṃbhogakāya emanation of Amitābha. He is depicted almost identically to Vajradhara: he stands in a vajra posture, arms crossed in front of the chest, holding a vajra in one hand and a bell with the other. The only difference between them is that Vajradhara is blue and Vajradharma is red.

His Holiness once mentioned that the red Vajradhara also appears in certain sādhanas composed by Mipham Rinpoche. But in *Wangdu*, Vajradharma is the saṃbhogakāya of Amitābha. So, in the *thangka* (scroll painting) of *Wangdu*, compliant with the secret intention of Mipham Rinpoche, the dharmakāya Amitābha is depicted above, the saṃbhogakāya Vajradharma is in the middle, and the nirmāṇakāya Padmasambhava is below.

There is plenty of reliable scriptural evidence supporting the claim that Vajradharma and Amitābha are the same entity. In the tantras, it is explicitly stated that Vajradharma is the manifestation of Amitābha: "The red light

beaming from Amitābha's forehead transforms into the red Avalokiteśvara, red light beaming from his throat takes the form of Padmasambhava,
the red light from Amitābha's heart turns into Heruka, and the red light
beaming from the tip of his nose becomes Vajrapāṇi." Some masters have
explained that Vajrapāṇi here is Vajradharma, and that Vajradharma is the
saṃbhogakāya of Amitābha, just as Vajradhara is the saṃbhogakāya form
of Samantabhadra.

Avalokiteśvara
Normally, it is better to follow the sequence of dharmakāya, saṃbhogakāya, and nirmāṇakāya. But, this practice is fundamentally a practice of
Avalokiteśvara. Furthermore, it is very difficult for ordinary human beings
to embark on the path of the dharmakāya and saṃbhogakāya buddhas. To
do so, one needs to receive the blessings of Amitābha and Vajradharma
through Avalokiteśvara. Therefore, here we first introduce Avalokiteśvara
before introducing Padmasambhava.

Avalokiteśvara assumes many different forms—with two arms, four arms,
eleven faces, a thousand arms, a thousand eyes, and so forth. The Avalokiteśvara here is very special. He is red in color and is holding a lotus flower in
his left hand, symbolizing compassion toward all sentient beings. His right
hand forms the mudrā of offering, symbolizing the removal of affliction and
suffering for all sentient beings.

The tantric teachings state that red light radiating from Amitābha transforms into Avalokiteśvara. It is also said in Karma Chakme Rinpoche's *Aspiration to be Reborn in the Pure Realm of Sukhāvatī* that light emanating from
Amitābha takes the form of Avalokiteśvara. Therefore, by praying to the red
Avalokiteśvara, both the Mahāyāna practice and the Vajrayāna practice can
be achieved. On the one hand, you can accomplish the magnetizing activity,
and on the other hand, you can attain rebirth in the realm of Amitābha.

In Han Chinese Buddhism, the practice of red Avalokiteśvara is rare, but
in Tibetan Buddhism, it is quite common. At Larung Gar, every thirtieth
day of the Tibetan lunar month, the saṅgha recites the *Gyalwa Gyamtso
Sādhana*, in which Gyalwa is depicted as a four-armed red Avalokiteśvara.
Reciting his name and mantra are tremendously beneficial to the dead.

We need to clarify that although *Wangdu* and Lerab Lingpa's *Profound
Practice of the Illusory Lasso of Avalokiteśvara's Nine Principle Deities* are
both practices of the magnetizing activity and both supplicate the nine
magnetizing deities, they are different from one another. In *Wangdu*, the

principle deity is a single-figure Padmasambhava, whereas in the latter practice, Padmasambhava is absent. There, the main deity is red Avalokiteśvara in the posture of sexual union. In his right hand he holds a copper hook, while in his left hand he holds a string of lotus flowers. He is embracing the Secret Wisdom Ḍākinī. His Holiness also commented, "Typically, Lerab Lingpa's sādhana of nine deities should include Padmasambhava. The reason why Padmasambhava is absent in this sādhana is unclear."

In *Wangdu*, it is very easy to count the nine deities. But in Lerab Lingpa's sādhana, they are not as obvious. We may count the nine deities of Lerab Lingpa's sādhana as follows: Amitābha, Vajradharma, Padmasambhava, Red Avalokiteśvara, Guhyajñāna, Heruka, Vajravārāhī, Kurukullā, Mahādeva. Here, Amitābha, Vajradhara, and Padmasambhava are present in an imperceptible way. First, the dharmakāya form of Amitābha, as chief of the Lotus family, is positioned above the head of Avalokiteśvara. Second, the saṃbhogakāya form of Vajradharma, transformed from Amitābha, is visible to the bodhisattvas whose perceptions are pure. Third, for ordinary sentient beings with tainted perceptions, the emanation of Amitābha is the nirmāṇakāya form of Padmasambhava.

Padma Gyalpo: The Lotus King Padmasambhava
"The Lotus King who reigns over all of saṃsāra and nirvāṇa" expresses that Padmasambhava has attained the ultimate accomplishment and, therefore, has control over all of saṃsāra and nirvāṇa and all animate and inanimate phenomena.

Padmasambhava is white in color with a hint of red, holding a vajra and a skull cup, with a *khaṭvāṅga*, or three-pointed trident, tucked under his arm. Usually, Padmasambhava is depicted with a consort, but it was the instruction of His Holiness not to include a consort. Instead, the khaṭvāṅga serves as a symbol of the ḍākinī consort.

The Lotus King Padma Gyalpo is one of the many epithets of Padmasambhava. According to his biography, when Indrabhūti of Oḍḍiyāna was on his way back home from a treasure-hunting voyage, he passed by a lake. At the center of the lake, he saw a noble-looking boy sitting atop a lotus flower. This boy was Padmasambhava. The king was very delighted by what he saw and brought the boy to his palace, where he was adopted as the king's own son and thus became a prince. Later, Padmasambhava granted empowerment to the king, and imparted secret teachings to him. Extremely delighted, the king offered all his wealth and retinue to Padmasambhava and honored him with the name Lotus King. Padmasambhava belongs to the Lotus family of the west. According to the tantric teachings, Padmasambhava is the emanation of Amitābha and Avalokiteśvara. It is also said in Karma Chakme Rinpoche's *Aspiration to Be Reborn in the Pure Realm of Sukhāvatī* that Padmasambhava originated from a beam of light that radiated outward from Amitābha's heart. Because he has gained control of saṃsāra and nirvāṇa, we should offer him our most devout prayers. Through invoking him, demonic forces and obstacles will be removed, and we will gain control of our body and mind.

Padmasambhava displayed incredible power and benefited countless beings across India, Tibet, and China. His deeds are so great and so numerous that they are beyond recounting. This is especially true in Tibet, where without Guru Rinpoche's influence, the harmonious merging and flourishing of Mahāyāna and Vajrayāna Buddhism could not have succeeded to the extent that it did. Tibetan Buddhism's prosperity in the world and the blessings of Padmasambhava are inseparable. In this dark age, Padmasambhava's teachings are showing their incredible power more than ever. In terms of the effects of transforming our mental afflictions, no other spiritual body of knowledge can compare to the teachings of Padmasambhava. To be more specific, if it were not for the blessings of Padmasambhava, even you, the reader, would not be able to be benefited by Tibetan Buddhism. Therefore, we should all be grateful to Padmasambhava.

Hayagrīva: The Overpowering Heruka
The "overpowering Heruka" refers to Hayagrīva and his power is to subjugate the entire world. Hayagrīva is a wrathful manifestation of Amitābha. While some Hayagrīva practices can be found in esoteric Buddhism in the Tang dynasty, it is in Tibetan Buddhism that one finds the greatest variety of these practices. Throughout the history of Tibet, it has been recorded that many people reached the ultimate accomplishment through Hayagrīva practices. In Dudjom Rinpoche's *The Nyingma School of Tibetan Buddhism: Its Fundamentals and History*, it is documented that Gyalwa Choyang, one of Padmasambhava's twenty-five heart sons, reached enlightenment by following the practices of Hayagrīva. Later, the great siddha Thangtong Gyalpo, who is considered to be the emanation of both Avalokiteśvara and Hayagrīva, also attained the ultimate accomplishment through this practice.

Hayagrīva is extremely powerful. Wondrous signs of accomplishment accompany the attainment of enlightenment through Hayagrīva. For example, a horse's head may grow from the crown of your own head and make a loud neighing sound, which resounds into the space above you, conquering Māra's obscurations from heaven, into the space below you, where it conquers all the obscurations in the realm of the *nāgas*, into the space to the right where all male demonic beings are destroyed, and into the space to the left, where all female demons are destroyed. In an age such as this when the Dharma is in decline, it is very necessary to practice Hayagrīva.

When I was a child, I had very strong faith in Hayagrīva. Back in those days, I would lead the yaks out to pasture every day. As I walked barefoot in the mountains, I would spin a small prayer wheel while reciting the mantra of Hayagrīva: OṂ VAJRA KRODHA HAYAGRĪVA HULU HULU HŪṂ PHAṬ. Anyone seeing me would think that I was a Hayagrīva siddha. We also had a few horses in our household. The local Tibetans believed that if we recited the Hayagrīva mantra, the horses would be safe from attack by wild animals. When my father entrusted these horses to my care, he asked me to recite the Hayagrīva mantra with diligence. I felt that since I had been entrusted with such an important responsibility, I had better recite the mantra as often as I could. In retrospect, I believe that although at that time I recited the mantra out of self-interest, I also sowed the seed of a good habit.

Guhyajñāna: Secret Wisdom Ḍākinī

The next deity is Guhyajñāna, also known as the Secret Wisdom Ḍākinī or Vajrayoginī. She is red in color and has one face with three eyes. In each of her four arms she is holding a flaying knife, a skull cup full of nectar, a trident, and a sword of wisdom. In the *yabyum* practices of Avalokiteśvara, she is his consort.

Guhyajñāna is a very important buddha figure in Tibetan Buddhism. Tibetan masters have said that no matter which buddha figure you practice, it is important to choose Guhyajñāna as a parallel practice. The guru yoga practice in Patrul Rinpoche's text *Words of My Perfect Teacher* instructs the practitioner to visualize themselves as Guhyajñāna.

Historically, many people have attained achievement through Guhyajñāna practice. Most of the eighty *mahāsiddhas* of India practiced Guhyajñāna. In Tibet, Guhyajñāna was practiced in the strictest secrecy and, even then, only by practitioners of the Sakya and Nyingma traditions. It was not until later that this practice passed to other sects. In the Sakya tradition, Guhyajñāna practice was transmitted to only one person at a time. Later, the requirements were lifted to allow from seven to twenty-one people of each generation to receive it through oral transmission. Today, the transmission of this practice is still very rare.

We should attach great importance to Guhyajñāna practice. If we can pray earnestly to Guhyajñāna, then her specific blessing will help us swiftly transform our lust into discerning wisdom and, as such, it will manifest itself in all worldly and nonworldly accomplishments.

Vajravārāhī

Vajravārāhī is also red in color, with one face, two arms, and three eyes. On the right side of her face is a swine's head. She holds a flaying knife in her right hand, and in the left hand she is holding a skull cup at her chest. A khaṭvāṅga is tucked under her left arm.

Vajravārāhī is portrayed with the head of a swine, which symbolizes the absence of dualistic labeling of phenomena as being either pure or impure. As pigs cannot tell clean from filthy and are indifferent to whether the food that they eat is clean or dirty, the swine's head symbolizes that Vajravārāhī has obliterated all conceptual thoughts of cleanliness and filth.

Vajravārāhī has many different forms. In addition to the red Vajravārāhī, there is also a blue Vajravārāhī and a black Vajravārāhī. Vajravārāhī is a practice common to each Tibetan lineage and, in particular, to the Kagyu tradition. Many Tibetan masters have personally seen Vajravārāhī herself. The biography of Venerable Longchenpa mentions that Vajravārāhī appeared to him quite often. Once, Longchenpa even asked Vajravārāhī why she would appear to him since prayers to her were not a specific part of his practice. Vajravārāhī also appeared to Jigme Lingpa on many occasions.

Mahādeva: Reservoir of Great Passion

The next deity is Mahādeva. Also red in color, Mahādeva is depicted with one face and two arms, with his left hand holding a skull cup in front of his chest, and his right hand brandishing a trident.

We may wonder why the expressions "supreme bliss," "king of desire," and "reservoir of great passion" are used to describe Mahādeva. This is because this deity can benefit all sentient beings by means of his great wisdom in which bliss and emptiness are inseparable.

In Vajrayāna, there are two Mahādevas: one is a worldly god, and the other is a manifestation of Avalokiteśvara. Some tantras document that Buddha Śākyamuni has, in the past, also taken the form of Mahādeva. Therefore,

Mahādeva is not an ordinary god but is a manifestation of an enlightened being. Relying on him, you can ripen your abilities to benefit beings and your abilities to magnetize. In order to benefit sentient beings, buddhas and bodhisattvas will manifest themselves in the forms of celestial gods. As such, it is difficult for ordinary beings like us to tell the difference. So, it is better not to jump to hasty conclusions when you hear the name of a celestial god. Historically, many people have attained enlightenment through the Mahādeva practice. In the biography of Guru Chowang, a treasure revealer of the Nyingma tradition, there are many fascinating stories of his personal encounters with Mahādeva.

Kurukullā: Enchantress of the Minds of All Living Beings without Exception

"Enchantress of all living beings without exception" means that Kurukullā can captivate the minds of sentient beings with creative methods. Kurukullā has a beautiful and majestic body that enchants those who behold her. She is red in color, with one face and four arms. She holds a bow and arrow with her two upper arms; and in her two lower arms she holds an iron hook and a lasso made of lotus flowers.

Kurukullā, an emanation of Tārā, is an enlightened manifestation of discerning wisdom. The power that she possesses is very uncommon. A Buddhist monk or nun who wants to maintain his or her untainted precepts should pray to Kurukullā devoutly, for she has the power to transform desire into the wisdom of great bliss and ensure that the practitioner's precepts remain immaculate. His Holiness gave very clear teachings in this regard: "Monks and nuns in a time when the Dharma is in decline may choose to exchange their extremely precious precepts for a moment of physical pleasure. This would be extremely shameful. By praying to Kurukullā devoutly, hardships of this kind can be completely dispelled."

For lay people who are experiencing difficulty finding a spouse, Kurukullā can be of help as well. It is for this reason that Kurukullā is known to some as "the personal deity of love." There are many single men and women who are having difficulty finding a partner, and a lot of them ask for help from their Tibetan lamas. These lamas, out of compassion for them, would suggest that they recite the Kurukullā mantra, OṂ KURUKULLE SVĀHĀ.

People who seek matrimonial harmony can also solicit help from Kurukullā. There is a story about a once beautiful but aging queen in ancient India who had over time lost the affection of her king. Determined to regain the king's affection, the queen sent a maid out on a mission to find an elixir that could reignite her husband's passion. The maid searched far and wide for the elixir with no result, until one day she met a beautiful red-skinned woman. After learning of the maid's mission, the red-skinned woman quickly prepared a particular type of food and gave it to the maid, telling her that if she could get the king to eat it, all of the queen's problems would be solved.

The maid returned to the palace and repeated the red-skinned woman's words to the queen. Afraid of the consequences of feeding this unidentified food to the king, the queen threw it into a nearby lake. (Another account of the story is that the queen, having lost the king's affection completely, was exiled and, therefore, couldn't give the food to the king.) A nāga who lived in the lake ate the magical food, was transformed into an image of the king, and in this disguise impregnated the queen.

When the king heard the news of the queen's pregnancy, he became enraged, and decided to punish her. The queen saw no alternative but to confess everything. Dubious, the king demanded that the maid summon the red-skinned woman to the palace. As she stood before him, the king immediately realized that this red-skinned woman was none other than the goddess Kurukullā herself, and, prostrating before her, asked for teachings that could help him surpass all desire. Through diligent practice, the king was eventually able to attain enlightenment, and thus it is said that the king was the first disciple in the human realm to hold the lineage of Kurukullā's teachings.

It is hoped that this story may encourage your faith in Kurukullā. In Tibetan Buddhism, there are many different practices related to Kurukullā. His Holiness Jigme Phuntsok Rinpoche has written a liturgy and praise of Kurukullā. When he visited the holy mountain of Samye Chimpu, he revealed a terma that contained a liturgy for Kurukullā practice.

The previous paragraphs have introduced each of the nine magnetizing deities. Each of them has extraordinary qualities, and if you pray to any one of them, you will receive incredible blessings. His Holiness once said, "If you don't have wealth, *Wangdu* can bring you wealth; if you want status, *Wangdu* can help you get status. Relying on this prayer, you can gain everything that you desire. If, however, due to having no control over your mind, you are unable to give rise to bodhicitta, emptiness, and other nonworldly accomplishments, reciting *Wangdu* with diligence will allow you to gain these qualities with ease." Therefore, whether it is to achieve your worldly or transcendent goals, you can pray to the nine deities and by relying on their blessings, all your wishes will come true.

HOW TO PRAY

Visualize the Qualities of the Vajra Body

Dancing in effortless bliss and emptiness with supreme and
    ordinary mudrās,
an assembly of vajra warrior ḍākas and ḍākinīs attract and
    magnetize.
Remaining always within the state of great equality of appearance
    and emptiness,
the dance of your vajra bodies shakes the three realms of existence.

This verse means that because the magnetizing deities have accomplished all supreme and ordinary mudrās, they have the ability to display dances in the dharmadhātu. The dance itself is a manifestation of the nonduality of appearance and emptiness. Residing in the great equality of the perfect union of appearance and emptiness, the dancing of innumerable vajra bodies cause the three realms of existence to shake.

Here, the word "mudrā" contains many layers of meaning; in this stanza it should be interpreted as quality and accomplishment. "Vajra ḍākas" indicate the male buddhas and bodhisattvas, namely Amitābha, Avalokiteśvara, Hayagrīva, and so forth, while "vajra ḍākinīs" indicates the female buddhas and bodhisattvas, such as Vajravārāhī, Guhyajñāna, and so forth.

Each sentient being has their own predisposition and capacity. To benefit sentient beings of different dispositions, enlightened beings manifest ḍākas and ḍākinīs. The reason they can assume different forms is due to the nature of phenomena being the inseparability of appearance and emptiness. Otherwise, this would be impossible to achieve, regardless of how powerful they were.

"Dance" is a figurative term, which in this case refers to the manifestation of buddhas and bodhisattvas. For instance, Avalokiteśvara can manifest in thirty-two different forms. Hayagrīva sometimes appears with one face and two arms and sometimes with one face and four arms and so on. The deities assume different appearances in front of sentient beings, much like a skillful dancer performing different dances for his or her audience.

"Shakes the three realms of existence" means benefiting sentient beings in the three realms of existence. The magnetizing deities manifest themselves in various ways to accommodate the perception of sentient beings in the three realms of desire, form, and formlessness. It should be noted that although the text only mentions nine magnetizing deities, in reality, there are countless magnetizing deities, each with an unlimited number of manifestations. For instance, though some deities may manifest with skin that is red in color, they may also manifest themselves as white, green, and so on.

So, to visualize and merge with the vajra bodies of the magnetizing deities, you should first understand the enlightened qualities of their bodies. In the realm of dharmadhātu that has no boundaries, the magnetizing deities display countless manifestations that cause the three realms to tremble, captivating sentient beings of the three realms and granting them temporary well-being and ultimate enlightenment.

Visualize the Qualities of the Vajra Speech

The sounds of laughter of your unimpeded speech reaches the
  three worlds.
You radiate red light rays that spread throughout saṃsāra and
  nirvāṇa.
Luminous essence of existence and cessation, you tremble and
  gather.

The Basic Meaning of the Verse
"Vajra speech" is a very broad term. In a narrow sense, it means the sound that the magnetizing deities make. In a broader sense, it means the sound of earth, water, fire, wind, and the sounds of all sentient beings. It can be said that all sound is the vajra speech of the magnetizing deities.

The magnetizing deities' vajra speech makes the sounds of laughter, such as "ha ha, he he, hey hey, and ho ho." With these sounds, they summon beings of the three realms; they are particularly able to call forward and subdue the demonic beings of the three realms.

"Existence" indicates deluded beings' three impure states of existence in saṃsāra. "Cessation" indicates enlightened beings' pure states in nirvāṇa. "Luminous essences" indicates the essence of the four elements of the inanimate world and the essence of living beings, such as the qualities of compassion and wisdom. The last two lines indicate that the mantra wheels at the throat (or heart) of the magnetizing deities radiate red light, which shines upon every corner of saṃsāra and nirvāṇa, vibrating and calling forth all the vital essences of both mundane and supramundane phenomena.

The Essence of All Worldly and Nonworldly Existence

Magnetizing has a wondrous effect. Through the practice of magnetizing, the essence and merit of all worldly and nonworldly existence is gathered and dissolved into one's own mindstream. For example, if you lack wisdom, you can gain it through the practice of magnetizing. Of course, magnetizing is different from what certain non-Buddhist sects describe as "harvesting energy." Some people believe that the reason that they are particularly skinny is because their *qi* has been sucked away by someone else. This, however, is not what magnetizing means. Although you will benefit from the magnetizing practice, no harm will be inflicted on others. Similarly, if we light a candle and hold it in our hand, its flame will not cause any other candle to be extinguished.

There is no need to mystify magnetizing. Worldly things can have very similar magnetizing effects. For example, some people are seduced by love, social status, wealth, fine food, and so on. Similar to the art of magnetizing, these are also means to entice people.

However, one must be aware that Buddhists do not magnetize for personal acquisition of fame or power but rather for the welfare of sentient beings. You cannot benefit sentient beings if you lack the necessary powers of enticement. Some lamas possess qualities of wisdom, compassion, and eloquence but seem to have great trouble expanding their religious influence. In spite of being very motivated to benefit beings, they fail to gather disciples around them. This is because they have not mastered the activity of magnetizing. People who have accomplished the art of magnetizing will spontaneously captivate others wherever they go. Therefore, if you wish to benefit sentient beings, not only should you possess the qualities of wisdom, precepts, and noble character, you should also be skilled in magnetizing.

Visualize the Qualities of the Vajra Mind

With your enlightened mind of great vajra passion,
you bestow the supreme and common siddhis.

With your vajra iron hooks and lassoes,
you bind all that appears and exists in supreme bliss.

Great Vajra Passion
The magnetizing deities, utilizing the great vajra passion of their enlightened minds, bestow all the supreme and ordinary siddhis that sentient beings desire. With their vajra iron hooks and lassoes, they bind the world of appearance and existence in the wisdom of great bliss.

"Great vajra passion" means the wisdom of discernment that is transformed from lust; it is a commonly used term in Vajrayāna. In *Chanting the Names of Mañjuśrī*, it is written, "Vajra passion, great passion." Passion in its ordinary sense is a kind of attachment. If you haven't realized the nature of your own mind, you can become entangled by it. When you have realized the primordial nature of the mind, passion is transcended into great vajra passion, which does not cause harm to oneself or to others. The same principle applies to the transcendence of anger, ignorance, and so on. As soon as you understand the true nature of these things, they can be turned into untainted wisdom.

The relationship between mental afflictions and wisdom has also been addressed by certain Mahāyāna sūtras that convey the ultimate meaning. The *Sūtra Requested by Kāśyapa* says, "Just as poison can be transformed into an elixir by the power of mantras, with creative means, passion can be transformed into wisdom."

Ordinary beings are constantly bound by desire, and constantly wanting something or someone, which causes a substantial degree of mental suffering. Such suffering is caused by not understanding the nature of the mind. If through pith instructions, you can understand the true nature of your mind, then all suffering and pain will dissolve into dharmadhātu. Therefore, everybody should devote their best efforts to realizing the true nature of the mind.

Vajra Hooks and Lassoes
In their hand, the magnetizing deities hold tools like iron and copper hooks, lotus lassoes, and so on. This can sometimes be misinterpreted. The magnetizing deities do not literally hook, tie up, and pull their subjects toward them like fishermen. You must understand that these instruments are merely symbolic of the deities' power to compel and enchant their subjects.

The implicit power of magnetizing can create skepticism among some. In reality, when a person who has never been interested in Buddhism meets a lama, he is often immediately captured by the hook of his compassion and wants to take refuge in the Three Jewels and, ultimately, becomes a person who is of benefit to Buddhism. This is the force of magnetizing.

When we interpret the Dharma, it is important that we hold the right view. For example, the sword in the hand of the bodhisattva Mañjuśrī is not used to harm or kill but is a symbol for the wisdom with which he eradicates the ignorance of sentient beings. The lotus blossom in Avalokiteśvara's hand is a symbol for his residing in saṃsāra while remaining untainted by its defilements, much like the lotus that sprouts from the mud but whose blossom remains pristine. Therefore, the objects that buddhas and bodhisattvas carry are not random but are symbols that each give rise to a specific karmic origination.

One important thing that needs to be understood is that magnetizing is a practice for the purpose of benefitting sentient beings. When benefiting sentient beings, bodhisattvas magnetize those who are drowning in the depths of saṃsāra by using their wisdom and compassion. Bodhisattvas dissolve sentient beings' minds into their wisdom of great bliss, transforming them from an untamed and rigid state into one of being calm and capable. Eventually, sentient beings are guided to realize the true nature of their minds.

The Practice of Wangdu

Because of the aforementioned reasons, we should practice magnetizing with diligence. When you chant and practice *Wangdu*, you can follow the instructions of the common or advanced tantric practices. Of course, uninitiated practitioners, or practitioners who are foreign to tantric practice, can practice *Wangdu* using the Sūtrayāna method. Mipham Rinpoche did not require people to strictly practice this prayer according to the generation or perfection stages. As long as we pray to the magnetizing deities with devotion, all animate and inanimate worlds will resonate. This will allow the essence of saṃsāra and nirvāṇa to be gathered into oneself.

For people who are new to dharma practice, the practice of magnetizing would definitely be of benefit. In this degenerate age, people have difficulty truly absorbing the Dharma because they lack inner strength; their path in learning the Dharma is filled with obstacles. If you are one of these people, by practicing magnetizing you will develop inner strength and be able to bring the Dharma into your mind more easily. Then, no matter what kind of obstacle you encounter, you will be capable of handling it.

If you want to accomplish magnetizing, you should first establish a connection with the magnetizing deities, which is to say that you should merge your body, speech, and mind with theirs. To merge with the deities' vajra bodies, Buddhist masters visualize their own body as the body of the magnetizing deity. This is the most effective method. If you are unfamiliar with such advanced practices, an alternative would be to carry the image of the nine deities with you and to make offerings to them.

In terms of speech, you should often recite the mantra of the nine deities and *Wangdu* in particular. The *Wangdu* prayer consists of the vajra words of Mipham Rinpoche. Reciting them even once brings forth vast merit. When you recite *Wangdu*, it is best to visualize as you chant. You can visualize a boundless red light emanating from the magnetizing deities, shining upon all sentient beings and benefiting them with the Dharma. You don't need to get too complicated with your visualization. Some people's imagination is overly active. They create unnecessary details in their visualization and may imagine a red lotus flower blossoming from the heart center of the magnetizing deities with a HRĪḤ on top in red letters, emanating light and so forth, even though there is no description such as this in the sādhana.

In terms of mind, you can visualize that your mind is inseparable from the wisdom of the magnetizing deities. Then you can observe the nature of your mind, directly understanding that the magnetizing deities are exactly the nature of your mind at this present moment. There are no other magnetizing deities apart from your own mind at this moment. If you can meditate like this, you will be able to swiftly and truly merge with the magnetizing deities.

The reason is as follows. The minds of sentient beings are no different from that of buddhas and bodhisattvas. Ignorant of this fact, people cling to the notion that they and buddhas and bodhisattvas are separate entities. The different levels of practice in Buddhism are designed to break such a discriminating notion. First, one visualizes oneself and a deity in a vertical relationship like that between a disciple and a lama. Then, in a more advanced stage of practice, we visualize that we are the equals of the deity, like the relationship that exists between friends. Last, we visualize that we are no different from the deity, like water that is poured into water.

Through such a visualization practice, we can eventually perceive our minds as the same as that of buddhas and bodhisattvas. It is very important to follow the gradual steps of visualization. Training our minds, much like refining gold, is a gradual process.

PRAY FOR THE ACCOMPLISHMENTS

Dancers in the play of a boundless web of illusions,
who fill space and overflow, like a vast outpouring of sesame seeds,
to the countless Three Roots, deities of magnetizing activity,
devoutly, I pray for your blessings to come down.
Grant me all of my heart's desires—the supreme and common siddhis!

An Infinity of Magnetizing Deities

"A boundless web of illusions" describes an infinity of magnetizing deities in dharmadhātu. When describing the maṇḍalas in Vajrayāna Buddhism, we often count buddhas and bodhisattvas in units of hundreds, thousands, tens of thousands, hundreds of thousands, millions, and billions. These numbers are figurative. In reality, buddhas and bodhisattvas are innumerable.

In the limitless dharmadhātu abide innumerable buddhas and bodhisattvas. *The Amitābha Sūtra* states that there are countless buddhas in each direction. "Nine" is only a symbolic number for the countless magnetizing deities.

"A vast outpouring of sesame seeds" illustrates just how many magnetizing deities there are. The magnetizing deities inhabit and fill all of space, one next to the other, conveying an image that is very much like an open sesame pod full of sesame seeds. Relatively speaking, magnetizing deities reside in the west; ultimately, however, they reside in every direction. Even in the tiniest molecule, there abide countless numbers of magnetizing deities.

We must keep an open mind when learning about Dharma. Only by doing so can we understand its incredible breadth. Even the common vehicle teachings depict states of infinity. For example, the sixteen arhats that protect Buddha Śākyamuni's teachings each possess both a limitless worldly and transcendent entourage.

Pray for Achieving Accomplishments

To the countless Three Roots, deities of magnetizing activity,
devoutly, I pray for your blessings to come down.

In praying to the Buddhas, the more devout we are, the stronger the blessings we receive. We should be so invested in our prayers that our hairs stand on end and tears stream from our eyes. Of course, it goes without saying that such devotion should be long-lasting. Some people are strongly motivated by the Dharma in the beginning, but when their initial enthusiasm cools, they grow more and more indifferent and unable to appreciate the merit of the Three Jewels and the guru. Though indifferent when hearing about the sufferings of saṃsāra, they brighten up immediately when the subject of delicious food comes up. This is not ideal, and we should develop a lasting conviction toward the Dharma over a preference for delicious food.

> Grant me all of my heart's desires—the supreme and common siddhis!

The supreme siddhi here indicates transcendent qualities such as the fruit of buddhahood. The ordinary siddhi refers to the eight worldly accomplishments, increased wealth, good health, longevity, and so on.

These days, it seems as though most people practicing Buddhism are rarely looking for supreme siddhis, just the ordinary benefits that can be useful in this life. One thing I want to remind everyone is that when you befriend a powerful person, you should ask that person to help only with the most important issues. Trivial matters are not worthy of their time. Similarly, when reciting *Wangdu*, if you are not looking for supreme benefits but instead recite it only for the ordinary purpose of dressing better, eating better, or sleeping better, this is not a worthwhile reason.

For those who have received the Mahāyāna teachings, these worldly qualities are as unreal as dreams and illusions. Regardless of how rich, how famous, or how high on the social ladder you are, everything will fall apart eventually. If you need more proof, just look at history. Worldly prosperity is transitory. Only transcendent merit has ultimate value. Therefore, we should seek transcendent qualities. Of course, there are many kinds of transcendent qualities. Each one of us has his or her own wish. Whatever you wish for, as long as you are diligent in your prayers, your wishes will come true.

Wangdu is the true wish-fulfilling jewel. If you recite this prayer diligently, not only will you gain all the qualities that you wish for, you can also remove all obstacles from your path. However, if you are faced with unavoidable karmic retribution that is the result of actions from previous lives, it would be difficult to expect immediate removal of such obstacles.

Once I was asked whether buddhas and bodhisattvas could save people from every kind of distress. If not, the questioner asked, then what is the use of praying? I told that person, when given the same dosage of the same medication, some patients are cured of their illness and others are not. Because the medication has no effect on some people, should it be rejected entirely? The same is true for the blessings of buddhas and bodhisattvas. Nobody says that they can solve each and every problem of every sentient being. The intricacies of karmic effect are extremely complex. By relying on the blessings of buddhas and bodhisattvas, some problems can be immediately solved, but other problems might not be. For problems such as these, praying is still the way that we can do our best.

Therefore, when we recite *Wangdu*, we are best advised to heed the teaching of His Holiness: "May the blessings of the magnetizing deities allow me to possess the quality of the three trainings throughout all future lives. Bless me so that I can benefit sentient beings through compassion in life after life!" Or, we should heed those of Samantabhadra: "With this merit, may I crush all mental afflictions, perfect all beneficial qualities, and benefit all sentient beings."

ACHIEVEMENTS OF CHANTING THIS PRAYER

This was composed on the first day of the seventh month of the Earth Hare year (1879) by one named Dhīḥ. Anyone who prays in this way will, without any doubt, accomplish all magnetizing activities exactly according to their wishes. This prayer may be written on red flags and flown in the air or used in prayer wheels powered by heat or wind. MAṄGALAM!

This text was written by Mipham Rinpoche in 1879 when he was thirty-four years old. "Dhīḥ" is the seed letter of Mañjuśrī and is the name by which Mipham Rinpoche refers to himself in this text.

It is made very clear here that not only accomplished masters but anyone who prays in this way will accomplish magnetizing activities. His Holiness Jigme Phuntsok Rinpoche also said, "Only people with sharp faculties can reach enlightenment by the profound tantric practice. Ordinary people might not succeed. But Mipham Rinpoche's *Wangdu* is different. As long as they have faith in the nine magnetizing deities, anybody can accomplish magnetizing activities."

Hanging Up Red Prayer Flags of Wangdu

When His Holiness was with us, prayer flags with *Wangdu* printed on them were flying on every roof at Larung Gar. Nowadays, one can easily find *Wangdu* flags in Tibetan areas. Even in some big cities in Han Chinese areas, people have the walls of their homes covered with *Wangdu* prayer flags. This provides an auspicious connection.

I would like to advise everyone to recite *Wangdu* diligently in the future and to hang up many *Wangdu* prayer flags. This will help in spreading the Dharma and also benefit local sentient beings. Many people today are suffering from paranoia, anxiety, and depression. If you can recite *Wangdu* or hang up *Wangdu* prayer flags, your body and mind can enjoy greater freedom, and happiness will spontaneously arise in you.

Be careful when hanging prayer flags. It is best to hang them somewhere high off the ground such as on a rooftop or a mountain. Don't hang them in your yard where people come in and out. Prayer flags are no different from the deities themselves. If they are hung in an inappropriate place and people step over them, this would be a considerable mistake.

Before you hang up the flags, they must be consecrated. If you can't find someone to consecrate them for you, sprinkle some rice left over from a previous consecration ceremony. If you don't have that either, recite seven times the mantra of dependent origination, which also counts as consecration.

Turning Prayer Wheels of Wangdu

It has also been explained by Mipham Rinpoche that apart from being made into prayer flags, *Wangdu* can also be made into prayer wheels powered by wind or fire. This will also help in accomplishing magnetizing activities. Of course, we can also make prayer wheels with *Wangdu* prayers that are hand spun.

Incidentally, there is a specific protocol to follow when making prayer wheels. You should not make prayer wheels without consulting the sūtra reference. His Holiness Jigme Phuntsok Rinpoche once commented, "When some people get ahold of the mantra of a buddha, they immediately put it in a prayer wheel. This is unreasonable. If you want to make prayer wheels, it would be good to make them with the MAṆI mantra because much scriptural evidence tells us that prayer wheels made with the MAṆI mantra are extremely beneficial."

Not long before His Holiness passed away, he repeatedly instructed his students to turn prayer wheels often, and he said with a strong sense of assertion that when a person is about to die, even if there is no one to recite prayers for them, as long as they have a prayer wheel next to them, they will not fall into the lower realms.

Anyway, we can make *Wangdu* widely known by means of prayer flags or prayer wheels. In this way, not only will our own body and mind become freer with many of our obstacles removed, but it will also help the Dharma to become more prosperous.

The Practice of Magnetizing at Larung Gar

Some dismiss this magnetizing activity as nothing more than myth or fiction, but the very example of His Holiness Jigme Phuntsok Rinpoche demonstrates how tangible the effects of magnetizing can be. All of his many great accomplishments would not have been possible without his accomplishment of the art of magnetizing. The very fact that so many people come to Larung Gar for Dharma study and practice is the result of his magnetizing activity. No one would come and settle in this freezing land of snow for no reason. I have personally experienced the effect of magnetizing on myself. Each time I go on a trip, I miss Larung Gar very much. As soon as I finish my business, I am eager to head straight back. This is inseparable from His Holiness's magnetizing activity. . . .

So, this is a true reflection of the power of magnetizing. At Larung Gar, we practice magnetizing every year at the Dharma Assembly of the Awareness Holders. During this time of the year, the mantra of the nine deities will be chanted by the full saṅgha for half a month. Such a practice taking place in a large assembly is extremely powerful. I once half-joked about shortening the duration of the Dharma Assembly, lest the Larung Valley run out of room for people to sit.

Before His Holiness passed away, he said, "In the future, if my disciples recite *Wangdu* often, the heart transmissions of the guru will continue." In *The Way of the Bodhisattva*, there is a story about a celestial being who cured a disease caused by the nāgas by building a large *garuḍa* tower. Many years after this celestial being had passed away, people still circumambulated the *stūpa* to cure the disease caused by nāgas. Similarly, even if you have never seen His Holiness Jigme Phuntsok Rinpoche personally, by practicing *Wangdu*, you can still receive the blessings of his mind transmission. When you have received his mind transmission, your own suffering will be dispelled and whatever kind of obstacle you encounter, you will face it with more ease and poise. You will be happy in your present life and, it goes without saying, in your future lives as well.

In 2011, I aspired to concentrate on practicing magnetizing activity. The motivation is simple. His Holiness Jigme Phuntsok Rinpoche had completely mastered the enlightened activity of magnetizing. I dare not say I want to achieve the same level of mastery as His Holiness, but as his disciple, I should at least follow the steps of the activities that he created. As a disciple of a guru who had mastered the art of magnetizing, it does not seem right to neglect this practice; I must endeavor with all my effort to continue his traditions. So, in recent years, I again and again encouraged Buddhist followers to recite *Wangdu* ten thousand times as a short-term target of their Dharma practice and an aspiration of contributing to the activities of spreading the Dharma.

4. The Unity of Religion and Tibetan Culture

Jann Ronis

Introduction

STARTING IN THE 1990s, Metrul Tenzin Gyatso, one of the second-generation leaders at Larung Gar, was engaged in thinking about the best way to modernize Tibetan culture. As a poet and polemicist, he laments a sense of dislocation among Tibetans in a 2006 collection of poetry, *Fleeting Thoughts betwixt Saṃsāra and Nirvāṇa*, and explores new horizons in the confluence between Buddhism and science in his 2011 book, *An Analysis of the Connection between Mind and Brain*. As a learned cleric-scholar engaged with secular discourse, he has followed in the footsteps of his teacher Khenpo Jigme Phuntsok and has also gone beyond him by responding to urban Tibetan secular intellectuals who criticize Buddhism as a regressive force in Tibetan society and culture. Especially influential for him was the great khenpo's *Heart Advice to Tibetans for the Twenty-First Century* (introduced in chapter 2). This tract served as an open letter of sorts to the youth of Tibet regarding the perceived weakening and adulteration of their behavior, values, and spoken language as the first generation of Tibetans to grow up in the post-Mao, open-market era. It was widely disseminated, periodically going in and out of print, and the khenpo's disciples still lecture and write about the importance of preserving Tibetan culture while also modernizing in pace with other nationalities.

Monastic Responses to Secular Critiques

Metrul Tenzin Gyatso is one of the Larung Gar leaders who is deeply concerned about the way forward for Tibetan culture and society. Two of his essays articulate his concerns with penetrating force: "An Analysis of the Development of Tibetan Culture When Religion Is Influential" (1998) and "A Rough Analysis of the New Era Essay, *A Call from Afar for Scrutiny*" (2002). These essays are not merely extensions of Khenpo Jigme Phuntsok's admonitions in *Heart Advice*. Indeed, the impetus for Tenzin Gyatso's 1998 and 2002 essays was not to comment on a general, inexorable decline in culture. Rather, Tenzin Gyatso was responding to a sensationalized and controversial attack on traditional culture by fellow Tibetans, who were by and large urban, educated, and secular, living in Chinese cities that border the Tibetan plateau. That is to say, his 1998 and 2002 essays were not intended to counter the seductions of a modern lifestyle and the rewards of assimilation; instead, they anticipated and responded to the vehement critiques of Buddhism and calls by Tibetan secular intellectuals to abandon almost everything Khenpo Jigme Phuntsok represented.

Metrul Tenzin Gyatso's opponents in the debate over Tibetan modernity were a group of Tibetan writers and intellectuals from Amdo dedicated to the elaboration of a secular-materialist ideology for modern Tibetans. Sometimes called the New Thinkers, these secular intellectuals offer an extreme prescription for the modernization of Tibet: the total abandonment of religious ways of thinking and acting.[1] For example, they attribute the weakening of Tibetan culture and vulnerability to foreign domination to the influence of Buddhism, particularly its nonviolent ethos. Their cultural hero is none other than Langdarma, the last of the Yarlung emperors who dismantled the Buddhist institutions sponsored by his forebearers, Songtsen Gampo and Trisong Detsen, who are considered by Tibetans to be bodhisattvas for their sponsorship of Buddhist temples, monasticism, and translations of the canon.

In his advocacy of a Tibetan modernity in line with Buddhist values, Metrul Tenzin Gyatso is part of the leading edge of Buddhist modernism at Larung Gar and a key figure there since the early 1990s. Born in 1968 in Mewa, Hongyuan County in Aba Prefecture (Sichuan)—a nomadic region that identifies as part of Amdo—he studied literature and the arts as a child and joined Larung Gar in 1987. Quickly emerging as a prominent disciple of Khenpo Jigme Phuntsok, in 1990 he became an officer at the monastery and is now one of the chief executives and religious leaders of the community. Needless to say, he also has a sizable flock of Han Chinese disciples across inland China.

Metrul Tenzin Gyatso has been writing about modern topics and issues since the 1990s. When I visited him at Serta in 2000, he presented me with a book on dream studies. This work on dreams must also be counted among the first well-reasoned writings on the topic of Buddhism and science to be composed in Tibet by a contemporary lama. In this chapter, I focus on two of his essays addressing the importance of Buddhism to Tibetan modernity and responding to critiques by secular intellectuals, namely "An Analysis of the Development of Tibetan Culture When Religion Is Influential," 1998, and "A Rough Analysis of the New Era Essay, *A Call from Afar for Scrutiny*" (2002). My translation of a long section of his 1998 essay can be found at the end of the chapter. These essays show how polemics are taking new forms in contemporary Buddhist literature and how sensitive Larung Gar leaders are toward the need for a modernist sensibility to infuse and inform traditional Buddhist teachings.

A New Kind of Polemics

The first of Metrul Tenzin Gyatso's essays, "An Analysis of the Development of Tibetan Culture When Religion Is Influential" was composed in early 1998,[2] a year before publications by the New Thinkers were disseminated widely in the official press, though some essays had already circulated. Thus, even before the first high-profile essays by Shokdung had shaken up public discourse throughout Amdo, Tenzin Gyatso was already sufficiently aware of and alarmed by the new ideas percolating to pen a medium-length article. Fittingly, this work does not refute any authors or essays by name, though twice it mentions "several recent essays." Throughout Tenzin Gyatso's piece, however, is the invocation of "educated young Tibetans." Indeed, he does not include any direct quotes but instead summarizes the views of the apostates who have been to Chinese universities. This work is written in the form of the modern essay, and its style of argumentation is incisive but articulated in everyday language. In other words, he leaves aside the typical syllogisms of traditional commentaries. Signaling an intended wide reach, initially it was published as a pamphlet and circulated for free.

Metrul Tenzin Gyatso's 1998 essay certainly did not change the minds of the New Thinkers or the media gatekeepers who promoted their writings. Indeed, their watershed moment was yet to come and broke the next year in 1999. In May of that year, an issue of the *Qinghai Daily* was dedicated to reflections on the relevance of the May Fourth Movement for the modern times. Shokdung and others published incendiary essays in this issue, and in the ensuing uproar, several public events were held in Xining for partisan debate on the issues. Shokdung's 1999 essays were primarily screeds against religion. I use the word *screed* not in order to bias my audience but because the level of discourse in them is simply not up to the standards of basic academic writing. Lauran Hartley writes about them, "[F]rankly, [they] are filled with internal contradictions, ambiguities, and slogans."[3] In 2001, consolidating his position as the main ideologue of the so-called New Thinkers, Shokdung published a book of new writings called *A Call from Afar for Scrutiny*.[4] Wu Qi has the following to say about it: "In it, the author advocated for rationality, essentially a culture based on logic. . . . Rationality is a key word used by the New Thinkers to attack opposing views because they think the characteristic of religion is superstition and irrational thinking."[5] However, one of the ironies of their critique is its lack of logical consistency. By contrast, as a cleric-scholar trained in the rigors of philosophical debate, Tenzin Gyatso's preemptive 1998 essay presents a strong bulwark against Shokdung's critique.

Tenzin Gyatso takes on Shokdung directly in his 2002 essay, a rebuttal of Shokdung's book titled "A Rough Analysis of the New Era Essay, *A Call from Afar for Scrutiny*." As far as I can tell, this work first appeared in a 2002 volume published by the Nakmang Institute.[6] The following year, in 2003, Metrul Tenzin Gyatso and Khenpo Tsultrim Lodro published a volume dedicated to refuting the assertions of the New Thinkers called *The Lion's Roar Guarding the Citadel of the Life Force of the Snow Mountains*,[7] and Tenzin Gyatso's rebuttal of Shokdung reappears there. Tenzin Gyatso calls this a "rough analysis" of Shokdung's book, but that is a drastic understatement. As Shokdung claims to model rationality for his Tibetan readership, Tenzin Gyatso articulates his takedown largely in the format of Tibetan debate. This work, therefore, abounds in syllogisms that take on Shokdung's primary claims. It treats a range of topics and includes chapters on taking refuge, overturning the habit of shooting one's arrow in the dark, Buddhism and science, a critique of trying to move forward with only one leg, and a defense of the doctrines of karma and no-self.

Conclusion

These two essays are comprehensive and forceful and must have given the traditionalists a number of good points to use when in debate with the New Thinkers. Indeed, many of Tenzin Gyatso's best arguments therein are still being used in present-day discourse that continues from the turn of the millennium debates that so enthralled Amdo. However, now twenty years later, public discourse in Tibet is very different. Since the period of the New Thinkers, the advent of the internet and social media, state development programs, and the post-2008 social unrest have brought into being conditions that could not have been envisioned by Metrul Tenzin Gyatso and others in the late 1990s. In the case of Larung Gar, the textual defenses of Buddhism and the importance of traditional culture continue to be produced. But, I would argue that their most compelling argument is their praxis: the massive social experiment to implement Buddhist virtues and innovate as a monastic institution. The self-designation of Larung Gar as a "city of Dharma" or, better yet, a "Dharma metropolis"[8] was not intended as an allusion to the large monastic seats of central Tibet. Rather, Larung Gar represents itself not as a megamonastery like Labrang to the north in Amdo but as a city—a modern city. The adoption of modern technology, the creation of a booming Buddhist-based economy, the elaboration of Buddhist modernism, and the success of Larung Gar as an ecumenical Buddhist institute prove the New Thinkers wrong on accounts of backwardness at the very least and provide an alternative vision for the future of Tibetan culture and the role of religion in society.

An Analysis of the Development of Tibetan Culture When Religion Is Influential

METRUL TENZIN GYATSO (1998)

In this land encircled by a white enclosure of snow mountains, Buddhism is prevalent. It would be impossible to separate religion from Tibetan people's attitudes and quotidian labor, or from the literate culture and folk customs. In Tibet, there is no way to conceive of a system of worldly activities that are completely independent of religion. The concept of "religion conjoined to politics"⁹ originated from this situation. There are many assertions about the exact contours and chronology of this concept. Nevertheless, generally speaking, the term "religion conjoined to politics" is a product of ancient Tibetan culture, and its correct meaning is governance carried out in accord with religion. Additionally, it denotes a condition in which secular authority is not misused but instead constrained by the values of goodheartedness, love, altruism, good manners, and honesty. When religion is conjoined with politics, the law is implemented in accord with religious precepts in a way that is unbiased and informed by karmic cause and effect. For this reason, commencing at the time of Dharma king Songtsen Gampo, many religious commandments such as the ten virtues were enshrined within state law.

So-called religious law is not something completely different from state law. Religious law is that which steers a person onto the correct path through having reformed the negative mental habits such as desire and anger in the mindstream of ordinary beings and the negative actions of body and speech that are produced by them. Whenever one cannot reform the mental states of anger, jealousy, deceit, conceit, and so forth, they serve as the basis for the unhappiness of self and others through undertaking many wrong deeds such as oppression, bellicosity, and dishonesty. Additionally, those negative mental habits will also cause society to become disordered such that there is no security or stability. If one can completely eliminate the negative mental habits, then the negative actions that are interrelated with them will automatically cease.

In the final analysis, the aim of religion is the taming of the mind. A person who is able to cease all misconduct does not need to struggle to uphold an additional set of completely distinct rules called "state laws" and, therefore, will be free of worry [about committing a crime]. Therefore, tradition speaks of the religious laws being a soft and loose silk knot. The religious law is the earthlike foundation of all the other codes of conduct or the chief of them all. The state laws are merely a factor for overcoming divisions and creating harmony within the religious code.

The state laws rejoice in and praise those who abide in religion and whose conduct accords with religion. The code of state laws is known as "the bulky and heavy golden yoke," because it uses strict punishment to forcibly control the behavior of people who cannot give up their bad nature no matter how much they are given religious training. Savage people, not abiding in the way of religion, have evil mindsets and engage in incorrect behavior such as bullying others, robbing, and killing.

Contemporary scholars, citing the canonical works of Hegel, Engels, and others, explain that conjoining religion with politics means that a single person serves as both king and religious leader, which began in Tibet with the seizure of political power over Tibet by Drogon Chogyal Phakpa. Partisans of this viewpoint say that from the beginning of the conjoining of religion with politics through to its abolition, unimaginable calamities occurred as a result of the fusion and not the separation of religion and politics. They suggest that internal disputes and the lack of growth of governance, economy, and science [in Tibet] were caused by problems such as religious powers usurping each other's monastic estates and subjects and the quarreling over political power by various sectarian traditions. Following this theory, many young people think that the primary reason Tibet has not been able to develop is related to the prevalence of religion in Tibetan lands. They have thereby fallen into rebellion and ignorance.

It is the case that there are formulations of religion conjoined with politics in which the roles of king and religious leader were assumed by a single person; that is not being refuted here. Nevertheless, in the context of Tibet's form of the conjoining of religion and politics, the explanations by Tibet's traditional scholars do not fit with this characterization even partially. Therefore, it appears that the equation of "religion conjoined with politics" and theocracy is from the outset a mistaken premise. However, if it were the case that religious and state power were located in one person, then now is the time to investigate the union of religion and society in Tibet. Basing ourselves on the historical documents of our ethnic group, we must examine the following: the definition of the term *religion*, the definition of *politics*, the modes of their conjoining, the need for conjoining them, and whether there are contrary assertions about this.

These days, it is not all right for us to minimize the calamities that have occurred in Tibetan history, and we must dare to acknowledge the hugely damaging results caused by them. Nevertheless, when it comes to articulations of the conjoining of religion and society expressed in the classics of the Tibetan tradition, the problems that have occurred historically should not be seen as the faults of the Dharma itself or of the union of religion and politics. In fact, it's just the opposite. It is illogical to conclude that the negative events that have occurred in the name of religion are the fault of religion itself, the inability to practice it properly, or the inability to implement a genuine form of the union of religion and politics.

Why is this? Because, as explained above, when the meaning of the conjoining of religion and politics is broken into its constituent parts, politics is expressed as the carrying out of governance in harmony with religion; and religion can be encapsulated in this quotation from Āryadeva's *Four Hundred Verses*,

> The tathāgatas have taught that
> Dharma, in brief, is nonharming.

If religion is well known to be altruism in terms of overcoming of malice and harming others and the cultivation of charity, then, henceforth, we will be able to know whether there is a basis for the emergence of those evil and disturbing behaviors within governance carried out in harmony with religion.

In particular, because in the Mahāyāna system the foundation of the Dharma is embraced by the tetrad of love, compassion, joy, and equanimity, and because the historical calamities that have occurred in the name of religion are the chief objects to be abandoned—such as favoritism, prejudice, self-interest, animosity, and envy—what possible connection could the Dharma have with aggression carried out for the sake of one's estate or peasants? Likewise, the Dharma states that considering some parts of the holy Dharma as excellent and some parts of it as bad is essentially the misdeed of abandoning the Dharma. If you carry out politics in accordance with the traditional interpretation of the Dharma, then sectarian persecution and favoritism obviously have no place. Even a young intellectual can understand this.

Nevertheless, it's amazing that these days many people are completely mistaken about this. Therefore, you must understand that those calamities that have occurred in history happened because of a misuse of the term "the conjoining of religion and politics" by people who were unable to practice Dharma or incapable of implementing a genuine form of this institution. Furthermore, those people were products of their times. In the final analysis, therefore, the calamities must be recognized as the faults of persons. At present, through historical studies that identify faults as faults, we can draw negative examples to learn from. This is a crucial point.

Many young people of the present day chase after other cultures and social systems and consider Buddhism and religion to be obstacles to the development of society. They identify Buddhism's seizure of an important role in old Tibetan society as the primary cause of the ethnicity's underdevelopment. They have contempt for and are vehemently opposed to the conjoining of religion and politics. Nevertheless, if they do not understand the meaning of "the conjoining of religion and politics," then how can they possibly disparage it? This situation is a case of the sun of refutation and presentation rising before the sky of the opponent has even dawned.[10]

The proposition that religion harms the development of society is at odds with reality. It goes without saying that when a nationality wishes to develop, it must reform its old, traditional ways of thinking. Even though it is like that, I find very unreasonable the assertion that we must discard all of our traditions wholesale without any discrimination as to good and bad. No matter how widespread religion might be in a given advanced country, this does not present any obstacles to social development. Since Buddhism has been identified as the only religion capable of marching forward shoulder to shoulder with science, what correct reasons or axioms are there to prove that Buddhism obstructs the development of society?

There are those who have identified Buddhism as being similar to other religions in opposing science in earlier times. Nevertheless, since the beginning of the twentieth century Buddhism—and, in particular, Tibetan Buddhism—has been recognized as the only religion capable of marching forward shoulder to shoulder with science. Einstein, the most famous scientist in the world and the formulator of the theory of relativity declared, "Even though there are many different religions, Tibetan Buddhism is the only one that can march forward shoulder to shoulder with science."[11] Even recently, many eminent scientists and experts on Buddhism have convened conferences to compare systems across a vast range of topics, including physics, biology, psychology, relativity, cosmology, methods for healing with the power of the mind, epistemology, dream studies, and death and dying. They have found many commonalities. In terms of the results of their experimentation, generally speaking, Western scientists have generated tremendous research findings about external reality, but not as much about the mind. For this reason, they have made the extremely laudatory determination that there are very valuable insights to be gained by others in Asia but also by those in the West from cultural exchange with the primarily Buddhist culture of Tibet.

Since the development of a people's mentality is an important measure of social development, why is Buddhism considered to be an obstacle to social development? If one says, "It's because even if religious beliefs and behaviors have had some positive effect on the development of the mind, religion is still an obstacle to the development of external reality." I don't see a single valid argument in that discourse. According to your own reasoning, because during the time of the three ancestral Dharma kings the Buddhist teachings became widespread, the society at that time should have declined. But the opposite is true. At that time, the Tibetan state and power spread beyond the borders and many small states in Asia were conquered by Tibet. Such a decline did not occur during this epoch. And yet, if there were a benefit to religion not flourishing, then it follows that there should have been unheard of progress during the suppression of the Dharma by Langdarma and especially during the Cultural Revolution, when not even the term *religion* was uttered. But it was just the opposite.

Before the Cultural Revolution, the causes and conditions for Tibet's underdevelopment in the external material sphere was mainly due to our not having studied or endeavored at science, technology, and life. How was religion responsible for that? Therefore, having identified the causes and conditions that have led to underdevelopment, we must exert effort at reforming them. But, I fear that this will instead turn into an occasion where all the bad things undergirding the lack of development will be heaped upon religion. By way of analogy, it's like a man with excellent eyesight who has a disabled leg and is trying to keep up with other people. Although he really needs to have his leg diagnosed and treated, instead he blames his eyes and damages them. This would be a cause for ridicule by all of the world.

There are an increasing number of foreigners who love Tibetan religion and culture, including the language. If the amount of those who are actually accomplished scholars continues to increase at pace, then there could come a time when Tibetans will have to learn their language from scratch from another ethnicity, beginning with the alphabet. I think it is a crucial issue that Tibetans be able to master their own civilizational inheritance. If you think about it, whether or not our minority's essential nature will be able to survive is closely related to having the power to preserve our primarily Buddhist culture and the excellent personality and conduct that are dependent on it.

It is obvious that there is no way to establish a form of Tibetan culture that is completely self-sufficient, unconnected to a Buddhist foundation. If the educated youth of Tibet imitate other cultures and, thereby, develop in several respects and even obtain some benefits from that, such a situation would not merit the spirit or the letter of "the development of Tibetan culture." It would merely be the proliferation of that extraneous culture. If Tibetan religious culture declines, then there is a huge risk that all the cultural forms that are connected to it and earlier good customs would decline. Ultimately, the essential nature of the minority would be obliterated. Therefore, because nobody wants the extinction of our civilization, along with the essence of our ethnicity, it is imperative to retain Buddhism as the foundation of the culture as a whole.

Furthermore, it is a serious mistake to identify our religion as merely a folk religion that involves offerings to gods and performing rituals. Because our religion possesses many amazing and uncommon profound points, we must have an educated certainty about it and a correct outlook, something that is not merely the compulsion to "keep your father's eating bowl clean."[12]

Einstein himself proclaimed, "If there is a religion that can assist science it would be Buddhism."[13] Therefore, it is possible to be interested in the development of the material realm without sacrificing our superior religious culture. Indeed, through identifying the method for developing the human mind as the values of good behavior, honesty, loving-kindness, altruism, and so forth, every Tibetan—by virtue of being Tibetan—should carefully consider karmic causality, conscientiousness, and shame. Be certain that if you practice in this way in your everyday life and view our religion as an indispensable condition for a happy life, you will spontaneously and gladly engage in it. Our religion and culture will benefit such a Tibetan person. Such an excellent personality type—disciplined through religion and culture—will become a model for the people of the world, bringing hope that Tibetan culture will benefit not only Tibetans but all of humanity. Even so, because the accomplishment of that goal is still a long way off, we Tibetans—and especially the youth—need to be one hundred percent committed to a common effort.

However, because of various obstacles, there is very little association between the young people with a modern education and those learned in the Buddhist classics. As a result, their views, feelings, behaviors, and so forth, have grown apart, and we are unable to decide on a unified objective for endeavoring in common for developing our religion and culture. Therefore, I feel that it is an urgent matter for the educated youth and monastically trained scholars of our ethnicity to become well acquainted with one another and exchange ideas.

Many scholars who have been to Buddhist academies are only contented by traditional culture. They have no respect for modern views and knowledge and are not concerned at all about the transformations occurring around the world or the changes happening within our society. Owing to the fact that they only respect the views and conduct of their own livelihoods, cut off from society at large, they have no way to bring about the energy necessary to modernize our ethnicity's religion and civilization. And, in turn, most young Tibetans who have received a modern education don't have even a sesame seed's worth of understanding about their exalted cultural traditions. They treasure only new knowledge and viewpoints, which are trivial. With the buzzwords *reform* and *innovation* constantly on their lips, they depend on the imitation of the meaningless cultures of others and are unable to adore the excellent traits of their own ethnicity.

It is obvious that monastic scholars with vast learning about traditional culture must acknowledge the fact of progress in the worldly realm. Massive changes are occurring and will continue to occur for both outer and inner phenomena. In a similar fashion, people's mentalities have changed in every manner. Under such conditions, I believe there is no impediment whatsoever to modifying explanations of the Dharma to suit the dispositions of modern people, provided that we do not lose the fundamentals of our system's triad of view, conduct, and meditation. Because the shifting tides of history and the changing face of society are incontrovertible facts, it is futile to challenge the irrefutable.

Regardless of how much science and technology develop, the Buddhist teachings need not be threatened by them. The notion that once a community reaches a high level of development, they will become irreligious is thoroughly contradicted by actual historical developments. This is made clear by the fact that, as explained above, in the most advanced countries these days, the numbers of people who admire Buddhism is increasing daily, and that among the most educated people, the number of people who are interested in or believe in Buddhism is also increasing.

Nowadays, there are many negative situations across the board because of the decline in Buddhist understanding on the part of Tibetan students. As a direct consequence of poor training in Buddhism, these days, a number of young people who have taken up the responsibility to research Tibetan culture assiduously ascribe their own intellectual deficiencies to the holy Dharma. They shamelessly and ostentatiously make many slanderous statements against Buddhism. For example, some of them say about the Buddhist doctrine of karmic cause and effect, "Buddhists are fatalistic about karma and, therefore, do not believe that through human agency people have the power to do anything innovative in the world." Additionally, they hold that people must adapt to their karmic lots in life and that it is pointless to try to make any attempts to effect any real substantial reforms in their conditions. Generally speaking, if the views and tenets of Buddhism are backed up by solid reasoning, then it is not the case that pointing out the religion's faults is out of bounds. Indeed, the Victor himself declared,

Monks and learned ones,
just as gold is burnt, cut, and rubbed,
examine my words carefully and
do not accept them simply out of respect.

Nevertheless, I believe that, speaking as a Tibetan, the denigration of the Buddhist teachings through making spurious criticisms is something to be embarrassed and ashamed of. Rather, it is very laudable that Buddhists reject the existence of a creator god and that, informed by the doctrine of karmic cause and effect, they use transformative techniques to improve the human mind. Indeed, contemporary philosophers and scientists also propound atheism. They extensively praise our tenet system of karmic cause and effect that is predicated on the rejection of a creator god.

We need to consider whether these polemical essays that directly and indirectly insult and denigrate religion are beneficial to society and the masses. From my perspective, these kinds of essays injure the religious sentiments of the Tibetan masses, the vast majority of whom have faith in the Dharma. Not only that, I worry that these essays threaten to worsen the deterioration of the attitudes and behaviors of the Tibetan people that is happening in the wake of the widespread decline of customs that promote noble conduct.

Even while the thunderous praise of Buddhism made by honest scholars resonates through the airwaves, some of our Tibetan youth are still unable to awake from the deep sleep of their stupidity. It's very depressing that they are trapped in backwardness and narrow-mindedness and do not have the intellectual capacity for understanding the profound nature of reality. However, I've heard that, recently, several graduate students from different schools have come to the Buddhist academies to have extensive conversations about Buddhist thought and the future of Tibetan culture. This is something to be very happy about. If we are able to continue holding such events on a regular basis, then, henceforth, I have hope that we will settle on a common objective for the advancement of Tibetan culture.

5. A Case for Animal Compassion

Geoffrey Barstow

Introduction

A second-generation leader at Larung Gar, Khenpo Tsultrim Lodro (1962–) has incorporated a deep concern for animals into his vision of Buddhist ethics. He personally adopted vegetarianism in 1998 after witnessing animal suffering during visits to a series of slaughterhouses in China and Tibet and has advocated for it consistently since then. In addition to his vegetarianism and anti-slaughter stances, the khenpo is also known for his life-ransoming activities,[1] sometimes buying millions of fish at a time from markets and releasing them into local lakes.[2] This concern with animals is part of an ongoing emphasis on ethical reform not only among ordained monks and nuns but also among laypeople. Khenpo Tsultrim Lodro's concern for modernizing Buddhist ethics is crystalized in what are known as the new ten virtues, a specific ethical code that the khenpo has promoted widely and includes an emphasis on practicing compassion toward animals.[3]

Khenpo Tsultrim Lodro is a senior student of the late Khenpo Jigme Phuntsok (1933–2004), founder of the Larung Buddhist Academy. He served for more than two decades as Larung Gar's dean of education,[4] playing a central role in shaping the development and growth of the Academy. The khenpo's profile, however, extends well beyond the confines of Larung Gar itself. Over the last two decades, he has emerged as one of the most popular and charismatic Buddhist teachers in Tibet. His written works are widely disseminated in print and online, and videos of his oral sermons are also widely shared. In addition to his Tibetan audience, Khenpo Tsultrim Lodro is also well known among Han Chinese practitioners of Tibetan Buddhism, and many of his works have been translated into Chinese.

Khenpo Tsultrim Lodro's emphasis on modernizing ethics, especially when combined with his willingness to engage and court a Han Chinese audience, has made him something of a controversial figure. In particular, his efforts to promote animal ethics have provoked a backlash among some Tibetan intellectuals.[5] In the eyes of these critics, Khenpo Tsultrim Lodro's emphasis on vegetarianism and his promotion of the anti-slaughter movement have been difficult for Tibetan nomads, many of whom rely on slaughtering animals as a primary source of income. One Tibetan friend of mine went so far as to say that Khenpo Tsultrim Lodro's concern for animal welfare was "destroying Tibetan culture."[6] Despite these critiques, however, Khenpo Tsultrim Lodro has remained steadfast in his attempts to reform the treatment of animals. Further, he remains one of the most important religious intellectuals in contemporary Tibet, and, despite his critics, his efforts at ethical reform remain widely influential across the Tibetan world.

Promoting Compassion for Animals

Khenpo Tsultrim Lodro originally delivered *Words to Increase Virtue*,[7] the work translated in this chapter, orally as a speech in 2003 during the annual festivities surrounding the Saga Dawa holiday.[8] It was later transcribed and widely distributed in publication, but the work's originally oral character remains. Khenpo Tsultrim Lodro speaks directly to "those here in this crowd" and repeatedly uses the first-person plural *we* directly, including himself among those who need to be concerned with this issue. Further, the text is clearly centered on the Larung Gar community. The only religious leader that Khenpo Tsultrim Lodro mentions, in fact, is his teacher Khenpo Jigme Phuntsok who founded Larung Gar and whose vision of animal ethics deeply informs Khenpo Tsultrim Lodro's own. Overall, then, this work gives its readers a sense of immediacy, as if they were personally listening to the khenpo speak.

This sense of immediacy is reinforced by Khenpo Tsultrim Lodro's rhetorical style. The khenpo is a proficient scholar, well regarded for his knowledge of Tibetan philosophical and other literature (as *Answers to Questions on Madhyamaka*—translated by Douglas Duckworth in this anthology— amply demonstrates). And yet, in *Words to Increase Virtue*, he eschews extensive scriptural citations, never once mentioning any of the many canonical texts that could be used to support his pro-vegetarian stance.[9] Instead, the khenpo appeals to his audience's emotions and common sense. He speaks of the suffering of animals in vivid and clear terms, seemingly encouraging his readers to have an affective response to these animals' experiences. "All their lives," he says, "animals slave without wages, and at the end they can do nothing but be killed." And such suffering, he emphasizes, is not animals' natural state, but is instead directly caused by human actions and, ultimately, greed. Domestic animals, he points out, do nothing but help humans. "People, however, don't help these animals at all. Instead, they do nothing but harm them. When an animal gets old and weak so that its body is like one big sore, people do not wait for death to act on its own, but tie up its mouth and kill it.[10] People who oppress and destroy animals like this are evil butchers, even though they think they have to do it." This is not a scholastic argument but is rather an appeal to his audience's ethical sensibility and, frankly, their shame over past misdeeds.

This argument rests on an assumption that slaughtering animals causes them to suffer. This assumption, in turn, rests on a belief that humans and animals experience the world in similar ways. The comparability of human and animal perspectives has been a topic of considerable debate in Western philosophy with some philosophers suggesting that humans and animals are fundamentally akin to each other and others arguing that humans and animals are wholly distinct. Contemporary philosophers have sought to understand Buddhist perspectives on this issue, though again there is little consensus, with some scholars insisting that Buddhism sees humans and animals as almost irreconcilably different and others arguing that Buddhism minimizes the human/animal distinction.[11] Khenpo Tsultrim Lodro clearly aligns with the latter position (along with, I argue, the bulk of the Tibetan intellectual tradition).[12] Early on in this text, he insists that humans and animals share a drive to avoid suffering, claiming that, "We are all the same in wanting pleasure and not wanting suffering." Later, he reinforces this position, explicitly asking his audience to use their own experience as a lens through which to understand animal suffering, "Think about a person. They would be happy to die several times with less pain than to die a single horrible death like that. Since animals are the same, it is very important to use a method that is quick and does not inflict much suffering at the time of death." For Khenpo Tsultrim Lodro, humans and animals share a fundamental approach to life, seeking happiness and avoiding suffering. Ignoring this kinship and prioritizing one's own pleasures, he argues, is the "delusion of humanity" and the reason we can wantonly cause so much animal suffering.

Another theme woven throughout this piece is the inescapable karmic repercussions of slaughtering animals and eating meat. Those who slaughter animals cause them to suffer greatly, creating powerful, negative karmic bonds between them. In the future, these bonds will return to the slaughterer in the form of "blood-debts that must be repaid." Overall, Khenpo Tsultrim Lodro concludes, "We have caused animals to suffer greatly, and by the power of this we ourselves will suffer in hell." Avoiding slaughter, therefore, brings about a twofold benefit. On the one hand, it relieves the animals themselves of the pain that accompanies the slaughtering process. On the other hand, avoiding slaughtering also benefits the person by alleviating the negative karma that accompanies killing.

While it is the act of slaughter that actually harms animals, Khenpo Tsultrim Lodro also makes clear that he sees meat eating as the primary reason for slaughter and, therefore, that vegetarianism is the best way to avoid harming animals. This point may seem obvious to a contemporary reader, but by making this claim the khenpo is wading directly into one of the most contentious debates in Tibetan discussions of meat eating. For many Tibetans, eating meat was ethically and karmically separate from the act of killing the animal. Perhaps most importantly, the seminal Geluk teacher Khedrup Je Gelek Palsang argued in his *Dusting Off the Sage's Teachings* that consuming meat that had already been slaughtered by someone else was, karmically speaking, wholly distinct from the actual act of slaughter.[13] According to this position, vegetarianism is not necessary because it is the act of slaughter that harms animals, rather than the consumption of meat. Other figures disagreed, of course, arguing that meat eating was the direct cause of animal slaughter.[14] To support this, advocates for vegetarianism often cited the *Laṅkāvatāra Sūtra*, which claims, "People pay money for meat, causing animals to be killed for profit. Both the killer and buyer own this sinful karma."[15] By identifying meat eating as the cause of animal slaughter, Khenpo Tsultrim Lodro clearly aligns himself with the latter position, and encourages vegetarianism as the best option for those who wish to prevent animal suffering. "If people didn't eat meat," he argues, "there would be no need for animals to die while experiencing such horrible suffering."

At the same time as he presents vegetarianism as the best way to relieve animal suffering, however, Khenpo Tsultrim Lodro also maintains an awareness that many of his listeners may find actually adopting vegetarianism to be a difficult task. There are many reasons that contemporary Tibetans might find adopting vegetarianism difficult, including established cultural norms, concerns about health, and the simple enjoyment of its taste. These difficulties are especially pronounced for Tibetan nomads, who compose a large portion of the khenpo's audience and who often depend on animal husbandry—including dairy and wool production as well as meat—for a significant percentage of their income. Whatever their reasons, it is clear that Khenpo Tsultrim Lodro does not expect all of his followers to immediately adopt full vegetarianism. Despite identifying meat eating as the reason for animal suffering, for instance, the khenpo focusses primarily on the act of slaughtering rather than meat eating itself. In doing so, he acknowledges that while vegetarianism is the ideal, it may be beyond the reach of many of those in his audience. Avoiding slaughter is, perhaps, a more realistic goal.

This implicit sense that Khenpo Tsultrim Lodro's advice can be adopted in different degrees is made explicit in another passage in which he presents a series of levels on which his anti-slaughter advice can be implemented. "This is not only about slaughtering for profit." He says, "It is also great if families abandon their personal slaughtering, either permanently or temporarily. If even this is not possible, you must definitely reduce the killing a little. At the least, if it is not possible to avoid slaughtering, you absolutely must not use such horrible methods as binding the nose or beheading." Here and elsewhere in the text, the khenpo articulates a moral vision in which individuals have a range of options for practicing nonviolence toward animals. Full vegetarianism remains the best, but if an individual feels that vegetarianism is not possible then they should avoid slaughtering their animals—particularly selling livestock to industrial slaughterhouses for profit. But, if even this is not possible, Khenpo Tsultrim Lodro sets the use of humane slaughter methods as a minimum.

Overall, *Words to Increase Virtue* articulates a powerful critique of meat eating and animal slaughter. At the same time, however, this critique is coupled with recognition of the fact that many Tibetans find vegetarianism difficult in practice and suggestions for alternate, less intensive practices for those who feel full vegetarianism is too difficult. This flexibility is interesting in part because Khenpo's critics sometimes accuse him of inflexibility and that he insists that all Tibetans become full vegetarians.[16] I have heard several Tibetans insist (often quite angrily) that the khenpo forces anyone who wants to be his follower to give up slaughtering and become vegetarian, including nomads who have no other economic basis. To their mind, he is placing unrealistic burdens on those who are devoted to him.[17] And yet, as this text makes clear, the khenpo's opposition to animal slaughter is actually quite flexible. In personal conversation, in fact, he has told me that he explicitly avoids asking nomads to become vegetarian, as he feels this step is too difficult for most of them. I cannot fully explain this difference between what Khenpo Tsultrim Lodro says and writes and how he is perceived by some Tibetans, except to point to the heated emotions and rhetoric that sometimes surround debates over vegetarianism as well as possible gaps between the khenpo's own stance and the implementation of his ideas by other monastics.[18] Regardless of what an individual thinks about this issue, however, it is clear that Khenpo Tsultrim Lodro's animal advocacy—found in works such as *Words to Increase Virtue*—has brought new intensity to a centuries old debate over animal ethics in Tibetan religious culture.

Acknowledgments

This translation is a modified version of a translation I first did in 2012 and which I published on my blog The Lost Yak. The original translation was done with the consultation of two lamas from Larung Gar who wish to remain anonymous but to whom I am very grateful. The present translation has been revised with the assistance of Catherine Hardie, who generously shared her own translation of this text with me in the summer of 2019, and with the assistance of Lama Gyaltsen of Corvallis, who generously assisted with some difficult passages. Thanks also to Holly Gayley for her editorial assistance and for including this work in this anthology.

Words to Increase Virtue

Khenpo Tsultrim Lodro (2003)

I bow to Noble Avalokiteśvara.

These days, we of the Snow Land butcher our cattle, sheep, and other animals for their warm meat, without even a trace of compassion. The killing has gone so far that some breeds have become scarce in some areas. Domestic animals are sent to butchers, where they experience untold suffering, not just because of the need for food and clothes, but also for the sake of purchasing guns and other unnecessary things. Their sufferings are becoming increasingly established, without anyone noticing. This situation makes me very sad, as their suffering is indeed spreading. Such actions, which cause the decline of both the humans and cattle of Tibet, are indeed very frightful. This much goes without saying.

Therefore, some years ago, we could not help but ask people to stop such practices.[19] The minds of many wise people were affected by this, and this has led to some improvement. At the same time, however, most people of this region continued to act as they did before. There has, therefore, recently been another appeal, offered to all those who have not thought this through and who have, therefore, not eliminated their misconceptions.[20]

Forcing cruel sufferings on animals is very improper. We are all the same in wanting pleasure and not wanting suffering. Those here in this crowd have all experienced suffering, and there is no difference at all between this and animals' experience of happiness and suffering.[21] This reasoning is enough for us here. As for others, anyone who merely sees this suffering with their own eyes will understand clearly. So, when you think about whether or not it is appropriate to subject animals to this suffering so that you can supply your tongue with pleasant tastes, you should also think about putting your own body and mind in their position. The implications are clear. If someone examines this issue in detail, how could they fail to see that brutal actions such as these are unnecessary? This is true even if that person does not believe in, or is unclear about, the certainty of karmic repercussions.

There are some difficulties that arise with this. Some personal comfort comes from taking the lives of others, such as a higher lifestyle, an increase in wealth, or a famous name. In truth, however, the price of our pleasant lifestyle is the blood, tears, and lives of other beings. For the sake of minor pleasures for ourselves, we trample the pleasures of others, totally obliterating them. Thinking of our own minor hardships, we do not consider the grievous suffering of others. Thoughts like these are the delusions of humanity. Destructive, harsh, and malicious thoughts are demonic. Therefore, you must cover your ears when you hear talk that promotes negative thoughts like these!

Cruel actions are motivated by base thoughts such as these. Therefore, in earning a living, be very afraid of wrong livelihood. Every morsel of food and every item of clothing are, at their root, derived from the tears of many animals. Worldly livelihoods, therefore, are achieved through cruelty and viciousness. Dying for the sake of kindness and gentleness would be a great joy!

These days, given that we live as humans in the world, it is no longer necessary to kill animals.[22] If you think about it, we all have other means of finding food and clothes, so how could killing animals be reasonable? Avoiding killing may cause us some slight difficulty. But surely it is suitable and worthwhile to accept those minor difficulties for the sake of animals' lives and happiness. In particular, our domestic animals have been very kind to us. In the spring, they plow the fields for farmers, amassing sins by killing insects. In the autumn, they help with the harvest. They continuously experience fear and anxiety, without a moment's leisure. When we have need, we load them ourselves. When we have no need, we loan them to others. In either case, animals perform domestic labor right up until they are too old to carry a burden, continually experiencing the innumerable sufferings of servitude. Throughout their lives, female yaks and hybrids nourish us with their milk, butter, and curd.[23] Until they die, sheep provide products such as wool and dung. They provide nothing but benefit to people and don't bring even the slightest harm.

People, however, don't help these animals at all. Instead, they do nothing but harm them. When an animal gets old and weak, so that its body is like one big sore, people do not wait for death to act on its own, but tie up its mouth and kill it.[24] Even enemies and murderers are not oppressed and tormented in the way that people treat domestic animals. All their lives, animals slave without wages, and at the end they can do nothing but be killed. What could be worse than this?

Therefore, we should all contemplate this. Those of you who are Dharma practitioners, examine this carefully with sound arguments and reject such actions. At the least, when your domestic animals have reached the end of their useful lives, grant them permission for a natural death. This is not a small kindness.

If we explain according to the holy Dharma, we see that, with absolutely no doubt, all of these beings were your parents in a previous life.[25] These parents of ours lack the roots of virtue required to obtain either release, birth in a pure land, or a human birth. For the time being, they also have not been born in the hells. By the power of attachment to their previous land, children, and wealth, they have taken birth in Tibet. Yet we do not recognize them in the slightest. Therefore, killing and selling our domestic animals for slaughter is nothing but killing and selling our own parents for slaughter.

Even if we only think in terms of our own benefit, killing like this is a great sin whose karmic repercussion is rebirth in the hells, accompanied by great suffering that can only be escaped at the end of a long period of time. If we do achieve a human birth, it will be short and plagued by disease. Even after that disease-ridden life ends, we will not be released; our children will have died young, and we will be reborn in a very unpleasant land. Beings in this land kill each other, and we will meet with five hundred blood debts that must be repaid. What we do ripens upon ourselves. The karmic fruition falls on our own heads. Is there anyone who has not created their own situation?

We have caused animals to suffer greatly, and by the power of this we ourselves will suffer in hell. Because we kill these animals, we will have a short life. Because we take away the dignity of these animals' lives, we will be reborn in an uncomfortable environment. In fact, at this point, there are none less powerful than these animals. But, you have a human body capable of controlling your actions, and karmic causes and effects are infallible, so be careful what you do![26]

This is not only about slaughtering for profit. It is also great if families abandon their personal slaughtering, either permanently or temporarily. If even this is not possible, you must definitely reduce the number killed a little. At the least, if it is not possible to avoid slaughtering, you absolutely must not use such horrible methods as binding the nose or beheading. For such animals, suffering is unavoidable, and, therefore, the killer's sin is also particularly large. If there were no malice between us and these animals, why would there be a need for such cruel practices? Think about a person. They would be happy to die several times with less pain than to die a single horrible death like that. Since animals are the same, it is very important to use a method that is quick and does not inflict much suffering at the time of death. Do not become indifferent!

These days, many animals die after having experienced immeasurable suffering. The reason for this is that people have the habit of meat eating. If people didn't eat meat, there would be no need for animals to die while experiencing such horrible suffering. Many sūtras and tantras explain that eating meat is a great evil.[27]

Through the power of previous karmic tendencies, meat eaters will be born as carnivorous animals and will again kill many animals every day. Since birth in an infernal realm is certain for such people, it is very important for both ordained and lay people to guide their next birth by taking a vow to never eat meat again, if this is at all possible. Let these activities be the earnest concern of those lords of compassion who uphold the teachings and those who are among the saṅgha!

As for this talk about Tibet, I have only spoken so that animals, especially those in our land, will have happiness throughout this and future lives. Therefore, I ask both the ordained and laypeople residing in the Dharma-upholding land of Tibet to please keep it in their hearts.

This was offered on Saga Dawa Duchen in the Water Sheep year of the seventeenth calendrical cycle [June 14, 2003] at Larung Buddhist Academy of the Five Sciences in the town of Serta. May it benefit those destitute beings who are helpless and protectorless!

6. Tibetan Buddhism and the New Science of Rebirth

Michael R. Sheehy

Introduction

In 1940 or 1941, the celebrated Tibetan modernist Gendun Chopel (1903–1951), while on sojourn abroad in India, concluded his travel log with an open letter to the Tibetan people in which he remarkably suggested that Euro-American science would provide evidence to validate Buddhist claims.[1] However prescient, his words were not published until fifty years after he wrote them.[2] Gendun Chopel's letter was a plea for Tibetans to regard modern science as an ally. Writing with the intent to inform Tibetans about the pervasive influence of science, his letter envisioned early twentieth-century Euro-American science-confirming Buddhist concepts including impermanence, the insubstantiality of phenomena, and dependent origination. Through cognitive science and psychology, he corroborated Buddhist epistemological insights, such as those proposed by the seventh-century Indian Buddhist logician Dharmakīrti, and demonstrated empirically the neurobiology of the subtle body as detailed in tantric physiology. Though there are precedents of earlier encounters between European science in Tibet traced back at least to the sixteenth century, it was Gendun Chopel's letter that sparked the curiosity for science amongst modern intelligentsia inside Tibet. Today, echoes of Gendun Chopel's call continue to be heard in writings from Tibetan authors inside Tibetan cultural regions of the People's Republic of China.

One example of such an author is the Amdo scholar and Tibetan language educator Dungkar Losang Trinle (1927–1997), whose writing after the Cultural Revolution made regular use of the Tibetan neologism *tsenrik*,[3] the term that is now consistently translated into English as "science." In

Dungkar Rinpoche's *Collected Works*, he employs the term *tsenrik* to discuss Tibetan medical science, psychology, and connections between the mind, body, and brain. However innocuous his usage of this term, it continues to have semantic resonance within Tibetan cultural constructions of science.

More recently within Tibet, there is a surge of science writings translated into the Tibetan language from both Chinese and English, enabling greater access to learning about basic science—including biology, physics, and neuroscience—and stimulating an emerging discourse on science among both Tibetan monks and laity. For instance, core sources published in the Tibetan language inside China include canonical science writings on the theory of relativity by Albert Einstein and Charles Darwin's *On the Origin of Species*. This is a marked change considering that until such recent translations, Tibetan scholars had limited access to scientific writings through reading Chinese- or English-language books.

If we widen the scope to include the Tibetan exile community, keeping in mind that there is limited circulation of such writings among the Tibetan readership in China, there are far greater Tibetan language sources on science. This includes numerous secondary school textbooks on chemistry, biology, physics, ecology, and the life sciences that have been published as part of the institutionalization of a science curriculum in the three main Geluk monastic universities in India. There are transcripts from Mind & Life Dialogues, conversations between the Dalai Lama and scientists on a range of topics—from quantum physics to cosmology and neuroscience—that have taken place since 1987, many of which are available in the Tibetan language. These resources have served as driving forces for the critical engagement of the Tibetan exile community with modern scientific thought. Yet, due to the lack of shared access to these resources, discrepancies in the translation of technical scientific terms and concepts have created a chasm between science knowledge among Tibetans in exile and within China.

Seeking to overcome this divide, there is a new generation of Tibetan scholars writing on science. These authors represent the full spectrum of viewpoints, from those who regard science as a rival of Buddhism to those who seek partnership with science. One such author is the scholar Khenpo Tsultrim Lodro (1962–), a monastic leader at Larung Buddhist Academy, whose voice is amplified in translation via the excerpts in this chapter from his seminal work on Buddhism and science, *The Mirror That Illuminates Existence: An Analysis of Past and Future Lives*.[4] The khenpo's fellow Larung

Gar leader Metrul Tenzin Gyatso (1968–) has also composed an influential work on neuroscience, *An Analysis of the Connection between Mind and Brain*.[5] Another notable scholar writing in China who has influenced the reception of science among young Tibetan readers is Chukye Gendun Samten (1964–).[6] In his work on Buddhist epistemology, he has a chapter on how Buddhist views are harmonious with modern science, expressing his sympathy with Gendun Chopel's view that science is an ally. Moreover, in Chokyi Gendun Samten's ambitious work on the foundations of Tibetan Buddhist intellectual culture for the twenty-first century, he makes explicit the connections that he sees between Tibetan Buddhism and science, building an argument on their mutual empiricism.[7] While there is an increasing number of authors writing on Buddhism and science, as scientific studies on Buddhist forms of meditation proliferate in North America, the predominance of works on the topic to date are written by Western authors with very few contributions yet made by native Tibetan authors inside China. If a serious dialogue between Buddhism and science is to advance, we need more Tibetan voices.[8]

Engaging Science in Tibet

Khenpo Tsultrim Lodro's work *The Mirror That Illuminates Existence*, translated here in part, is exemplary of a particular strain of the Tibetan cultural discourse on contemporary experimental science. First published in 2003, *The Mirror* is found in the first volume in the khenpo's multivolume *Collected Works* and has been published as a separate paperback. The work is concerned with providing scientific proof for life after death in dialogue with Tibetan Buddhist understandings of rebirth. It was published along with several of his briefer writings that discuss Western science, local histories, and ethnographies of death in Tibet, alongside his research on rainbow body.

Articulated through an authoritative intellectual voice from inside Tibet, *The Mirror* makes evident compelling dynamics of the Buddhism and science dialogue, demonstrating both potentials and tensions indicative of the exchange. In fact, the central topic of this work—that there is proof for rebirth—strikes at the heart of this tension; that is, for there to be an even playing field for dialogue, based on mutual empirical grounds, significant portions of Buddhism have been historically bracketed and redacted from the exchange. Redacted content is what the Dalai Lama in Mind & Life

Dialogues calls "Buddhist business."[9] This dialogical tactic of bracketing metaphysical content has been employed because many Buddhist doctrines, including rebirth, karma, and enlightenment do not easily conform to scientific understandings.[10] In bold fashion, the khenpo removes these brackets by positioning rebirth, one of Buddhism's most cherished tenets, in direct interchange with evidence-based research from Western scientists. In so doing, he seeks to reconcile the new global epistemology of science with Tibetan Buddhist philosophical views that credit the atemporal and immaterial, giving the reader a fascinating glimpse into the reception of science in contemporary Tibet.

The Mirror defies normative genre conventions and, in many ways, is representative of a new kind of Tibetan literature. What makes this work distinct among Tibetan writings to date is that the khenpo directly engages research from Western authors, quoting extensively from medical and psychological literature that is not only inaccessible to the majority of his readership, but that presents ideas from a very different cultural worldview. Presentation of worldviews outside the purview of Tibetan readers is not itself an unfamiliar convention. For instance, there is the well-established genre of philosophical tenets that is typically structured to include a section on non-Buddhist views, often Indian or Chinese, set up like straw men to be refuted. The khenpo conforms to this genre structure in a separate, complementary work, *A Brief Presentation of Ancient and Modern Thought from the Eastern and Western World*, citing science as one of the tenets of thought to refute.[11]

Khenpo Tsultrim Lodro organizes *A Brief Presentation of Ancient and Modern Thought* into three sections: (1) philosophy, (2) science, and (3) Buddhist thought. In the first section, he presents a sweeping overview of thought from the pre-Socratics to contemporary philosophers, subsuming Western philosophy into two main camps, (a) the materialists and (b) the idealists. In the second section, he gives a brief history of science, citing precursors in Egypt and key thinkers in the Scientific Revolution, and concludes with mention of the Apollo 11 spaceflight in 1969 and the launch of the Hubble Space Telescope into orbit in 1990.[12] This history is followed by a succinct twofold presentation divided first according to science of the subtle physical world (in which he discusses the early science of atomic theory, the theory of relativity, and quantum mechanics) and second according to the science of the coarse physical world in which he discusses astrophysics and astronomy.[13] In the third section, the khenpo concludes by subsuming these disparate fields of science within existing Buddhist philosophical systems, raising questions to critical readers about the oversimplification of science in Tibetan terms.[14] In contrast to this work, which utilizes an established genre structure to situate science in polemical discourse with Buddhism, *The Mirror* is progressive in its engagement of science, making use of this foreign worldview to convince its readership of its own Buddhist beliefs.

The New Science of Rebirth

In *The Mirror*, the khenpo takes risks by employing the empiricism of science to validate the Buddhist belief in rebirth. Rather than invoke Buddhist arguments for rebirth based on inferential evidence, which would be familiar to Tibetan scholars, he draws from first-person accounts recorded by Western researchers to suggest scientific proof of past and future lives. For the khenpo, as a Buddhist scholar, his concern is discerning a view that aligns with what is real, and for him, such a view is based on evidence. As he makes explicit, a primary intent in authoring *The Mirror* is to provide direct evidence for his readers that rebirth is not simply a Buddhist belief, but that it is verified by those who have no Buddhist orientation, thus validating rebirth beyond the scope of religious bias or blind faith.

Following the logic that consciousness is what continues beyond life and, therefore, cannot be a material attribute of the body, the khenpo puts forth a fourfold argument for why consciousness is not contingent on the brain.[15] First, the cerebrum, the principle anterior part of the brain, cannot be a precondition for an analytical mind because there are documented cases of persons born without a cerebrum who have demonstrated analytical cognition.[16] Second, while the brain does produce certain mental phenomena, consciousness cannot be contingent on it because when consciousness leaves the body, as reported in near-death and out-of-body experiences, consciousness is not connected to the brain. Third, since consciousness is not a physical organ that will be altered if it is hindered or defective, even if the brain is altered, the continuity of consciousness cannot be affected. Fourth, while there are neural correlates to consciousness, the correlations do not mean that the brain produces consciousness, based on the logic that consciousness could have existed prior to a brain. This fourfold argument is the khenpo's response to the predominant physicalist view that implies that when the body dies, consciousness ceases. The khenpo argues against this view and cites research to bolster his argument from those whom he calls the "new scientists." These new scientists understand that "consciousness can be separated from the body, and it has the capacity to exist independently."[17]

To demonstrate that consciousness can abide without a body, he draws extensively from the work of Raymond Moody (1944–), a medical physician and philosopher who has written several books that describe out-of-body experiences (OBE) and near-death experiences (NDE). Moody's books include *Life After Life* and *The Light Beyond*, both of which the khenpo had access to read in Chinese translation and which he quotes extensively, as is evident in the excerpts translated. Moody is among this band of new scientists who include Michael Sabom (1954–), the American cardiologist and near-death researcher; Charles Tart (1937–), the American parapsychologist and a founder of transpersonal psychology; Sir John Eccles (1903–1997), the Australian neurophysiologist who was the 1963 Nobel laureate for his work on synapses; Sir Charles Scott Sherrington (1857–1952), the British neurophysiologist who was the 1932 Nobel laureate for functions of neurons; Roger Wolcott Sperry (1913–1994), the American neuropsychologist who was the 1981 Nobel laureate for his split-brain research; Donald MacCrimmon MacKay (1922–1987), the British physicist known for his work on brain organization; John von Neumann (1903–1957), the Hungarian mathematician and contributor to quantum mechanics; and Ian Stevenson (1918–2007), the Canadian-American psychiatrist known for his near-death studies and reincarnation research.

While each of these figures are referenced, and their prestige is leveraged to stress their authority, the khenpo's main sources for *The Mirror* are books by Moody and Stevenson.[18] His rhetorical strategy is to present empirical proof of past and future lives through scientific research findings, yet the body of work by Moody and Stevenson is not based on third-person measures but rather first-person reports. Although this distinction may not be obvious to his readers, these are starkly different methods than a scientific study. Owning this, Moody writes in *Life After Life*,

> I am fully aware that what I have done here does not constitute a scientific study. And to my fellow philosophers I would insist that I am not under the delusion that I have "proven" there is life after death.[19]

What these accounts do provide, however, is evidence-based understandings of life after death according to anecdotal data, which contributes significantly to the khenpo's rhetoric, as well as to the growing body of phenomenological research on disembodied and post-life experiences. After discussing a succession of evidence for past lives, based on remembrance and hypnosis, the khenpo returns to examine how consciousness and the physical body can exist separately. From this, he draws parallels between scientific research and the Tibetan concept of bardo, an interval between states, which he uses to segue into his presentation on *The Tibetan Book of the Dead*. In this section, included in translation here, the khenpo juxtaposes excerpts from this fourteenth-century Tibetan instructional text on the process of dying with out-of-body first-person narratives from Moody's books.

The Tibetan Book of the Dead, in its manifold incarnations, has held a special place in the Western imagination of Tibetan Buddhism since its first publication in 1927, and the khenpo's inclusion of it for this readership is clearly strategic. It should also be noted that in *Life After Life*, Moody's 1975 debut book, Moody writes about parallels of his research with *The Tibetan Book of the Dead*:

> He notices that he is still in a body—called the "shining" body—which does not appear to consist of material substance. Thus, he can go through rocks, walls, and even mountains without encountering any resistance. Travel is almost instantaneous. Wherever he wishes to be, he arrives there in only a moment. His thought and perception are less limited; his mind becomes very lucid and his senses seem more keen and more perfect and closer in nature to the divine. If he has been in physical life blind or deaf or crippled, he is surprised to find that in his "shining" body all his senses, as well as all the powers of his physical body, have been restored and intensified. He may encounter other beings in the same kind of body, and may meet what is called a clear or pure light.[20]

Moody finds "striking parallels" with his research on the near-death experience and *The Tibetan Book of the Dead*, as he does in the Bible, Plato's *Phaedo*, and writings by the Swedish mystic Emanuel Swedenborg (1688–1772).[21] Without coincidence, the themes mentioned here by Moody—incorporeal tunneling, instantaneous teleportation, hypersensitivity—are reflected in the section translated, as they were selected by the khenpo from

The Tibetan Book of the Dead. Having established proofs that consciousness can exist independent of corporality and after bodily death, as suggested in the passages that Moody quotes, the khenpo elaborates on Tibetan understandings of gestation and embryology, signaling rebirth.

With artful Buddhist argumentation and tactical juxtaposition of a classical Tibetan text alongside first-person accounts recorded by Western researchers, the khenpo absorbs the threat of science, thereby situating Tibetan Buddhist ideas on an equal playing field. He further downplays scientific refutations of rebirth and dismisses them as "wrong view."[22] By doing so, the khenpo broadens the potentials of an encounter between Buddhism and science by creating new dialogical spaces based on logic and first-person data, and at the same time, accentuates the tensions of disparate epistemologies and cultural views that are inherently alive in the dialogue.

Reception of The Mirror in Tibet

The Mirror is wildly popular among Tibetan intellectual youths. Along with his writings on social ethics and vegetarianism, this work has established Khenpo Tsultrim Lodro as a leading Buddhist modernist in Tibet. The khenpo wrote the work for Tibetan students who attend Chinese colleges and are steeped in scientific materialism as their predominant worldview.[23] In order to understand *The Mirror*, it is vital to understand that his intended audience is educated millennial ethnic Tibetans living inside Tibetan cultural regions of the People's Republic of China, both monastic as well as lay, who view science as a global source of authority. The khenpo conceives his discourse as a communication to this younger generation of Tibetans who do not necessarily have a firm understanding of their own Buddhist philosophical tradition, nor are they proficient in contemporary scientific thought. With this audience in mind, *The Mirror* is masterfully crafted in its literary style and rhetorical tone.

While the Buddhism and science dialogue has historically been framed as a calculated interchange of ideas across two distinct intellectual traditions, the dynamic is as much an exchange of expertise as an intercultural experiment. The khenpo recognizes this dynamic, and he capitalizes on the reality that social pressures on Tibetan intellectual discourse are fundamentally different inside China than they are in India or the West; hence, the nature of the Buddhism and science interface is definitively distinct from what has developed in forums such as the Mind & Life Dialogues.[24] This also indicates that the Buddhism and science dialogue is broader than historically imagined to date and that the inclusion of Tibetan scholars inside Tibetan regions of China widens the scope of this dialogue.

For the khenpo, the stakes are high. While he knows that rebirth—the central topic of *The Mirror*—is inconsequential for Western scientific thinkers, he realizes it is an understanding that is deeply embedded in the Tibetan cultural imagination. His task is not only to persuade a new generation of scientifically minded Tibetans that rebirth is true, but by drawing on the authority of science, the khenpo seeks to subsume its insights into a Buddhist framework.[25] To do so, he adopts a rhetoric that suggests scientific proofs support the discoveries of Buddhism. *The Mirror* concludes with a plea to the Tibetan reader to learn science in order to better understand Buddhism.

Acknowledgments

For their help with questions about the Tibetan text, the translator is grateful to the author Khenpo Tsultrim Lodro and Khenpo Dza Tsering Tashi of Larung Gar, and for her editorial feedback, Catherine Hardie.

The Mirror That Illuminates Existence: An Analysis of Past and Future Lives

KHENPO TSULTRIM LODRO (2003)

Within the single wisdom maṇḍala of the two knowledges,
the perfect Sovereign of Sages conquers the two benefits,
utterly relinquishes the taints of the two obscurations,
and gazes directly at the very nature of what's knowable—
the two truths.

His eloquently spoken teachings are a treasury of ambrosia
that always bring joy to those who are fortunate.
At the end of time, may those who are obscured by the darkness of
perverse thinking
and wearied by the ways of rebirth maintain their vision of unity.

For beings frightened in the great ocean of saṃsāra
who thrash around the foamy wave crests of birth and death,
while powerlessly dragged by the fierce winds of karma—
this was composed for those of you who wander like this.

THE BUDDHISM AND SCIENCE DIALOGUE

Over the course of the last three hundred years, having relied on the influence of the new sciences from the Western world, we have simply failed to embrace a mentality that discerns what is destructive from what is constructive. Now, at the end of the twentieth century, there is the understanding that the progress of external development alone is not satisfactory.[26] Recognizing that material development alone is not satisfactory, research has turned its focus to understanding the difficult points about being human, including birth, death, and the mysteries of the innermost mind. On these topics, of all the peoples on earth, the culture of the Tibetan people has been considered to be a profound apex and is praised time again by unbiased scholars, as will be explained below.

Since scientists have faced such difficult issues, a dialogue and debate has emerged between learned scholars of the new sciences of the West and contemplative scholars from Tibet. In 1987, a few leaders of these new sciences of the progressive West met with Tibetan contemplative scholars for a dialogue that continued for six days.[27] In 1989, there was a second dialogue in America.[28] These dialogues continued in 1990 and 1992. These leaders of the new sciences said that the understandings that emerged from these dialogues were like discovering a new island in the ocean. Rather than either side claiming victory, these dialogues were held in the spirit of mutual respect and learning. This is really an occasion to celebrate!

In recent decades, it is quite possible that some have thought that our teachings of Tibetan Buddhism are old and backward, and that these teachings would never be very effective in modern scientifically developed countries. It is clear that, by failing to keep their own wisdom apace with the transitions and changes of their opponent's religion and by holding on to the backward thoughts of a few in the past, such people have simply failed to fathom the depths of our own ancestors' culture.

DENYING REBIRTH CONTRADICTS MILLIONS OF PEOPLE

Nowadays, all around the world, both East and West, thousands of people remember their past lives, and most of them provide quite strong evidence in terms of their truly unique recollections. These are educated people who test and analyze and are proponents of contemporary science. These people who recall their previous lives are from different countries, geographic regions, ethnicities, religions, and cultures. They are a diverse group of individuals. We are in no position to merely refute their beliefs as we please or dismiss them all to be liars or believers in fiction or blind faith. Furthermore, consciousness can be separated from the body; it has the capacity to exist independently on its own. There are cases where people perceive their own body lying on a nearby bed. There are endless descriptions of experiences like this from all over the world. Some scientists have begun to research this subject.

In particular, the scholar who has most extensively studied this subject and had such astonishing direct personal experiences is Dr. Raymond A. Moody (1944–). In the year 1970, he studied the recollections of rebirth among 150 people and wrote the following in his book *Life After Life*: "Let me say at the very beginning that, on grounds which I will explain much later, I am not trying to prove that there is life after death, nor do I think that a proof of this is presently possible."[29]

However, as his studies continued and became more extensive, his view developed significantly. In 1988, he wrote in one of his books, *The Light Beyond*, "I strongly believe that after humans pass away, something exists, because when people almost die their consciousness goes on separately from their body. These are near-death experiences (NDE)."[30] Moreover, there were subsequently numerous doctors who studied these experiences and affirmed Moody's view to be correct.[31]

CONSCIOUSNESS AND THE BRAIN: INCONCLUSIVE PROOFS

To observe a mutually beneficial relationship between some aspects of the brain and consciousness, and to argue, merely on this basis, that consciousness in its entirety derives from the brain—that it does not exist prior to but is brought into existence by it—is highly inconclusive. Proof remains inconclusive that consciousness depends on the brain, is a conditional function of the brain, and a manifestation of the brain. That the brain is the causal nexus for consciousness cannot be definitively proven.

First, if having the cerebrum part of the brain is merely seen to be the precondition for an analytical mind, then people without a cerebrum must have no analytical capacity whatsoever. Without a cerebrum, it follows that it would be impossible to have this function. Without it, there is consequently no consciousness to assert. Even so, there are people who do not have a cerebrum who nevertheless have a very acute analytical mind.[32] For this reason, not only is it not conclusive that a cerebrum is the precondition for consciousness, but there is no direct proof in so much as anything relies on it.

Second, while the brain does generally produce some specific phenomena of the mind within the mindstream of an individual, it is not conclusive under all conditions. When someone dies, for instance, their consciousness continues in the bardo interval between lives. Even when someone has not died, their consciousness can still depart from their body. When someone leaves behind their whole flesh-and-blood body, how could they possibly take their brain with them even though it is clear that they still have their analytical mind? This is known and proven all over the world.

Third, some argue that just like when someone's eye is defective, the perceptual awareness of their eye is hindered, and in this same way, they argue that if the cerebrum is altered, their individual consciousness changes. They state that the brain is like the subliminal ground consciousness that has the capacity to create the simultaneous supportive conditions for coarse consciousness.[33] However, regardless of what changes are made to the brain, they are not capable of affecting the existence of consciousness. These arguments are like seeing a grain of rice cooked in a pot and saying that all the rice is cooked. The logical conclusion is to understand that this is simply false. This proves nothing.

Fourth, the mere fact that there are correlates that can be observed between certain features of the brain and consciousness suggests that the essence of consciousness, without prior existence, is produced by the cerebrum part of the brain. This, however, cannot be definitively established. If we understand that a result is produced from causes and conditions, we must make sure that it definitively did not exist prior to those causes and conditions, and that it cannot be proven to come about anew from something else. However, we cannot definitively prove that consciousness did not exist prior to the cerebrum.

REBIRTH IN THE *TIBETAN BOOK OF THE DEAD*

According to instructions in the *Tibetan Book of the Dead*, there are practices that directly describe experiences of rebirth. These instructions from the *Tibetan Book of the Dead* are practices for the mental body while traversing the intermediate state of the bardo, detailing the circumstances in which beings in the bardo of the in-between hear words that connect them to their later rebirths. For the most part, in different countries around the world nowadays, people who have near-death experiences directly experience the diffusion of their mental and bodily constituents, as described in the instructions. Yet, since these people only die for an instant before coming back to life, what they experience are the first stages of the process but not the later ones. From the instructions, it reads,

> Hey, fortunate one! At the time when your body and mind
>   are separating,
> phenomenal reality will manifest as subtle, lucid, pure appearances.
> These experiences of a brilliant, naturally dazzling light may
>   frighten you.

What are called "clear light" and "radiance" are said to each emerge for all humans during their experiences at the moment of death. This is tantamount to not only seeing, but completely recognizing. This is what people have said.

At first, the light is not very bright. Then, suddenly, it is extremely clear and very bright. This is said to transform into visions of light that are clearer than any in this world and like nothing ever experienced. Again, from the bardo instructions, it reads,

> Hey, fortunate one! Listen, again. Furthermore, you are with complete, unimpeded senses, which means that even though you may have been blind, deaf, or crippled while you were alive, now while in the bardo interval, your eyes see images, your ears hear sounds, and so forth. Your senses are flawlessly clear and refined. In this way, your senses are said to be complete. Recognize these as signs that you have died and are wandering in the bardo.

This is how what happens is described. Professor Moody wrote in *The Light Beyond*,

> On Long Island, a seventy-year-old woman who had been blind since the age of eighteen was able to describe in vivid detail what was happening around her as doctors resuscitated her after a heart attack. Not only could she describe what the instruments used looked like, but she could even describe their colors.[34]

As discussed earlier, the expert cardiologist Dr. Michael Sabom (1954–) conducted a close evaluation of thirty-two patients.[35] Of these, twenty-six patients were able to similarly describe accounts of how their consciousness departed from their body while they were in the emergency room.[36]

Furthermore, Moody writes in his book *Life After Life* that "people must be amazed."[37] He writes that many doctors have said that there are patients with no prior medical knowledge who, after they are brought back to life, are able to describe the emergency procedure by which they were resuscitated exactly as it happened. They are able to do this notwithstanding that the doctors clearly considered they were dead during the emergency resuscitation procedure.

Also, in the bardo instructions, it reads,

> Hey, fortunate one! You are "unimpeded," which means that you are a mental body, and your awareness is separated from its support. You no longer have a physical body. So, now you have the ability to travel freely without being impeded. You can travel through rocks and mountains, earth and stones, walls and buildings, and even Mount Meru. However, while you can now travel back and forth through Mount Meru, you cannot go through your mother's womb or the vajra seat.[38] These are signs that you are wandering in the bardo.

This is how what happens is described:

> . . . a woman who suffered a respiratory arrest and was carried to the emergency room, where a resuscitation attempt was made.

> > I saw them resuscitating me. It was really strange. I wasn't very high; it was almost like I was on a pedestal, but not above them to any great extent, just maybe looking over them. I tried talking to them but nobody could hear me, nobody would listen to me.[39]
> > The doctors and nurses were pounding on my body to try to get IVs started and to get me back, and I kept trying to tell them, "Leave me alone. All I want is to be left alone. Quit pounding on me." But they didn't hear me. So, I tried to move their hands to keep them from beating on my body, but nothing would happen. I couldn't get anywhere. It was like—
> > I don't really know what happened, but I couldn't move their hands. It looked like I was touching their hands and I tried to move them—yet when I would give it the stroke, their hands were still there. I don't know whether my hand was going through it, around it, or what. I didn't feel any pressure against their hands when I was trying to move them.[40]

And the description continues,

> People were walking up from all directions to get to the wreck. I could see them, and I was in the middle of a very narrow walkway. Anyway, as they came by they wouldn't seem to notice me. They would just keep walking with their eyes straight ahead. As they came real close, I would try to turn around, to get out of their way, but they would just walk *through* me.[41]

And Moody states,

> Likewise, though the doorknob seems to go through his hand when he touches it, it really doesn't matter anyway, because he soon finds that he can just *go through* the door. Travel, once one gets the hang of it, is apparently exceptionally easy in this state. Physical objects present no barrier, [and movement from one place to another can be extremely rapid, almost instantaneous.][42]

Also, the bardo instructions reads,

> Hey, fortunate one! You are now "endowed with the strength of the magical powers of karma" which has nothing whatsoever to do with your enlightened qualities or magical powers of meditative absorption, but rather is strength that arises from your karma. These are magical powers according to your own karma. In a second, you can encircle the four-continent universe as well as Mount Meru. Simply by being mindful, you can arrive in a flash at any place that you wish. You can do this with the strength that a normal person uses to merely stretch out and draw back their hand. If you are not mindful, you'll forget to use your various magical powers. Don't be concerned with your ability to manifest this or be mindful of all that. The fact is, you now have the ability to manifest without being impeded.

Even though one is instructed to recognize what will appear in the preceding manner, these experiences manifest in all sorts of ways. There was one woman who reported having such an out-of-body experience:

And whenever I would look at a person to wonder what they were thinking, it was like a zoom-up, exactly like through a zoom lens, and I was there. But it seemed that part of me—I'll call it my mind—was still where I had been, several yards away from my body. When I wanted to see someone at a distance, it seemed like part of me, kind of like a tracer, would go to that person. And it seemed to me at the time that if something happened anyplace in the world that I could just be there.[43]

Again, someone else reported, "From any single direction, when I wanted to go there, I could very quickly. If I wanted to go, I would go. If I wanted to arrive, I would go and be there."

The bardo instructions tell us that consciousness without a support is able to suddenly manifest itself in any location it wishes and can steer itself around fluidly. While I have heard accounts of people who have experienced these phenomena, to date I have not heard of anyone who has displayed magical powers other than what is mentioned in the instructions. Again, it reads,

Hey, fortunate one! You will "see with the pure divine eyes of your same species," which means that you will see those beings who are going to be reborn as your same species while you are together in the bardo interval. For instance, if you are going to be born as a god, you will see those same species. Gods will see each other. In this same way, those who are going to be reborn as one of the six species will see their similar species.[44]

And,

Hey, fortunate one! You have a phantom body in which you will encounter places and close relatives as if in a dream. However, though you may try to talk with these near relatives, they will not reply.

A great many people's experiences at the time of death correspond with these descriptions. As they describe it, once consciousness separates from the body, immediately or shortly thereafter, the presence of many other consciousnesses can be seen. It appears as if they are coming to accompany the dying person.[45]

There is an account from a woman who was having difficulty giving birth and who described an out-of-body experience. She said,

It was immediately after delivery that I had a severe hemorrhage and the doctor had a difficult time controlling it. I was aware of what was happening as, having been a nurse myself, I realized the danger. At this time, I lost consciousness, and heard an annoying buzzing, ringing sound. The next thing I knew it seemed as if I were on a ship or a small vessel sailing to the other side of a large body of water. On the distant shore, I could see all of my loved ones who had died—my mother, my father, my sister, and others. I could see them, could see their faces, just as they were when I knew them on earth. They seemed to be beckoning me to come on over, and all the while I was saying, "No, no, I'm not ready to join you. I don't want to die. I'm not ready to go."

Now, this was the strangest experience because all this time I could see all the doctors and nurses, too, as they worked on my body, but it seemed as if I were a spectator rather than that person—that body—they were working on. I was trying so hard to get through to my doctor. "I'm not going to die," but no one could hear me. Everything—the doctors, the nurses, the delivery room, the ship, the water, and the far shore—was just sort of a conglomerate. It was all together, as if one scene were superimposed right on top of the other.

Finally, the ship almost reached the far shore, but just before it did, it turned around and started back. I did finally get through to my doctor, and I was saying, "I'm not going to die." It was at this point, I guess, that I came around, and the doctor explained what had happened, that I had had a postpartum hemorrhage, and that they had nearly lost me, but that I was going to be alright.[46]

Like this, while you are transitioning in the bardo, it is possible to encounter phenomena such as these.

7. Answers to Questions on Madhyamaka

Douglas Duckworth

Introduction

A COMMON MISCONCEPTION is that Buddhism on the Tibetan plateau was wiped out during the Cultural Revolution and that it is a relic of a past golden age. Yet, the embers of a strong Buddhist institutional tradition were rekindled in the 1980s with new leadership in China, particularly in the regions of eastern Tibet, where Buddhism has flourished anew. Larung Gar represents one such institution that has flowered on the Tibetan plateau since its founding in 1980, producing a uniquely modern and vibrant Buddhist culture that, despite its precarious position, continues to represent and uphold a robust scholarly tradition well into the twenty-first century.

Classical Indian Buddhist texts are studied in the curriculum at Larung Gar alongside commentaries from different Tibetan monastic traditions. While the Nyingma tradition, and the works of Mipham Rinpoche (1846–1912) in particular, have a prominent place in the course of study, several major texts from different Tibetan sects are studied together in this unique institution. One of the main successors of Larung Gar's charismatic founder, Khenpo Jigme Phuntsok (1933–2004), is Khenpo Tsultrim Lodro (1962–), whose writings have kept up the institution's reputation for high-quality scholarship.

In the last volume of Khenpo Tsultrim Lodro's three-volume *Collected Works*, published in 2007 when he was forty-five years old, there are several short texts he wrote on a range of specialized topics within Buddhist philosophy. In one of these texts, *Some Reflections on the Sources of Knowledge*, he discusses differences between Mipham Rinpoche and Sakya Paṇḍita (1182–1251) in their respective presentations of varied topics related to epistemology (*pramāṇa*). In another text, *Contemplations on the View: An Offering Cloud That Delights the Old Sage*,[1] he offers historical and philosophical contemplations on the view of mental non-deliberation of the Chan monk known to Tibetans as Heshang[2] in light of his own Nyingma tradition's associations with this view. In other texts compiled in this volume, he expounds upon assorted topics ranging from the three vows,[3] the Vinaya or monastic code, the three knowledges from the *Ornament of Manifest Realization* (*Abhisamayālaṃkāra*), spelling and grammar, differences between self-emptiness (*rangtong*) and other-emptiness (*shentong*), differences between Prāsaṅgika and Svātantrika, and more.

A major topic that Khenpo Tsultrim Lodro treats in the text translated in this chapter is the difference between Prāsaṅgika and Svātantrika. The distinction between these two strands of interpretation has a prominent place in a voluminous Tibetan literature on the philosophy of the Middle Way. Etymologically, the difference between these two lines of interpretation is simply that Prāsaṅgikas are those who use *reductio ad absurdum* arguments, or arguments that just show the absurdity of a claim, and Svātantrikas are those who use autonomous arguments or arguments that are formally structured valid inferences that establish a philosophical claim. There is a lot of discussion in Tibet around what, if anything, is of significance in this difference.

The translation below focuses on the issue of how Prāsaṅgika Madhyamaka is to be understood. It is an abridged version of a short work Khenpo Tsultrim Lodro composed in the genre of responses to questions, titled *Answers to Questions on Madhyamaka*,[4] which is a representative example of a classical tradition of Buddhist scholarship that continues on the Tibetan plateau in the twenty-first century.

Distinguishing Svātantrika and Prāsaṅgika

In his *Answers to Questions on Madhyamaka*, Khenpo Tsultrim Lodro poses nine questions in verse, followed by prose responses. His first question is:

Those in the Sakya and Geluk traditions have a lot to say
about the differences between Prāsaṅgika and Svātantrika arguments,
but how does Jamyang Mipham Gyatso
assert the difference between them?[5]

His answer discusses five distinctions drawn out from the way that Mipham distinguished between Prāsaṅgika and Svātantrika arguments, in terms of the respective ways of claiming the logical subject, what is negated, the assertion of what is established, the reason, and the example. His response bears the mark of Mipham's late nineteenth-century vision for Buddhist scholarship in the Nyingma tradition and enacts a style of creative commentarial prose that has been typical of Buddhist scholarly literature in Tibet for centuries.

He elaborates most fully upon the first distinction, regarding how a logical subject is respectively understood in the contexts of Svātantrika and Prāsaṅgika. While Svātantrikas accept a commonly appearing logical subject when presenting an argument for emptiness, Khenpo Tsultrim Lodro says that there are no commonly appearing logical subjects for Prāsaṅgikas in those contexts. He cites Mipham's *Eliminating Doubts*,[6] a response to a critique of his commentary on the *Ornament of the Middle Way* (*Madhyamakālaṃkāra*), which says,

> Since from the perspective of pure vision, nothing whatsoever is perceived that is seen from a perspective infected by distortion, this establishes that there are no commonly appearing subjects.[7]

Thus, for him, a Prāsaṅgika viewpoint represents the culmination of the realization of emptiness, or pure vision, not just the path that leads to this realization. In the culminant perspective of pure vision, no contents of distorted perception serve to ground a debate on the nature of things, and this is the case with not just a logical subject shared between a Prāsaṅgika and a realist (who holds that things intrinsically exist), but even a logical subject for Prāsaṅgikas themselves.[8] Thus, any inferences establishing the nature of the ultimate, including those proving emptiness, are simply held from the perspective of others for Prāsaṅgikas.

Khenpo Tsultrim Lodro also cites Mipham's *Light of the Sun*,[9] another text written in response to a critic of one of his commentaries, this time his commentary on the ninth chapter of *The Way of the Bodhisattva* (*Bodhicaryāvatāra*). There, Mipham says that the reason why the logical subject in a debate on the ultimate appears in common for a Svātantrika is that:

> Svātantrikas explain with an emphasis on the categorized ultimate due to the essential point that they accept the ultimate as

a mere emptiness of true existence and the conventional as epistemically warranted.[10]

As for Prāsaṅgikas, in contrast, he cites the same text that says,

At the time that Prāsaṅgikas explain with an emphasis on the uncategorized—the great Madhyamaka free from assertions—it is in the context based upon ultimate analysis; nothing is maintained to be established on its own even conventionally, and all that appears is ascertained in accord with the sacred domain of meditative equipoise free from constructs and without reference.[11]

Thus, the reason for there being no commonly appearing logical subjects in the unique context of Prāsaṅgika discourse on the nature of reality is due to the fact that this context undermines the presuppositions of any conceptually framed truth. And, it does so by enacting the culmination of analysis as nonconceptual rather than representing it as an ultimate truth of emptiness that it proves.

For the second distinction between Prāsaṅgikas and Svātantrikas, Khenpo Tsultrim Lodro presents a difference between them in terms of what is negated. He says that in the context of a Svātantrika analysis of reality, a negation must be qualified with an operator, like *ultimately*, but this is not the case in the unique context of Prāsaṅgika, where both of the two truths, the ultimate and conventional, are negated without qualification.[12] Thus, when presenting a statement about the nonarising of phenomena, there is no need to qualify it such that phenomena are held to not arise ultimately, precisely because nothing is held to arise at all in a unique Prāsaṅgika context. This is because distorted phenomena are not observed from the perspective of pure vision, which is the culmination of analysis that this context represents. Khenpo Tsultrim Lodro states that when the quality of the logical subject is understood well—as appearing in common or not in the respective contexts of Svātantrika and Prāsaṅgika—then the necessity of qualifying the object of negation or not will be understood perforce. He thus defers to the first distinction, saying that there is not a lot more to be said here.[13]

Khenpo Tsultrim Lodro's third distinction between Prāsaṅgika and Svātantrika is in terms of the assertion of what is established. While the process of negation may appear to be the same for Prāsaṅgikas and Svātantrikas, the difference lies in what is held after the negation. The difference, he says, is that Svātantrikas hold assertions after establishing an absence of true existence, whereas nothing is asserted for Prāsaṅgikas after this negation.[14] The Prāsaṅgika stance regarding the way things are in reality represents the culmination of analysis and thus remains beyond affirmation and negation. This is the context of noble silence—inexpressible.

Khenpo Tsultrim Lodro presents the fourth and fifth ways that Prāsaṅgika and Svātantrika are distinct in terms of how reasons and examples are understood to function in an argument. He takes on these last two features together and says that the difference in both cases lies in the fact that, for Svātantrikas, a reason and an example are accepted by both parties of a debate, whereas these elements of an argument are put forth primarily in the perspective of an opponent for Prāsaṅgikas.[15] In this way, his fourth and fifth features marking the Svātantrika-Prāsaṅgika distinction again resemble the first, concerning the status of commonly appearing logical subjects, and follows that same logic. Thus, what distinguishes Svātantrika from Prāsaṅgika is whether or not the elements that compose an argument on the nature of reality are accepted by both parties. For a Prāsaṅgika, nothing is accepted in this context—not even emptiness.

Khenpo Tsultrim Lodro concludes the first of nine questions by way of summary, reiterating the essential point of the Svātantrika-Prāsaṅgika distinction: a Svātantrika holds that arguments with threefold criteria established by a source of knowledge are accepted by both parties,[16] whereas a Prāsaṅgika maintains that an argument with the threefold criteria holds only for the opposing party of a debate.[17] He concludes by pointing out that the distinction here is not merely a formal, linguistic distinction, but is an indispensable part of understanding the view of emptiness, free from proliferations.[18]

His second question asks,

> Is there a difference or not
> between a Mādhyamika's unique reductio and
> a reductio in a logician's argument?[19]

His answer is "Yes, there is a difference," stating again that a Prāsaṅgika's unique form of argument is acknowledged only by the other party in a debate, not for oneself.[20] A Prāsaṅgika's gaze in a debate on the nature of reality thus can be said to be like that of an anthropologist, one who just offers a description from the vantage point of "the natives" of saṃsāra but does not assent to the reality of a native's worldview.

Khenpo Tsultrim Lodrö's third question reiterates a point he made earlier, when he poses the following question:

> Is it not a contradiction that
> Candrakīrti's commentary *Introduction to the Middle Way*
> (*Madhyamakāvatāra*)
> makes a claim to nonarising,
> yet our tradition of great Madhyamaka is without claims?[21]

Here again, he deals with the status of claims in Prāsaṅgika, reiterating that there are no claims demarcating the ultimate in Prāsaṅgika. Thus, a claim to ultimate nonarising can only be made to the extent that it is a provisional, instructive claim; that is, when it is a claim acknowledged only by others.

In the relationship between Svātantrika and Prāsaṅgika within this tradition inherited from Mipham, Prāsaṅgika represents the highest view, where neither are claims made nor are distorted objects perceived, and, further, where no distinctions are held between two truths. Svātantrika, by contrast, represents all the discursive contexts of the path to understanding this view in which the two truths (ultimate and conventional) are established by sources of knowledge, claims are made to the ultimate truth of emptiness and the conventional truth of appearance, and assertions are made about conventional truth that contradict mundane conventions. In this way, Prāsaṅgika and Svātantrika can be seen to mutually supplement each other.

Khenpo Tsultrim Lodrö's fourth question touches on the nature of the debate between Candrakīrti and Bhāviveka in the first chapter of *Clear Words* (*Prasannapadā*), and his fifth concerns which stage of the path the afflictive obscurations are eliminated.[22] Here again, he appeals to Mipham's interpretation on this issue, while glossing over conflicting interpretations of other Sakya and Geluk scholars. He does so by appealing to a special intention behind these alternative interpretations, such as those of Tsongkhapa and Gorampa, by saying that their words must be free from faults given that they are great scholars who are bodhisattvas with experience and direct access to teachings from the Buddha.[23]

Khenpo Tsultrim Lodrö's sixth question asks,

The conventional is said to accord with the world in Prāsaṅgika; how is this "world" to be understood?[24]

He answers that the "world" is not to be understood only to refer to the perspective of others, but also to the world that includes a Prāsaṅgika's view, the world unanalyzed that appears in the incontrovertible way of dependent arising. Thus, while Prāsaṅgikas make no claims to the ultimate (from their own perspective), he says that they do hold claims about the world in terms of conventional truth. Nevertheless, in another text, *A Beginner's Guide to the Reformulation of a Reductio*, he adds that a Prāsaṅgika's claims about the conventional are not like those made by Svātantrikas.[25] Presumably, this is because such claims are made in the context of no analysis; that is to say, they are not ontologically committed to claims made that accord with the ways of the world.[26]

Khenpo Tsultrim Lodrö's seventh question asks,

An object viewed in common by different beings
is which of the two truths?[27]

This question reflects a question Mipham asked in his celebrated *Beacon of Certainty*, a text that is also structured around responses to questions about Madhyamaka. There, Mipham posed a question about whether or not there are commonly appearing objects among the six classes of beings. Drawing from Mipham, Khenpo Tsultrim Lodrö answers this question by saying that there is a common object observed, yet it is not a discrete object. Rather, he says that the common object is none other than the unconditioned, empty and luminous nature of mind, otherwise known as buddha-nature.[28]

Nevertheless, just as there are no common logical subjects conceived in the context of an inference into the nature of reality in Prāsaṅgika, there are no discrete objects at all perceived in common by different beings either. While Khenpo Tsultrim Lodrö makes clear his commitment to a common basis of appearance in the world that he refers to as buddha-nature, he does not claim that any discrete objects appear in common for different beings other than what is simply acknowledged in mundane convention. Thus, while he accepts a common basis of reality, at the same time, he denies any shared logical subjects in the context of ultimate analysis and any discrete bases of perceived appearances shared by ordinary beings in the world.

Apparently, due to this bivalence (of accepting a common basis of reality on the one hand, while denying discrete bases of perceived appearance shared by ordinary beings on the other), he claims that the view he outlines can be expressed without contradiction as either other-emptiness or self-emptiness.[29] In other words, the basis of reality he sketches for the great Madhyamaka can be seen either as a ground of an inconceivable reality (i.e., buddha-nature) or as an abyss that defies any conceptual delineation around discrete kinds (i.e., emptiness).

In his eighth question, Khenpo Tsultrim Lodro makes an explicit link to another of his Nyingma predecessors, Longchenpa (1308–1363), when he responds to the following question:

> In his commentary on the *Treasury of the Abiding Reality*,
> Longchenpa said that Heshang's words were right,
> yet were not understood by narrow-minded people.
> Does this not conflict with Mipham's view?
> And who are these narrow-minded people?[30]

In his response to this question, he refers his readers to his *Contemplations on the View: An Offering Cloud that Delights the Old Sage*, another text in the volume that explicitly focuses on this topic and a place where he adds nuance to how the role of mental nondeliberation is to be understood in the writings of Heshang, Kamalaśīla, and Longchenpa.

In his ninth and final question, Khenpo Tsultrim Lodro returns to the debate in the first chapter of *Clear Words*, and asks whether or not it is necessary to reformulate a reductio in the form of a probative argument, which is an argument that proves a thesis rather than simply undermines a false claim.[31] He says that it is not necessary to reformulate reductios in the unique Prāsaṅgika context for the reason mentioned above (that Prāsaṅgikas need not accept the terms of a debate that are acknowledged only by an opponent).[32] He also says that it is not only unnecessary to formulate a probative argument in the context of ascertaining the consummate (or uncategorized) ultimate, but that it is inappropriate to do so because in that context, neither are assertions of nonexistence made after negating existence nor are assertions of nonconceptuality made after negating conceptuality.[33]

Conclusion

Khenpo Tsultrim Lodro presents Prāsaṅgika as the summit of the Madhyamaka view. Unlike a Svātantrika argument that is formulated to prove emptiness, a Prāsaṅgika argument does not and cannot prove emptiness; rather, it represents emptiness from the perspective of its realization. Significantly, a Prāsaṅgika argument does so performatively by enacting it through the linguistic form of a reductio. That is, the unique feature of a Prāsaṅgika argument is that it employs a linguistic device that puts emptiness on display by showing rather than stating what a consistent linguistic system that espouses emptiness actually looks like. It does so by turning the linguistic system on itself and imploding it by the rules of language acknowledged only by others—the others who have bought into the rules of the linguistic system. In other words, a Prāsaṅgika argument is not couched in a language that presupposes the intrinsic nature that it explicitly denies. Rather, it enacts the deconstruction of any presupposed nature that undergirds the system in the first place.

Nevertheless, just as a Prāsaṅgika's reductio is important to reveal the radical nature of emptiness in the final analysis, probative arguments found in Svātantrika discourse can also play a role to maintain the boundaries of truth claims, to distinguish between two truths (ultimate and conventional), and to make arguments to challenge distortions embedded in the status quo. Thus, we can see that Khenpo Tsultrim Lodro follows Mipham by positioning the probative arguments of Svātantrika in a way that they have a significant place in a consistent Madhyamaka system. This is because both Svātantrika and Prāsaṅgika supplement each other in this presentation, and, arguably, neither is sufficient on its own to maintain a coherent, consistent, and complete Buddhist philosophical system.

Khenpo Tsultrim Lodro carries the torch, in style and in content, of Mipham's vision to illuminate the relevance of Nyingma scholarship in a creative philosophical synthesis. He thereby continues a lively tradition of Buddhist scholarly writing into the twenty-first century. As we can witness in his work, Buddhist high culture on the Tibetan plateau is alive and well; it is not just a relic of a past golden age, at least not yet.

Abridgement of Answers to Questions on Madhyamaka

Khenpo Tsultrim Lodro (2007)

Herein lies difficult points on the meaning of the profound Madhyamaka that have often been debated by scholars of the past and present. On issues that are not very clear in the textbooks of our tradition, questions are posed and are then followed by a concise answer.

Question One

Those in the Sakya and Geluk traditions have a lot to say
about the differences between Prāsaṅgika and Svātantrika arguments,
but how does Jamyang Mipham Gyatso
assert the difference between them?

According to the tradition of the omniscient Mipham Gyatso, there are five differences between the arguments of the Prāsaṅgika and the Svātantrika: the differences between the logical subject, what is negated, the assertion of what is established, the reason, and the example. Svātantrikas have not eliminated fixation upon two separate truths, so they emphasize the categorized ultimate.[34] For this reason, they do not negate a commonly appearing logical subject, and maintain it as the subject of an argument.

The meaning of "commonly appearing" is something like a form held to just appear in common in the unreflective cognitive streams of both parties of a debate. Svātantikas need to accept this because they maintain that things truly exist or exist by virtue of their own characteristics. This does not appear in the perspective of a Prāsaṅgika, so it is not accepted. *Dispelling Disputes* (*Vigrahavyāvartanī*) says,

> If anything were really established in perception,
> there would be something to negate or affirm.
> Yet there is no such thing, so I am without fault.[35]

Prāsaṅgikas emphasize the uncategorized ultimate, the indivisibility of the two truths. Thereby, Prāsaṅgikas are free from all assertions of existence and nonexistence, without holding "merely this exists and just this does not." For this reason, even mere appearance is negated in this context. Thus, the *Light of the Sun* says,

> It is widely held that the difference is that in the Svātantrika system, the object is held to exist by virtue of its own characteristics, while Prāsaṅgikas do not accept this. When Svātantrikas explain with an emphasis on the categorized ultimate, due to the essential point that they accept the ultimate as a mere emptiness of true existence and the conventional as epistemically warranted, they ascertain Madhyamaka in accordance with postmeditation certainty together with assertions.[36]

And,

> At the time that Prāsaṅgikas explain with an emphasis on the uncategorized—the great Madhyamaka free from assertions—it is in the context based upon ultimate analysis; nothing is maintained to be established by virtue of its own characteristics even conventionally, and all that appears is ascertained in accord with the sacred domain of meditative equipoise free from constructs and without reference.[37]

Eliminating Doubts says,

> Since from the perspective of pure vision, nothing whatsoever is perceived that is seen from a perspective infected by distortion, this establishes that there are no commonly appearing subjects.[38]

I will elaborate a bit here on whether or not mere appearance is negated when the ultimate is ascertained in Prāsaṅgika and whether or not Svātantrikas must accept that things are established by virtue of their own characteristics. Others say that Prāsaṅgikas, too, do not negate mere appearances, but rather they just negate true existence with respect to things like pots. This claim indeed has a great purpose, but . . .

To summarize, those who claim that mere appearances are not negated from a perspective that investigates the ultimate have a hard time establishing why Svātantrikas assert true existence. These are the most critical points in the philosophical systems of Prāsaṅgika and Svātantrika, so it is important to fully scrutinize them and understand.

The second difference has to do with what is negated. The object of negation for Svātantrikas is simply what is ultimately existent, so it is necessary to qualify what is negated with *ultimately*. The object of negation for Prāsaṅgikas involves both of the two truths, so it is held that there is no need to qualify the object of negation. The *Beacon of Certainty* says,

> To qualify an object of negation with
> qualifiers like *truly existent* is
> acknowledged in Svātantrika texts, but
> in terms of ultimate analysis,
> what is the point of these qualifications?[39]

Others say that the many occurrences of an object of negation being qualified with qualifiers like *truly existent* in the Buddha's Word and Prāsaṅgika texts should be understood to apply as well to when qualifiers are not used. And for this reason, they say that there is no difference between Svātantrika and Prāsaṅgika in terms of the object of negation being qualified or not.

Our position accords with Prāsaṅgika texts like the "Wisdom Chapter" of *The Way of the Bodhisattva* and the commentary on the *Four Hundred Verses* (*Catuḥśataka*), where it is known that the object of negation is qualified in some contexts, namely, when making distinctions in postmeditation. During an analysis of the ultimate, however, not only are no qualifiers used, but making qualifications is not appropriate, as is stated in *Clear Words*. In summary, there is not a lot more that needs to be said: if you know well the meaning of whether or not there is a commonly appearing logical subject, then you also know whether or not a qualifier needs to be applied to an object of negation.

The third difference concerns the assertion of something that is established. Svātantrikas make assertions that establish things (like nonarising) after refuting things (like arising). Prāsaṅgikas, however, do not make any such claims and do not assert anything like nonarising as an implication of negating something like arising. The *Raplen Rejoinder*[40] states:

> The systems of Svātantrika and Prāsaṅgika are not able to establish simultaneously the meaning of nonconceptuality by negating each referent object, along with all entities that appear, with

arguments such as the argument that negates the arising of the four extremes and the argument of being neither one nor many. Although they appear to be the same in the way of direct negation, they should be distinguished in the end by the criterion of whether or not they make assertions about the ultimate in their own system.[41]

The fourth and fifth differences have to do with the arguments and examples. Svātantrikas use arguments and examples that are established from the perspectives of both parties of a debate. Prāsaṅgikas, however, put forward arguments and examples that are mainly established from the perspective of an opponent, as described in the *Lamp of Wisdom* (*Prajñāpradīpa*) and *Clear Words. Eliminating Doubts* says, "The process of refuting the argument and the example is described by Candrakīrti."[42]

When elaborated in this way, there are five differences, but these can be condensed to the essential point: Svātantrikas accept arguments with three modes[43] established by reliable sources of knowledge for both parties of a debate, while Prāsaṅgika arguments are established with three modes according only to an opponent's claims. . . .

QUESTION TWO

Is there a difference or not
between a Mādhyamika's unique reductio and
a reductio in a logician's argument?

There is a difference between these two because the unique argument of Prāsaṅgika Madhyamaka, as explained above, is a threefold reason, entailment, and contrapositive posited only in the perspective of an opponent. In the context of a logician's reductio argument, by contrast, for the most part the reason is accepted by the opponent, while the entailment is accepted by both parties through a reliable source of knowledge. Furthermore, sometimes both the reason and the entailment are established simply by allegation but are not established by both parties through a reliable source of knowledge. For instance, in the case where someone believes that sound is apprehended by the eyes and generally accepts that being apprehended by the eyes entails being permanent, it is said, "It absurdly follows that sound is permanent because it is apprehended by the eyes." In this case, the mere sound is held to be commonly appearing, and thus is not like a Prāsaṅgika's reductio.

QUESTION THREE

Is it not a contradiction that
Candrakīrti's commentary *Introduction to the Middle Way*
 (Madhyamakāvatāra)
makes a claim to nonarising,
yet our tradition of great Madhyamaka is without claims?

It is said that generally in Prāsaṅgika texts there is just a lack of assertion or claim. This is explained by some scholars to mean that there is no truly existent thesis, but that there is a thesis of a lack of true existence. Others say that there are no autonomous claims, but that there are claims that are reductios. Both of these assertions are found in texts of the omniscient Mipham, but I think there is no contradiction in maintaining the latter here because, as was explained above, whereas there are no autonomous claims made, there is no problem when such claims are made based on merely the perspective of others.

QUESTION FOUR

When proponents of Svātantrika in the end
assert the uncategorized,
why did Candrakīrti undermine
contexts when the categorized is merely expressed?

This question is evidently in reference to Candrakīrti's rebuttal of the critiques of Buddhapālita in the *Lamp of Wisdom*, and an extensive refutation of Svātantrika. . . . Just a critique of autonomous arguments is expressed by means of showing that it is not reasonable for logical subjects to appear in common, for an object of negation to be qualified with the qualifier *ultimately*, or for the reason and example to be established for both parties of a debate. Yet there is no explicit refutation there saying that it is inappropriate to express the categorized ultimate. . . .

QUESTION FIVE

Our tradition claims that both the afflictive and cognitive obscurations
are removed on the seven impure grounds,
while just the cognitive obscurations are removed on the pure
    grounds.
What are the reasons and scriptures that support this?

... There is both reason and scripture that supports that cognitive obscurations are removed on the seven impure grounds. Only cognitive obscurations
being removed on the pure grounds is known from the *Sūtra Explaining the
Intent* (*Saṃdhinirmocanasūtra*) and the root text and autocommentary of
the *Introduction to the Middle Way*.

In this way, those like Rongton and Gorampa claimed that there are no
afflictive obscurations to be removed on the seven impure grounds. Others
like Shākya Chokden, Lord Tsongkhapa and his sons, Gyaltsap Je and Khedrup Je, accepted that there are. Lord Tsongkhapa and his sons claimed that
there are no cognitive obscurations removed there, while most early scholars
accepted that there are. The way to not fall to either of the two extremes is
revealed in Mipham Gyatso's tradition.

Previously, there were incredible scholars who were great bodhisattvas
residing on the grounds, like Tsongkhapa and the omniscient Gorampa.
They listened every day to limitless doctrines in the presence of many buddhas, and practiced their meanings, so how can what they have said have
faults? Even if their literal words seem to be undermined, there is certainly
an inconceivable purpose and basis in another intention there. Thus, it is not
possible for there to be any faults with respect to the meaning. . . .

QUESTION SIX

The conventional is said to accord with the world in Prāsaṅgika.
How is this "world" to be understood?

Here, the word *world* does not refer solely to those whose minds have not
been influenced by philosophies. Rather, it is to be understood in terms of
whatever appears to any unimpaired mind without reflection or analysis[44]
regardless of whether or not it has been influenced by philosophies. As the
omniscient lord of Dharma, Mipham, says in his writings,

The statement "I speak from the perspective of the world"[45] does not foist all conventions upon the perspectives of others. Rather, the conventions of Prāsaṅgika are also included in the world; the world should be understood to mean these incontrovertible appearances of dependent arising.

Also, he says in *Shedding Light on Thusness*,

The meaning of "the way of the world" does not merely refer to the perspective of others. This is because it is accepted as the incontrovertible appearance of dependent arising for everyone, both for oneself and others, and just this appearance is accepted without analysis in terms of its ultimate status.[46]

Furthermore, master Candrakīrti said,

What is apprehended by the six unimpaired faculties is understood by the world.[47]

This way of identifying the world is also accepted by Lord Tsongkhapa and sons as well as by Rongton and Gorampa.

QUESTION SEVEN

An object viewed in common by different beings is which of the two truths?

The consummate observed basis is the mode of reality that is the unconditioned, empty, and clear nature of mind, which has the name buddhanature. The *Beacon of Certainty* says,

Since in our system
there is no basis at all
delimited as appearing or empty,
all that appears is equality.[48]

Thus, in terms of the two truths delineated in terms of authentic/inauthentic experience, it is only the ultimate truth, and in terms of the two truths delineated as appearance/emptiness, it has aspects of both of the two truths.

One might ask, "How is buddha-nature the consummate observed basis?" The *Sublime Continuum* (*Uttaratantra*) states,

> In the way that the earth abides in water, water in wind, and
> wind completely abides in space,
> while space does not abide in wind,
> water, or earth;
> in the same way the aggregates, constituents, and faculties
> abide in karma and afflictions, karma and afflictions
> constantly abide in a distorted mind
> and a distorted mind
> completely abides in the purity of mind,
> while the nature of mind
> does not abide in any phenomena.[49]

It says that the aggregates and the like come from karma and afflictions, and karma and afflictions come from a distorted mind, which comes from the luminous and clear nature of mind. Thus, the consummate basis of all entities is this luminous and clear nature of mind. . . . As well, it states that entities that arise do so within the luminous and clear nature of mind. When they disintegrate, they disintegrate within that expanse, and they remain within that nature now. This nature pervades all things like water pervades every drop; thus, it is the nature of all things and is held to be the commonly observed basis.

Some people call this "other-emptiness." Whether this is called "self-emptiness" or "other-emptiness," I think there is no contradiction. In reality, it is this in general that is the viewpoint of the tantras and the sūtras that are definitive in meaning, and in particular, it is the viewpoint of the middle and last wheels of doctrine. Specifically, there is a lot that can be said about how this is the single essential point, without contradiction, of the view of the great accomplished scholars and practitioners of the Sakya, Geluk, Kagyu, Nyingma, and Jonang. Yet, I will not elaborate here. When what is commonly observed in a temporary context is set forth, it lies within conventional truth, because, as such, it is necessarily a domain of confined perception.

QUESTION EIGHT

In his commentary on the *Treasury of the Abiding Reality*, Longchenpa said that Heshang's words were right, yet were not understood by narrow-minded people. Does this not conflict with Mipham's view? And who are these narrow-minded people?

This has been answered in a text I have written called *Contemplations on the View: An Offering Cloud That Delights the Old Sage*. Please consult this.

QUESTION NINE

Master Bhāviveka said to Buddhapālita that his reductios must be reformulated as probative arguments, by which his own position would be contradicted. Does Bhāviveka himself claim that his own reductios necessarily be reformulated as probative arguments?

. . . It is said that the reformulation of a reductio as a probative argument is something that others, those with assertions, accept. For us who have no assertions whatsoever, only the internal contradictions of other's claims are revealed by reductios. For this reason, when nothing at all is asserted, what is there to be contradicted?

The way that these problems are expressed and are responded to are extremely key points to the Svātantrika and Prāsaṅgika philosophies. This way of explanation has been criticized a lot by scholars in the new schools, and these criticisms do serve a purpose. Nevertheless, I see not a single one of these critiques that actually hits the main point. Therefore, a lot of great scholars in India and Tibet accept this way of explanation, which is the unerring viewpoint of Candrakīrti. You can know this just by reading *Clear Words*. It is extremely important to ascertain the meaning of equality, so you should know this in detail from *Clear Words* itself.

8. LIBERATING LIVES

CATHERINE HARDIE

INTRODUCTION

RESCUING AND FREEING animals whose lives are in imminent danger—otherwise known as life liberation, life release, or ransoming lives[1]—is an ancient mode of compassionate action found in many Buddhist cultures. Both China and Tibet have long-standing traditions of life liberation, practiced both as a common act of spontaneous compassion and as a full-fledged ritual custom.[2] The life liberation ritual serves three purposes: to rescue and prolong the life of the imperiled animal, gifting it a state free from fear; to sow the seeds of liberation in its mindstream; and as a natural consequence, to create merit for the practitioner and anyone to whom they might wish to dedicate it. The merit generated by liberating lives is considered to be powerful and efficacious, especially for curing illness, extending life, and purifying karmic defilements.

Throughout the Buddhist revival in mainland China during the reform era,[3] life liberation has reemerged as a vibrant arena of moral practice and lay sociality.[4] Among Sinophone (or Han Chinese) networks of Tibetan Buddhist followers, life liberation activities have been particularly popular owing to their status as a culturally familiar and uniting activity for practitioners of all backgrounds and a compelling vehicle of religious outreach for the Tibetan lamas who preside over them. In a variety of scopes and sizes, life liberation activities have become a fixture of collective practice in the Sinophone Tibetan Buddhist milieu.[5]

Against this backdrop, the practice of life liberation has evolved as a dynamic field of cross-cultural and cross-regional activity. The majority of rituals conducted in Han Chinese regions involve setting free small captive animals, such as birds, fish, and sea creatures into natural habitats.

Another common practice involves the ransom of Tibetan livestock bound for slaughter in eastern Tibetan areas or major neighboring Chinese cities, such as Chengdu or Lanzhou. Once those animals—usually yaks and sheep—have been purchased and blessed, they are transported to pastoral Tibetan communities where local households or monasteries care for them until their natural death. Contemporary life liberation practice in the Sinophone Tibetan Buddhist scene thus blends a range of customs, styles, and scales, spanning urban and rural settings, and, in the instance of livestock for slaughter, linking Han Chinese and Tibetan participants in networks of meritorious activity.

While the enthusiastic embrace of life liberation within the Sinophone Tibetan Buddhist milieu owes much to the shared, deep-rooted tradition of releasing lives in both the Chinese and Tibetan Buddhist worlds, efforts by contemporary Tibetan lamas to promote the practice have also strongly influenced its favorable reception. One of the most powerful streams of contemporary life liberation advocacy has issued from the Larung Buddhist Academy of the Five Sciences. In the two decades since Larung founder Khenpo Jigme Phuntsok sponsored a nationwide life liberation campaign, Larung Gar's major second-generation Chinese-speaking khenpos have continuously promoted the importance of liberating lives through impactful teachings, writings, and outreach activities among Han Chinese lay audiences.[6]

It should be emphasized that the animal protection advocacy of Larung leaders has not been confined to Sinophone Buddhist circles alone. Compassion for animal suffering and respect for all sentient life in general form part of the intergenerational ethos of the Larung school (a convenient shorthand for the Larung institution-lineage nexus) and campaigns advocating animal-focused practices of compassion have been undertaken throughout its entire sphere of religious and social influence. Larung leaders are renowned not only for championing life liberation, but also for promoting vegetarianism and opposing the practice of selling livestock into slaughter.[7] Yet, while their opposition to livestock sale for slaughter has chiefly targeted Tibetan communities, their life liberation advocacy has been directed more comprehensively, albeit not exclusively, at Han Chinese audiences.[8]

Larung Second Generation's Life Liberation Advocacy

The two essays translated in this chapter, by Khenpo Sodargye and Khenpo Sherab Zangpo, respectively, are significant contributions to the efforts of the Larung second-generation khenpos to propagate life liberation in mainland China. Both khenpos' essays draw on core themes in traditional Buddhist life liberation advocacy—the preciousness of life, the meritorious benefits of saving beings, and the karmic perils of killing.[9] At the same time, both essays vigorously address the contemporary state of life liberation practice in mainland China.

Ironically, as many PRC-based Buddhists have perceived a heightened need for ethical interventions in human-animal relations in the face of skyrocketing domestic meat consumption and the massive growth of mechanized slaughter and related industries, life liberation has received increasing censure. The past decade has seen mainstream media and online forums awash with critical voices—both secular and Buddhist, Chinese and Tibetan—arguing that life liberation activities all too often run counter to Buddhists' avowed goal of protecting life.[10] Notwithstanding an underlying compassionate motivation, critics contend that modern-day life liberation has been variously shown to detrimentally impact local ecosystems, fuel the very animal breeding industries that endanger animals in the first instance, disregard animal welfare, and create human disturbance.[11] In the face of irresponsible or naive behavior on the part of some life liberators and a stream of public criticism, staunch proponents of the practice, including the Larung school, have felt an acute need to address its problems and defend its legitimacy.

The following essays are examples of their responses to these issues. "Discussing Life Liberation Again"[12] was originally a live teaching delivered at Larung Gar to a Han Chinese monastic and lay audience in late 2009. Like the majority of Khenpo Sodargye's teachings, it was filmed for online dissemination and later transcribed and edited. The resulting text, upon which the following translation is based, was then incorporated as a chapter in *Life Salvation* (Ch: *Shengsi Jiudu*), a book of the khenpo's collected teachings on refraining from slaughter, life liberation, and assisting others in the dying process. It can also be found on his Wisdom and Compassion website (Ch: *Zhibeifowang*), where it is intended as an educational resource for lay Buddhists.

Khenpo Sodargye (1962–) is a Tibetan Buddhist educator, translator, writer, philanthropist, and spiritual master, and one of Khenpo Jigme Phuntsok's principle Dharma disciples. With a social media following of more than two million, he is also the Larung second generation's most high-profile teacher among Han Chinese audiences in the PRC and beyond. Born to a nomadic family in Sichuan Province's Draggo County, Khenpo

Sodargye completed a post-middle-school teacher training education prior to becoming a monk in 1985 and joining the Larung saṅgha under the tutelage of Khenpo Jigme Phuntsok. From 1987, he served as Khenpo Jigme Phuntsok's Chinese translator and in the 1990s, accompanied him on two major international teaching tours. In the past three decades, he has overseen the rigorous scholastic training of hundreds of resident Chinese monastics and, since the mid-2000s, has invested tremendous energy in popularizing lay Dharma education and engaging in youth outreach. Not only has he pioneered the use of the internet to teach Sinophone lay audiences, he has also published a series of best-selling popular Buddhist titles, lectured widely at leading universities in China and overseas, and founded the World Youth Buddhist Studies Symposium.[13] He has also been highly active in social and educational philanthropy in eastern Tibetan areas.

In this essay, Khenpo Sodargye reaffirms the roots and importance of life liberation in the Larung school and offers authoritative guidelines for conducting it appropriately. The very reason he considers it necessary to discuss life liberation again, he states in his opening, is because, from his observations, "many things are not as they should be." While underscoring that life liberation is a practice of "unsurpassed merit," he warns of "adverse consequences" if it is performed improperly.

Beginning with an overview of the origins of life liberation in the Larung school, Khenpo Sodargye places his own advocacy efforts, and those of his fellow khenpos, in the charismatic legacy of Khenpo Jigme Phuntsok (known to his disciples by the epithet His Holiness the Wish-Fulfilling Jewel).[14] Though acknowledging a history of life liberation practice in the Larung community dating back to 1987, Khenpo Sodargye makes clear that it was not until 1997—when Khenpo Jigme Phuntsok dreamt of his root master, Thubga Rinpoche, extolling to him the benefits of releasing lives— that a "large-scale, nationwide" campaign was launched in earnest. Revealing the depths to which he was personally inspired by the atmosphere at the time, he recalls vowing inwardly that "in my remaining years, even if I could save only one living being, I would spare no effort."

Turning his attention to the importance of life liberation, Khenpo Sodargye directs his remarks primarily at "newer monastics and lay practitioners," who may be unfamiliar with the merits of the practice. In what may be seen as his signature style of preaching to Sinophone audiences, he deftly draws on an eclectic range of modern and ancient sources of both Buddhist and non-Buddhist provenance, shifting easily between memorized scriptural quotations, engaging anecdotes, and plain-speaking discussion. Notable is Khenpo Sodargye's effort to situate life liberation as a theme and practice within a religio-cultural confluence of Indo-Tibetan Buddhism, Chinese Buddhism, and Confucianism. This variety of Sino-friendly nonsectarianism has been well received by contemporary Han Chinese Buddhist audiences.[15]

The third and most substantial section of Khenpo Sodargye's essay addresses "current problems" in the popular practice of life liberation— behaviors which, in his repeated use of the phrase, are "not in accord with the Dharma." While this expression is sometimes used simply in the sense of "inappropriate" or "improper," his intended meaning in this context is that contemporary life liberation practice often fails to conform to the standards and requirements of authentic Mahāyāna Buddhist principles. The ten best-practice guidelines that Khenpo Sodargye sets forth pertain to issues including the way in which the animals are ritually consecrated and released, the motivation of life liberators, environmental and animal welfare considerations, and miscellaneous misunderstandings that impact the effectiveness of the life liberation process. One might note that while avoiding causing ecological harm is given clear importance, it is only one of the many matters that life liberators acting in accord with the Dharma must consider. Equally consequential, for example, is that animals are correctly blessed, ensuring their contact with the Dharma and ultimate liberation.

In Defense of Liberating Lives

Published in 2013, four years after the essay above, Khenpo Sherab Zangpo's "Even If You Can Only Save One Life, It Is Also Worthwhile"[16] forms part of a longer book chapter titled "The Equality of Life," which, in addition to addressing life liberation, touches on themes of nonharming, vegetarianism, and helping living beings. This chapter is part of a volume of Khenpo Sherab Zangpo's collected teachings, *Life is Play* (Ch: *Shengming Zhe Chuxi*), which is currently available in print and digital formats as well as on his Bodhi Continent website (Ch: *Putizhou*). Sections from the book, including this essay, have been reposted widely on numerous Chinese language Buddhist websites and on social media.

Khenpo Sherab Zangpo (1963–) is an eminent PRC-based Tibetan Buddhist master, a close second-generation disciple of Khenpo Jigme Phuntsok, and one of the Larung school's primary voices among Han Chinese constituencies. Born in Dege, Kham, he was tutored by monastic mentors throughout his childhood and commenced systematic studies of Buddhist philosophy in 1976. After receiving full ordination as a monk in 1984, he traveled to Larung Gar and was accepted as a student by Khenpo Jigme Phunstok. Three years later, he received his khenpo degree and assumed teaching and administrative responsibilities within the Larung community. In 1994, he founded Tashi Triling, a retreat hermitage in the Dege region, and has continued to significantly invest in the growth of this community and the development of a number of nearby monasteries. The past decade has seen him intensify his outreach activities among Han Chinese lay Buddhists by embracing online technology for teaching purposes. He has also published four well-received books in Chinese on the study and practice of Buddhism[17] and is an important conduit of the Larung school in the contemporary Sinophone Tibetan Buddhist milieu.

Whereas Khenpo Sodargye's "Discussing Life Liberation Again" is primarily concerned with reforming shortcomings in life liberation practice, Khenpo Sherab Zangpo's essay focuses on rebutting prevalent criticisms of the activity. Employing concepts and terms such as *production chains* and *ecological balance*, his counterarguments manifest an expert quality capable of resonating with urbane Buddhist readers, equipping them with persuasive grounds to defend the practice.

Insofar as life liberation's potentially negative ecological impact is concerned, Khenpo Sherab Zangpo does not attempt to defend the practice of all life liberators. Rather, by explaining that "*we* [emphasis mine] do our utmost to consider the microecology of the release site, pay attention to the matching of species and the balancing of their numbers, and make sensible arrangements and plans," he maintains that it is possible to conduct life liberation in a way that causes minimal environmental impact—as his network evidently strives hard to do. Similarly, in countering the common criticism that life liberators care only about the merit-bearing ritual act of releasing the animals and are indifferent to their ongoing safety and well-being, he emphasizes "For a long time *we* [my emphasis] have consistently paid attention to the follow-up work of liberating lives."

Notwithstanding his advocacy for carrying out life liberation with scrupulous attention to its manifest consequences for the animals involved, Khenpo Sherab Zangpo firmly resists a reduction of the practice to a secular conception of animal rescue, wherein the ultimate objective lies in simply ensuring their survival. "That animals be free and far from immediate danger is important," he explains, "but we also aspire for these beings to be fundamentally free from death and suffering."[18]

Thus, Khenpo Sherab Zangpo also underscores the importance of blessing the animals in a correct manner. In addition, he stresses the necessity of performing a proper dedication of merit in order to bring about a positive karmic result for all involved. While acknowledging the meritorious power of collective life liberation activities for all who participate, he makes clear that the benefit is greatest for practitioners who undertake the entire process with great sincerity, compassion, and the altruistic intention to benefit others. If practiced to its fullest potential, he writes, life liberation can fulfil the six perfections (*pāramitās*), thereby constituting a comprehensive method of Buddhist cultivation.

As life liberation activities in mainland China have become subject to increased criticism and regulatory measures in recent years, calls by Chinese and Tibetan Buddhist leaders to unite wisdom with compassion in releasing lives have become widespread. The Larung school has been a vanguard proponent of this approach. In seeking to steer a path between promoting life liberation and assimilating valid contemporary criticisms, its second-generation khenpos have consistently advocated a best-practice approach to releasing lives. Their responsiveness to modern scientific discourse and secular-style concerns, however, has not led them to downplay life liberation's ultimate religious objectives or abandon a traditional presentation of its benefits. As the following essays show, Larung life liberation remains firmly grounded in the principle of karmic causation, belief in past and future lives, and faith in the worldly efficacy of virtuous action. Ritual dimensions remain important, as do the benefits of life liberation events in collective religious life. With respect to life liberation, therefore, the Larung school's "modern" stance may be seen as combining two vital aspects: an emphasis on reason, progressive reform, and ethical accountability on the one hand and a firm insistence on traditional religious values on the other.

Acknowledgments

I would like to extend my sincere thanks to Venerable Changsheng and Gu An for helping me to clarify the meaning of several challenging phrases in the essays below and to Wayne Hardie and Will Spiegelman for proofreading and offering constructive feedback on my translation manuscript.

Discussing Life Liberation Again: Remedying Things That Are Not in Accord with the Dharma in the Practice of Life Liberation

Khenpo Sodargye (2009)

Today I will be talking once again about life liberation. Life liberation is something with which every Buddhist is relatively familiar. Over the years, many centers, monasteries, and individuals have taken part in this virtuous practice in different ways. So why do I wish to discuss it again? Recently, I discovered that people everywhere are performing quite a lot of life release. However, in the course of doing so, many things are not as they should be, so I would like to make some recommendations. Since releasing lives is of unsurpassed merit, it should be done in a way that perfectly accords with the Dharma; otherwise, it can lead to adverse consequences. Therefore, I would like to use this time to have a simple conversation with everyone about knowledge relevant to life liberation.

Genesis of Life Liberation Advocacy

For me, liberating lives is the most joyful and compelling thing in my life. Whenever it comes to life liberation, just thinking about the many lives of beings that can be saved makes me do my utmost to overcome any physical, psychological, or life difficulties. Trifling feelings of cold or hunger are not worth mentioning.

Our earliest life liberation was in 1991 when we started releasing yaks and sheep in Tibetan regions and loaches, fish, birds, and so on in Han regions. The reason we came to this idea was that in 1987 on our way to Wutai Shan, we witnessed deplorable scenes of killing in vegetable markets, and some of the monks then made a vow to release lives together. Looking back now, however, due to our lack of familiarity with the environment in Han regions, our life liberation practice at that time was in many ways not mature. Only later, by 1991, could the life liberation activities we held in many places be considered acceptable. Every year, we ransomed many yaks in Tibetan areas. In every city, we visited Han areas. If causes and conditions were sufficient, we would begin by teaching everyone some Buddhadharma and then launch them into life liberation; all along, this was how it was.

Our real advocacy of nationwide, large-scale life liberation, however, originated with a dream of His Holiness the Wish-Fulfilling Jewel. On the eighth lunar day of April in 1997, His Holiness had a dream, but what was different about this dream, compared to his lucid dreams in the past, was that it was very much like the dream of an ordinary person. In his dream, His Holiness went to an unfamiliar place where he saw his root guru, Thubga Rinpoche, seated upright on a Dharma throne giving Buddhist teachings to a saṅgha of tens of thousands. His appearance was one of extreme majesty, and his voice and smiling countenance were exactly the same as they were prior to his passing forty-two years earlier. With matchless joy, His Holiness thought to himself, "Over these last few days the Academy's entire saṅgha has been doing Yamāntaka practice together in order to vanquish the human and nonhuman hindrances that beset Buddhism and the Academy. Yet, while we possess the ability to destroy these forces, we lack the ability to liberate them, so there is inevitably some doubt in my mind as to whether this is ultimately of benefit or harm. I will seize this opportunity right now to seek the lama's advice."

After His Holiness confessed the doubts in his mind, Thubga Rinpoche said in a kindly tone: "This current practice is extremely sublime. Regardless of whether you are able to liberate demonic beings, as long as you recite the liturgy and conduct the subduing with samādhi, mantras, hand mudrās, and pure aspiration, the merit is inconceivable and will greatly benefit sentient beings. You have really performed a great liberation of lives." His root guru then went on to describe the various beneficial qualities of liberating lives.

Knowing that life liberation would please his teacher and thus make him happy, His Holiness said to his guru: "Since returning from Singapore the year before last (1995), I have released at least one hundred million lives in Han China." Upon hearing this, Thubga Rinpoche pressed his palms together and praised him continuously: "Virtuous son! Virtuous son! You really are the Wish-Fulfilling Jewel for the degenerate age, the sun of the degenerate age!" Repeating this three times, he then conferred a four-line instruction by way of a vajra song:

> In awakening to the ambrosia-like nature of reality,
>   deep, tranquil, nondiscriminating, luminous, and unconditioned,

one gains the capacity to deliver limitless beings
with skillful means adapted to those to be tamed.

Thereafter, Thubga Rinpoche presented His Holiness with a statue of
Yamāntaka and, calling him close, touched his forehead to his own in a blessing. His Holiness was overjoyed; his feeling was just as it was when his root
guru had blessed him in the same way the day before he had passed away. At
that moment, His Holiness awoke from his dream. The hour hand on the
clock had just touched five in the morning. When it was light, His Holiness
discovered a Yamāntaka statue in his room that had never belonged to him.
The statue in his dream with the deity and consort, however, had turned
into a single deity whose original single face and two arms had become three
faces and six arms. The color was also different.

With this auspicious connection, His Holiness instructed us that in the
age of degeneration, among all virtuous deeds, life liberation is the sole
cause of delight for buddhas, bodhisattvas, and root gurus. Moreover, he
urged Buddhist groups in all parts of China— including Vajrayāna Dharma
assemblies, monasteries, and lay Buddhist associations, as well as monastics,
householders, and believers everywhere—to release lives widely. From then
on, under the energetic advocacy of His Holiness, life liberation events were
launched with vigor and vitality across the country with gratifying results.
Senior khenpos and major reincarnate lamas from our academy proceeded
one after another to Han Chinese or Tibetan regions to release lives. Even
ordinary monks and lay practitioners at the academy, when they traveled
to a city, made every effort within their ability to join the ranks of those
rescuing living beings.

Given the five turbidities[19] that overflow the present era, that His Holiness the Wish-Fulfilling Jewel had such power and charisma is truly incredible. From that time on, I made a silent vow of aspiration in my mind that
in my remaining years, even if I could save only one living being, I would
spare no effort. In order to encourage both myself and others to collectively undertake this virtuous activity, in June 1997 I wrote an essay titled
"The Beneficial Qualities of Life Liberation: Marvelous Ambrosia Rain"[20]
in which I expound the benefits and advantages of renouncing killing
and liberating lives. This essay revolves around the themes of killing and
karmic retribution; confession of past killing; the foremost importance
of great compassion; meat eating and vegetarianism; the boundless benefits of releasing lives and the role of life liberation in attaining liberation

and rebirth in Sukhāvatī; and so on. At the same time, I also wrote essays titled "What Is the Most Precious Thing?"[21] and "Letter Urging Friends to Release Lives"[22] and compiled a recitation liturgy to be used for life liberation. Despite not having much ability, I thought that within a limited scope these writings and methods might have some effect and perhaps be of help to a very small number of sentient beings.

IMPORTANCE OF LIFE LIBERATION

Many Dharma friends sitting here have always been very interested in releasing lives, and many lamas, when they travel to Han Chinese areas, also approach life liberation as a matter of prime importance. This is especially worthy of joy. However, some newer monastics and lay practitioners may be unclear about the merits of life liberation and the importance of this practice for present and future lifetimes, so it is necessary to give a brief introduction on these matters today.

Why is liberating lives so extremely important? In this world, all beings, irrespective of whether they are human or animal, cherish their own lives beyond compare. The lives of all beings are equal. Nowadays, however, notions like this are relatively scarce. The concept of equality between human beings is accepted. Especially in the twenty-first century, so long as one is human, one has the right to life, the right to speech; on this there is global consensus. But what is it that humanity lacks the most? It is the concept that animals also have a right to existence. Animals also crave life and fear death; it is just that they cannot speak.

We cherish our own lives, and, in fact, animals are just the same. This is a concept many Buddhist practitioners in both Tibet and China fully understand and to which they do not just pay lip service. If seasoned practitioners with compassion were to witness someone get shot by a gun, they would find it difficult to bear. By the same token, if they were to witness an animal being killed, that act would give rise to the same kind of unbearable compassion. The Chan master Hanshan said, "Humans cherish their lives, and creatures cherish their lives. Releasing lives is in harmony with the will of heaven and in accordance with the Buddha's decree." It is not only Buddhists who understand this principle; even kindhearted, worldly people disapprove of the barbaric conduct of taking lives and eating meat. For example, in his speeches on vegetarianism and nonviolence, the Indian vegetarian Gandhi always emphasized that all beings have a right to existence, and animal life is as precious as human life.

There are many recorded teachings in the Buddhist scriptures on protecting and releasing lives. The earliest is in the *Golden Light Sūtra* (*Suvarṇaprabhāsa Sūtra*). Long ago, when the Buddha was born as Jalavāhana, the merchant's son, he saw that a pond had dried up and thousands of fish would be scorched by the sun and die as a result. He borrowed twenty elephants from the king, filled leather bags with water, poured it into the pond, and resuscitated the fish. After doing so, he gave them food and recited to them the name of the buddha Ratnaśikhi (also called Ratnasambhava). Upon hearing the Buddha's name, the fish were reborn in the Trayastriṃśa Heaven. In the *Miscellaneous Jewels Sūtra* (*Saṃyuktaratnapiṭaka Sūtra*), it is recorded that a novice monk who had only seven days to live noticed a breach in a pond on his journey home. Realizing countless ants would soon drown, he gave rise to heartfelt compassion, filled his monastic robes with earth, blocked the gap in the pond wall and rescued all the ants. With this act, the novice monk's life span was transformed as he attained the karmic fruit of prolonged life. *The Medicine Buddha Sūtra* (*Bhaiṣajyaguru Sūtra*) says, "The positive karma generated by liberating lives allows beings to overcome hardship and prevents their future suffering." For this reason, if people who find themselves afflicted by suffering and karmic obstacles are able to practice life liberation, it may be possible for them to avert disaster and change their fate, turning misfortune into blessings. If they are frequently encouraged to release lives, even persons who are incurably ill may unwittingly experience miracles.

Therefore, among all unconditioned Dharma practices, meditating on emptiness is of inconceivable merit, and among all conditioned Dharma practices, the merit of liberating lives is unequaled. The faults of killing are too numerous to mention. I often quote Nāgārjuna's teaching in the *Great Treatise on the Perfection of Wisdom* (*Mahāprajñāpāramitā Śāstra*): "Among all karmic sins, killing is the gravest; among all virtues, abstaining from killing is the foremost." Once I read a book that said "liberating lives is the foremost," but when I later checked the original text of the *Great Treatise on the Perfection of Wisdom*, I saw it is in fact "abstaining from killing is the foremost." Nevertheless, there is a difference in the relative merit of "abstaining from killing" and "liberating lives." *The Commentary on the Aspiration of Sukhāvatī*[23] says that while abstaining from killing is of definite merit, if in addition to this, one is able to diligently release and protect the lives of sentient beings, one will naturally obtain all kinds of happiness in this lifetime.

As Buddhists, we often hold celebrations of various kinds in our everyday lives, including at the new year, at the time of other festivals, for weddings, the birth of children, and the opening of new businesses. On such occasions, there is nothing more positive than releasing lives. Many lay Buddhists frequently ask: "This year someone in my family is getting married; please, teacher, give them your blessing. What is the most important thing they should do?" I always answer: "Liberate lives. If they are able to release lives, with this sublime causal connection, their future family is bound to be harmonious and happy. Conversely, if for celebration's sake they kill countless living beings such that their dining tables are totally covered with freshly slaughtered life, due to the heinous karmic sin, their future will certainly not hold good results."

In the past in Tibet, every year each family would kill one or two yaks. Even so, many people greatly feared the law of karma and would desperately chant prayers and confess their wrongdoing. In cities today, however, everything people eat and drink is bound up with killing beings—it is really terrible! Therefore, as Buddhists, in addition to releasing lives, what we eat and drink should be based on a vegetarian diet. Stepping back, if you are just not able to be vegetarian, then you should at least abstain from ordering live creatures to eat and try to live a simple life. Some time ago, I read an essay by Einstein called "What I Believe," and in it he says, "I believe that a simple life, both physically and mentally, is beneficial to everyone." I thought about it later, and really it is true: the simpler a person is, the happier they are, and the more complicated a person is, the greater price they have to pay. For example, if you eat an especially sumptuous meal, not only do you have to spend a lot of money, but you also need to sacrifice the lives of more innocent beings than you could pay back even in countless lifetimes. Some monastics and lay Buddhists complain about having to do Vajrasattva heart mantra recitations. Yet, if we think about it, how many beings have we consumed since we were young? Just this amount alone warrants us doing confession practice night and day. If we do not, how could these beings fail to return and demand repayment at the time of our death?

There is nothing more precious in this world than life, while killing beings for the sake of one's own momentary appetite is the cruelest thing. Buddhist Master Lianchi said: "The most important thing in the world is life; the cruelest act in the world is killing" and "Liberating lives is not merely Buddhist;

all Confucian gentlemen invariably observe this practice." The concept of abstaining from killing and liberating lives is not followed by Buddhists alone, but is vigorously advocated by many other religions, chiefly Confucianism. Of course, as we have analyzed in the past, these religions are mainly concerned with protecting the lives of human beings; their scope does not extend to all sentient beings. Therefore, everyone should be clear about the vastness and supremeness of the Buddhist concept of compassion. On this basis, we should treat all beings equally and protect them equally. When this compassion reaches a certain level, even if you see a small creature whose life is threatened, you will do your utmost to help and rescue it.

In today's world, when various vulnerable communities are hit by disaster, governments will make every effort to lend a helping hand. Yet, while thousands upon thousands of animals around us are being killed every day, many so-called compassionate figures are not in the least bit concerned and pay no attention. Sometimes, therefore, it seems human behavior is quite terrible. Why is it that today we have an outbreak of infectious disease, tomorrow an earthquake, snowstorms the day after that, and various natural and man-made disasters occurring one after another? In actual fact, these occurrences are also related to the reckless taking of lives by human beings. If this bloody behavior continues to spread, it will inevitably provoke the wrath of heaven and the fury of men, and nature will retaliate against humankind such that human beings' living space will become increasingly narrow and limited.

Regrettably, however, many people in big cities nowadays have no compassion at all. In order to protect their own interests, they do not hesitate to kill countless sentient beings and even consider it fitting and proper. In order to change this wretched situation, we need to promote life liberation. Even if you do not have the financial means or opportunity to frequently do so, once or twice a year is fine.

The Chan master Zhigong said: "The merit of releasing lives is boundless," and he quoted a teaching from the Buddhist scriptures to broadly explain this rationale. Hanshan also said: "One compassionate thought of saving a life is a thought of Guanyin. If one releases lives every day, one's compassion will increase daily, and if one perseveres at length all these thoughts will flow into Guanyin's ocean of compassion." It is thus clear that other insignificant acts of virtue cannot compare to the practice of life liberation.

For this reason, there are many eminent lamas from our academy who have devoted themselves to life liberation for their entire lives. For example, Khenpo Tsultrim Lodro sets aside a fixed period each year to release lives in the Han region and has not broken this practice in more than ten years. This truly fills one with praise.

As for myself, in the past I also wanted to take out a month each year to do life liberation. However, for various reasons, I just could not set aside such a long period of time. No matter what, however, every autumn I still try my best to go out and release lives. This year I have already released one thousand yaks and sheep. In the future, as long as I still have one breath left in me and a little ability, prior to abandoning this body, what I really wish to do is to release lives.

Nowadays, with the support of many great bodhisattvas in Han Chinese areas, life liberation in all its aspects enjoys conducive conditions and conveniences. For this reason, I hope Buddhist believers everywhere actively take part in this virtuous activity. Just imagine if you were a cow under a butcher's knife facing imminent slaughter and at that moment someone saved you and returned you to nature—how would you feel in your heart? Or imagine you were a prisoner sentenced to death and at the moment you were about to be executed someone found a way to rescue you—how happy would you feel? How grateful would you be toward your rescuer? I believe the answer goes without saying.

Whenever I release lives and see how the fish and loaches swim away freely in the water, and how the little birds fly eagerly into the blue sky, my mind feels greatly at ease. Even though my body cannot fly, it is as if my heart was soaring happily with the birds in the sky; that kind of feeling is truly wonderful. Therefore, releasing lives is an especially happy thing. In the future, when causes and conditions are sufficient, I hope everyone is able to organize some life liberation events over a slightly longer period. However, if you simply lack the ability or conditions to do so, just purchasing one life and releasing it is fine, too.

There once was a student I knew well. When he was in middle school, high school, and college, every time he received pocket money he would go straight to the market and buy some fish to release. He persevered with this practice for many years and moved many teachers and classmates. Due to his virtuous motivation and actions, his surrounding karma was extremely wonderful, and last year he passed an examination to go to America. Not long ago, I heard that, while studying there, he is still doing his utmost to release lives within Christian and other religious groups.

Indeed, sometimes it is not necessary to be an eminent monastic with great means; so long as there is kindness in one's mindstream, it can be put to use at any time. It is just like a small lamp; while maybe not as bright as a headlight, it still has the ability to dispel darkness. Therefore, regardless of what kind of person you are, you should pay greater attention to releasing lives.

I often think that there is nothing more precious in this world than life. While some people say the Buddhadharma is the most precious thing—and, in a sense, this is indeed true—at a critical juncture, ordinary mortal beings are perhaps still more likely to choose their own lives as being most precious. Therefore, everyone must respect life and care for life. Animals also have a right to existence. Even if we can only help one being, we should go all out to do so.

The Dharma friends belonging to the fourfold sangha²⁴ who are present here have spared no effort in supporting and assisting with life liberation, charity, and so on, for many years, and I would like to express my heartfelt gratitude for this. We do positive deeds together with the goal that all beings receive benefit, not just for the sake of our own health. Of course, the beneficial qualities of releasing lives are inconceivable—prolonging life in this lifetime, strengthening the body, bringing success in business and well-being to families, purifying karmic sin for future lifetimes, being reborn in the western paradise of Sukhāvatī, and the realization of one's true nature. These are indisputable facts, but our focus is more than just these things—it is the lives of sentient beings.

The lives of beings are more important than anything else, and if it they can be protected from being killed, the karmic fruits are truly unsurpassed. Conversely, if a person intentionally kills another being, the karmic sin is difficult to purify. Sometimes, when I am ill, many people urge me to see a doctor, but I always think, "Has this been caused by an act of killing in a past life? If so, just doing a few simple virtuous deeds in this lifetime is not sufficient. If I killed another person, it is my turn to pay with my life. Were I just to give that person a few dollars and do a minor good deed [on their behalf] and expect to be able to resolve everything, then, let alone that person, I doubt even their relatives would agree!" Therefore, everyone must make an aspiration not to be reborn as a killer in all lifetimes to come.

As it happens, even if every aspect of our practice is really lacking, as monastics, at least we will not accrue the negative karma of killing. If we had not left home, we would barely have been able to avoid killing when socializing with people from different walks of life. Even if the act of killing is not committed by oneself, acts of killing indirectly committed for one's own sake also accrue immeasurable karmic sin. This negative karma is destined to ripen upon oneself, so it is imperative to pay attention to this!

CURRENT PROBLEMS

These days, many lamas all over the country are encouraging everyone to release lives, and many disciples are doing so. Originally, I thought everyone was releasing lives quite satisfactorily. However, after making multisided observations, it seems the conduct of many is somewhat not in accord with the Dharma. Therefore, as a result of this conversation, I hope, when people liberate lives in the future, the following mandatory principles are observed.

All beings to be liberated must be released under the blessing of the Three Jewels.
I also mention this in the liturgy booklet. Before releasing the lives, it is necessary to bless all the animals using the supports of the Three Jewels, such as *Liberation on Hearing*,[25] *Liberation on Wearing*,[26] the *Prajñāpāramitā Sūtra*, the *Heart Sūtra*, and the *Diamond Sūtra* or Buddha images and prayer wheels. For large-bodied animals, like yaks and large birds, it is necessary to touch these supports to their heads; for animals with small bodies, like loaches, small fish, and sparrows, they should be waved over their crates. In short, every sentient being must receive the blessing of the Three Jewels.

All beings to be liberated must drink some consecrated water.
The *amṛta* pills [from which this water is made] must come from a pure source. If they originate from someone with broken vows or impure *samaya*, not only do they carry no blessing but as they have an inauspicious energy, they are extremely harmful to sentient beings. Therefore, it is best to use Guanyin pills, liberation pills, life release pills, and so on, that have been bestowed by eminent masters. Steep these amṛta pills in water. For fish, this water should be poured into their buckets; for birds, it should be sprinkled over them or a way should be devised to make them drink some of the consecrated water. The tantric scriptures frequently mention liberation on sight, liberation on touch, and liberation on taste. This is liberation on taste—attaining liberation after tasting. In the past, every time I liberated yaks, there would be several that were really fierce and difficult to approach. But I had to find a way and would spend a long time catching them, opening

their mouths, and pouring in some consecrated water. Only by tasting it in this way can they be liberated.

Prayers should be recited in close earshot of the animals to be liberated.
As for which prayers to recite, the best are the seven Medicine Buddha names, the names of the eight great bodhisattvas, the mantra of dependent arising, and *Samantabhadra's Prayer for Excellent Conduct*, and so on, found inside "The Beneficial Qualities of Life Liberation." These days, many life liberation liturgies—while I dare not say they are completely inappropriate—are produced to promote certain individuals, and whether or not they are of great benefit to sentient beings is difficult to say. Therefore, all Dharma friends, when you release lives in a collective and organized way, I ask that you be sure to recite our liturgy. I am not saying that ours is in accord with the Dharma and theirs is not—this is not what I mean. In the past, I have compared a lot of liturgies; there would have been no need for me to compile another one if other liturgies were suitable. However, after making detailed observations, in order to answer to the needs of all sentient beings, we merged the life liberation essentials of sūtra and tantra and produced this integrated liturgy.

Nowadays, when many people release lives, their behavior is strange and puzzling. I have witnessed many life liberation scenes where there are people not reciting the Buddha names properly but lighting incense and circling around, taking yellow cloth and fluttering it about, and even singing on the side. They explain they are doing this "so all beings give rise to joyous minds." Different places have different customs, and some of these customs are utter folk practices with no relationship to Buddhism at all. We spend so much money on releasing animals, but, if it is done like this, it is difficult to say whether or not the animals will be able to attain liberation. So, I am afraid that the life liberation ritual also warrants our attention, including those conducted by monastics from some monasteries. I am not saying they are all improper, but there are still problems in certain places. When you release lives in the future, therefore, I hope your conduct is properly in accord with the Dharma.

Actions should be gentle.
There are some lay practitioners who, when they release lives, carelessly toss the fish through the air without the slightest compassion. This is definitely

not acceptable. According to the *Commentary on the Treasury of Abhidharma* (*Abhidharmakośabhāṣya*),[27] causing other beings to give rise to great panic in their minds will result in becoming demented or insane in a future life. Therefore, you should pay attention to this point.

Motivations should be pure.
When a person releases lives, they should want to release lives; they should not just go through the ritual motions. As for using life liberation as a pretext to collect donations or to seek out certain kinds of people—there is just no need for this. Of course, when liberating lives, every person's motivation is different; there are some who take part for the sake of good health and longevity, some for beautiful looks, and others who do so purely out of curiosity. Once there were some people in Sichuan who wanted to go and release lives. I asked them why, and they replied, "We've heard Longquan Lake is really fun and that there is a farmer's homestead where you can relax on the return trip. It sounds really pleasant!" Releasing lives with this kind of mentality has no meaning. We should be generating great compassion to benefit and wholeheartedly help all beings. Only in this way does liberating lives and reciting the names of the buddhas and bodhisattvas have real meaning.

Life liberation is best done in person.
Some people think, "It is fine if I just donate some money for life release, I do not necessarily have to attend in person." This is a lazy excuse. In fact, if you attend life liberation in person, recite the liturgy collectively along with everyone else, and release the beings back into nature using your own hands, the merit is definitely much greater than if you just donate some money. Although rejoicing in other's good deeds is meritorious, according to the *Treasury of Abhidharma*[28] and the *Vinayasūtra*,[29] doing virtuous deeds oneself is more sublime. Therefore, when causes and conditions are sufficient in all their aspects, liberating lives is best done in person.

Have concern for the environment when releasing lives.
Some people who do life liberation never consider the impact on the surroundings. For example, they release snakes in places that are densely populated by humans and cause a lot of trouble. Given that today there are barely any sparsely populated areas as there were in ancient times, many issues need to be considered. There was once a news report that told how a group of people doing life liberation released more than a thousand snakes

into the countryside. Every day, at midday and again in the evening, the snakes would crawl inside villagers' homes. A lot of chickens were killed, people did not dare to sleep at night, and there were even old ladies who were frightened to tears. Of course, some people say that poisonous snakes should not be released because they are harmful to humans. But this way of speaking is also incorrect. After all, snakes *are* living beings; it is only that their reincarnation is brought about by anger and malice. Therefore, they are still deserving of our protection.

When choosing a life release location, observe what kind of environment the animals to be released will be able to survive in.
For example, there are many kinds of aquatic creatures, some of which live in fresh water and others that live in seawater. If, just seeing it is a fish, you casually release it into the ocean, maybe it will not be able to survive there and will die instantly. Dead fish floating on the surface of the water is also a kind of environmental pollution. So, before releasing lives, first make inquiries regarding the kind of environment the animals are suited to and be sure to pay attention to this when you are buying them.

Do not release lives on fixed dates.
Many people often liberate lives on Buddhist commemorative days that fall on April 8 and June 4, or on the tenth, fifteenth and thirtieth of each lunar month. In doing this, it is very easy for fishmongers and others to catch on to your patterns. I heard it used to be the case in the Lhasa area that on the fifteenth and thirtieth of each lunar month, many animals to be killed would appear in the streets and their prices on those days would be particularly high. While, normally speaking, there is great merit in doing positive deeds on the Buddha's birthday and the anniversary of the Buddha's enlightenment, if it bears on the lives of sentient beings then we do not necessarily have to do so on these days. Otherwise, some businesses may take advantage of the opportunity to raise their prices and deliberately catch a lot of animals.

Dispelling Several Common Misunderstandings

Some people think, "Real life liberation means rescuing animals from under the butcher's knife. Therefore, animals should be purchased from markets." While this way of thinking is fine, there is definitely a large price differential.

If you go to a wholesale market, a pound of loaches might cost fifteen yuan (in the past, when we first started releasing lives, loaches were three yuan per pound), whereas if you were to purchase them at a regular market you would pay twenty yuan. The animals on sale at regular markets are very pitiable, and if you are willing to pay a high price you can purchase them, but the fish mongers there are really rotten; after they have sold one tray they will go back to the wholesale market and get another tray, and on their return will continue slaughtering. If this happens, our money gets wasted and we end up not being able to rescue many beings.

Some people have no experience in liberating lives and, although they weigh the fish at the time of purchase, when they are delivered to the life release location, they do not weigh them again. Some fish mongers are extremely cunning and remove some of the fish [after the transaction] and place them back on sale and only deliver the remainder to the life release location. When they arrive, if the fish were actually weighed, it is possible not even one-half would be remaining. Therefore, those without any experience will encounter many problems to begin with. If you are doing life liberation over a long period, you need to pay even more attention to these issues. Even if you are not doing long-term life release, in dealing with people at markets you still need to observe matters with wisdom, asking: "What will be the results of releasing lives? How can certain links in the overall process be monitored?" Otherwise, without you realizing it, a lot of money will be wasted.

Some people think, "Life liberation money should not go directly to fishmongers. Otherwise, once they get money they will just buy and kill more animals." This argument is not correct. Given these fish and loaches are [goods that can be converted into] money to begin with, even if the fishmonger does not sell them to you, he can still sell them to other people. Therefore, there is perhaps no need to argue too much about this type of thing.

Nowadays, some people in Tibetan areas say: "Slaughtering yaks is fitting and proper; doing so can stimulate economic development and improve living standards in pastoral areas." This argument is unreasonable. Developing productivity does not necessarily entail killing; there are many other avenues, such as learning knowledge, running factories, manufacturing handicrafts, and so on. Killing is an activity that generates karmic sin. Even if one can make money doing so, it is a very despicable industry. However, many people today understand neither the concept of compassion nor the harmonious effect of liberating lives on nature and blindly promote the "theory of getting rich by killing." This is quite lamentable.

To sum up, nowadays there are some people whose practice of life liberation from beginning to end is not so proper. They spend all their money in a hurry but do not end up saving many beings. Even if they do rescue some, they fail to enable them to make an auspicious connection with the Dharma of liberation. Therefore, everyone must pay attention to these principles when releasing lives in the future.

At present, there are some groups that have not liberated lives even once in the past two or three years. This is not very good. When I travel outside to places like Shanghai and Shantou, there are some lay practitioners who release lives every day—they truly are amazing. There are also lay practitioners who release lives every week or every month. We might not be able to manage this, but, even without this kind of ability, releasing lives once or twice a year should be no problem. Some time ago, I wrote a letter requesting students to release lives several times each year, but I am afraid this instruction has not been followed. In actual fact, in other matters I do not require you to follow my instructions, but in so far as benefiting beings and propagating the Buddhadharma are concerned, if my advice is valuable and meaningful, I hope everyone will consider it and try to keep it in their hearts. This would be beneficial to both self and others!

Life Liberation: Even If You Can Only Save One Life, It Is Also Worthwhile

Khenpo Sherab Zangpo (2013)

Among all forms of virtuous action, the Buddha said that the merit and benefit of saving the lives of sentient beings is the greatest. If we ourselves were in danger of being killed and someone saved us, their act would necessarily elicit our infinite gratitude—other forms of assistance cannot compare to the kindness of saving lives. This is the case for other beings as well as humans.

My beneficent guru, His Holiness the Wish-Fulfilling Jewel, only had to see an animal suffering or being harmed and he would be grieved to the point of tears and do everything he could to rescue it. Under the positive influence and guidance of our teacher, we disciples, wherever we go, make earnest efforts to release life and promote the bringing of freedom, happiness, and fearlessness to rescued animals, as well as the giving of compassion, warmheartedness and faith to those who release lives.

In 1997, His Holiness was leading the Larung Gar saṅgha in the collective practice of Yamāntaka. Before the dawn of April 8, he dreamed of his own root master, Thubga Rinpoche. Thubga Rinpoche said, "This practice is truly sublime and of great benefit to sentient beings; you've really performed a major life liberation" and then went on to describe the various meritorious qualities of releasing lives. Knowing that [news of] life liberation would please his teacher, His Holiness reported to him: "Since returning from Singapore the year before last I have released at least a million lives in Han China." Hearing this, Thubga Rinpoche was overjoyed and praised him many times with hands pressed together: "Virtuous son! Virtuous son! You really are the Wish-Fulfilling Jewel for the degenerate age, the sun of the degenerate age." Then, by way of a vajra song, he conferred a four-line teaching,

In awakening to the ambrosia-like nature of reality,
deep, tranquil, nondiscriminating, luminous, and unconditioned,
one gains the capacity to deliver limitless beings
with skillful means adapted to those to be tamed.

Afterwards, His Holiness instructed us that in the age of degeneration, life liberation is the Buddhist practice most pleasing to buddhas, bodhisattvas, and root gurus, and he urged his fourfold saṅgha to release lives widely and to practice this marvelous path. He then gave twenty thousand yuan to several disciples, one of whom was me, expressly to go to Han China to release lives. With this beginning, his disciples began to carry out large scale life liberation in various places on an ongoing basis. . . .

When you have money, don't waste it; liberate as many lives as possible. People who do not have much money can still liberate lives in accordance with their means and do their best to rescue beings. So long as one's aspiration is pure, the amount of money you spend does not matter and the merit is the same. Liberating lives is not just something we do at holy places or on Buddhist festivals; we should rescue beings as fate decrees, regardless of when or where. It is best, of course, to practice life liberation on a long-term basis. Releasing lives is an effective way of eliminating hindrances and quickly increasing the accumulation of merit and wisdom. It not only benefits the released beings but also increases one's own this-worldly fortune and yields fruits of health and longevity. It is also an important auxiliary condition for attaining rebirth in the western paradise. Therefore, we should diligently help living beings to be free from dangerous situations. We must do so because our virtuous aspirations and actions today will help us in the future when we, ourselves, are in danger. We should generate an aspiration for all beings to be reborn in the western paradise. If it isn't possible for us to be reborn there ourselves, then no matter where we are born in the future, we should aspire for all lifetimes to come to benefit all beings and never harm them.

Around us are many relatives, colleagues, and friends, who, for various reasons, have not yet taken refuge in the Three Jewels but rush about day and night for the sake of their purported happiness and well-being. Despite their pursuit of happiness and well-being, however, everything they do is the cause of suffering. While some people may have already taken refuge in the Three Jewels, their behavior often is not in accord with the Dharma. As far as possible, we should try to exert influence over such people through our actions and allow them to see the power of virtuous conduct from the changes in our own behavior and minds. If our actions are able to lead them to arouse just a tiny amount of faith in the Dharma and even go so far as to release a single being in this lifetime, then according to the doctrine of the infallibility of karma, this will definitely benefit them in present and future lifetimes.

In the process of liberating lives, we often encounter obstacles. For example, just after releasing some fish, someone hears about it and comes rushing with a fishing net or rod to catch them, or someone deliberately creates an incident to prevent the life release from taking place. When these types of situations occur, do not give rise to resentment and quarrel with people but plead with tactful words and actively seek solutions. We cannot demand everyone understand and support life liberation. Indeed, while many people in Han Chinese areas might not oppose releasing lives, it can at least be said that they do not understand or support it. This is because the education they receive does not include concepts of life liberation, equality of life, and so on. Learning new knowledge and changing preconceived ideas are very difficult.

Some people think that frequent life liberation activities have created new market demand. They believe that because some vendors specialize in buying, selling, and catching animals for life liberation, if we did not release lives then situations like this would not arise. In actual fact, among those animals at local markets, slaughterhouses, and farms that are destined for human dinner plates, only a handful can be rescued. Since this proportion is negligible, if farmers, slaughterhouses, and market holders or vendors were counting on supplying life liberation for their business, they would go bankrupt very quickly. They would hardly be so naive. Regardless of whether or not life liberation is carried out, farmers will over-cultivate, slaughterhouses will excessively slaughter, and vendors will buy, sell, and kill. Only if the majority of people in society popularly and consciously reduce the demand for meat products can the scale of killing of and trading in animals be decreased. Otherwise, the modest life release activities of a small number of people are unlikely to have an impact on the breeding and slaughter industries and such large chains of relevant production.

Even if individual vendors see life liberation as bringing them a "business opportunity" and increase their stock levels due to this unanticipated demand, releasing these lives will not cause harm or suffering to anyone. Of course, were it the case that cattle, sheep, fish, shrimp, and so on, were living freely and happily on their breeding farms to begin with and only because of life liberation were slaughtered and transported to markets, then criticizing life liberation for inflicting suffering on animals would be justified.

However, in reality, this is not the case: if life liberators did not fortuitously purchase these cattle, sheep, fish, and shrimp, they would be slaughtered as planned since the purpose for which they are bred is to be eaten. Life liberation does not cause slaughter; it permits a few lucky animals to be spared from the pain of being brutally killed. If people really want to criticize from the standpoint of animals, they should blame the people who slaughter, capture, breed, trade, wear, and feed on animals for their own benefit, appetite, or vanity, and not those who protect and release captive animals.

Furthermore, during the life liberation process we do our utmost to consider the microecology of the release site, pay attention to the matching of species and the balancing of their numbers, and make sensible arrangements and plans. Some people say that life liberation will destroy the ecological balance. I do not know why these people cannot see the way excessive expansion of modern farming, animal husbandry, and slaughter-related industries are causing unprecedented water pollution, soil desertification, species extinction, breakage in the natural food chain, and the prevalent abuse of antibiotics and new diseases in humans and animals. The animals we release are mainly purchased from markets and slaughterhouses. Prior to this, most of them were crammed into breeding farms. We only take meat away from human mouths and not from animals in nature. There is no question, therefore, of us destroying the food chain.

When we release fish and shrimp into rivers and oceans, some people worry this will cause trouble for the aquatic environment. In fact, regardless of how great an effort we make, we can only release a limited quantity of animals. Even if, due to occasional oversights, we have an impact on certain bodies of water, the effects are extremely limited. Many waters are actually very susceptible to pollution due to a scarcity of fish in the water. It seems that people should be more concerned about the serious and irreversible damage to water resources caused by industrial emissions, urban sewage, and excessive aquiculture.

For a long time, we have consistently paid attention to the follow-up work of liberating lives. It is not the case, as some people think, that we only concern ourselves with the [ritual] form of liberating lives without caring whether the released animals live or die after the ceremony is over. Every time we liberate lives, we do our best to find a safe location and prevent the released animals from being captured again. For example, we do not release fish into fishponds or at fish farms. These are dedicated places for raising fish and shrimp for people to catch and kill. If the animals are released in these places, they will be soon caught and sent to markets and restaurants. Nor are waterfowls released in mountain areas or fish released in waters that are polluted or in which they could not survive. Factory-reared chickens and ducks pose more difficulty to release, so in some places lay Buddhists have raised funds to buy land, establish life release parks, and house these animals. The period each year when autumn turns to winter and people start to fatten animals and give them extra nourishment is when cattle and sheep are slaughtered in large numbers. We go to the slaughterhouses and purchase cattle and sheep and transport them back to Tibetan areas where we entrust them to honest and reliable herders to care for them until their natural deaths. The herders are very happy to do this. First, they participate in liberating lives and thereby accumulate roots of merit. Second, while taking care of the cattle and sheep, they can make use of the cow and sheep milk to produce dairy products and improve their livelihoods.

Some people think spending money to liberate animals that will eventually die, or die when they are released, is a waste of money. It is indeed the case that released animals cannot avoid death and that we are unable to locate a release site where they will never die. Nevertheless, we cannot not liberate lives for these reasons. If the released animals are able to survive to the end of their lifetimes and die naturally, the suffering they experience will be far less than being slaughtered one lifetime after another or being disemboweled. Even if they die shortly after or in the process of being released, it is still a thousand times better than being slaughtered for food and hacked to death before their consciousness has departed their body. For this reason, liberating lives not only helps animals gain freedom from the temporary suffering of the fear of death, but more importantly, chanting the life liberation liturgy and allowing animals to hear the Buddha names and mantras becomes the cause of their future liberation from saṃsāra. No matter how the money is spent, it is not wasted. Everyone has their own views on this. Many people actually increase their own suffering by spending money. If this is not considered a waste, then neither should spending money to help reduce the suffering of other beings.

Apart from those animals in markets and slaughterhouses soon to be turned into human food, there are many sentient beings waiting for someone to lend them a helping hand, such as animals whose living habitats have been lost due to environmental degradation, and beings in our midst that are frequently ignored, such as stray cats and dogs, people suffering from diseases who require economic, material, spiritual, and other forms of help, children who cannot attend school due to poverty, old people with no one to care for them, and so on. All phenomena are dependently arising, and helping other beings also depends on causes and conditions. Although we may wish for all beings to be free from suffering and enjoy happiness, in practice we can only act in accordance with prevailing causes and conditions and do our best to help within the scope of our abilities. Regardless of whether human or animal, we should help to the best of our ability every sentient being requiring assistance that appears in our field of vision.

There are some people who see others releasing lives and dismiss it as not very worthwhile. They say it would be better to use the money to help people in poverty. When a poor person actually appears in front of them, however, they prefer to rescue disaster victims rather than the poor and say it would be better to use the money to help the physically ailing. When someone else does this, however, they do not rejoice but say something different again. In short, no one is as smart as they are, and despite wanting to practice generosity, by always waiting for the ideal time to do so, they end up neither helping animals nor helping humans. Rather than allowing afflictive habits of greed and jealousy to make trouble, criticizing other people's good deeds, and damaging one's own karmic fortune, it would be better to practically help, even if it is just one being. This would be more beneficial to oneself than talking high-mindedly.

When we are liberating lives, we frequently encounter people who rejoice in and support our actions. The drivers who assist us in transporting cattle and sheep back to Tibetan areas actively offer to do so for free or at a discount. The people at the slaughter yards are also very happy that they can still make money without having to kill. It would seem most people who kill beings as a profession are not convinced killing is a pleasant thing. When the trucks transporting the cattle and sheep arrive in Tibetan areas, people along the road see the multicolored prayer flags on the trucks and the colored fabric strips tied to the horns of the cattle and sheep. They know these are life liberation vehicles and greatly rejoice. In Han regions, when we go to the market to purchase aquatic animals, we often encounter vendors who are supportive, too. They either donate a few fish to be released, or help us carry the animals we purchase, or give some money so that we can liberate lives on their behalf. Every time this happens, we greatly rejoice in their virtuous thoughts and actions. They also seem to be very happy. It is probably the case that in the midst of this completely new human interaction and human-animal connection, they also feel a kind of happiness they have never before experienced. If those who pass by or observe people performing life liberation are able to give rise to a joyous mind and even positive feelings toward the Buddhadharma, it will leave an imprint in their mindstreams, which, just like seeds planted in a field, will bear fruit when future causes and conditions are ripe.

Many people may not be aware that their every kind thought and positive act, even if small and fleeting, is sure to serve as a bright light of rescue in their long night of saṃsāra, a time of danger. This knowledge—that even a hurried passerby can be benefited—is what enables us to continue persevering with releasing lives, no matter what difficulties and misunderstandings we encounter in the process.

Liberating lives is not simply rescuing animals from under the butcher's knife or cages and securing their survival. Of course, that animals be free and far from immediate danger is important. But we also aspire for these beings to be fundamentally free from death and suffering. When we release lives, therefore, we recite the Buddhist life liberation liturgy so the released animals can make an auspicious connection with the Buddhadharma, sowing seeds in their mindstreams.

Naturally, it is excellent if a monastic can lead the recitation of the liturgy but, if not, laypeople can still release lives. Life liberation is ideally carried out in accordance with the three excellences. Put simply, this means generating a proper aspiration prior to releasing the animals, wholeheartedly reciting the liturgy and Buddha names for the benefit of these living beings during the release, and dedicating the merit in accordance with the Dharma. We now have a proper life liberation liturgy, *Life Liberation Recitation Liturgy* (Ch: *Fangsheng Niansong Yigui*) and audio recording; it would be best if everyone used this as a guide when chanting the liturgy. At the same time, we need to sprinkle consecrated water on the life-release animals and, ideally, bless the crown of their heads with objects such as a liberation-on-wearing amulet, buddha image, or scriptures. If you simply lack these conditions, you should at least recite the buddha names and mantras. The buddha names, mantras, and so forth, we recite enter into the beings' ears and sow seeds of liberation in their consciousness. After hearing these sounds, some beings' roots of virtue will rapidly mature, and they will henceforth attain positive rebirths.

Buddhist practice can be encapsulated in the six perfections. Life liberation, properly performed, also fulfils the six perfections. Specifically, these are:

1. Generosity. Life liberation itself is the gift of fearlessness. Exerting a positive influence over living beings with the Buddhist liturgy and allowing them to gain temporary and ultimate benefit is also the gift of Dharma. Offering wealth so living beings may escape suffering and attain happiness is also a form of material generosity.

2. Ethical discipline. Liberating lives in accord with the Dharma enables beings to attain temporary and lasting benefit. This is in line with the core of the Mahāyāna precepts, which is to benefit all beings. While releasing lives, trying our best to avoid injuring or frightening the animals is consistent with the precept against doing harm to sentient beings.

3. Patience. If you encounter hindrances in the process of liberating lives, you should not be resentful but actively and patiently seek a solution. Life liberation frequently also requires us to endure tiredness, hunger, cold, and heat. These are all forms of patience.

4. Diligence. Willingly and joyously take part in liberating lives.

5. Meditative concentration. When releasing lives, regardless of whether you are transporting animals or doing other activities, or whether you are chanting, visualizing, praying, or practicing compassion and bodhicitta, you should be conscientious and undistracted throughout.

6. Wisdom. Comprehending the sublime merit of liberating lives is a form of wisdom. Going one step further, with the view and experiential understanding of the emptiness of subject, object, and action, liberating lives is an even greater form of wisdom.

When the animal release is completed, it is necessary to properly perform a dedication of merit. We should dedicate the merit of liberating lives to the beings of the six realms of existence, with the wish that all beings be free from suffering, obtain happiness, and ultimately achieve buddhahood. Dedicating merit in this way allows us to gain the sublime benefits of releasing lives. At life liberation events, I sometimes hear people say they wish to dedicate the merit to their parents for the sake of their good health and long life, or their own family's harmony, and so forth. I think if your parents and family members have not already achieved enlightenment, then they are necessarily still among the beings of the six realms. In this case, dedicating our merit to all sentient beings naturally includes them. There is no need, therefore, for people to worry that by dedicating merit to the beings of the six realms one's own parents won't receive benefit.

The capacity of a single person to liberate lives is limited. If we do so collectively, however, our capacity for and merit in benefiting beings is amplified. I daresay the amount of merit gained by participating in a single collective life liberation event would be difficult for an ordinary person to achieve with an entire lifetime of effort. This is especially the case if buddhas and bodhisattvas with enlightened realization take part in liberating lives: our ordinary aspirations will mingle with the wisdom of great beings such that inconceivable merit is attained. Collectively liberating lives is thus a skillful method for rapidly accumulating vast merit.

With regard to various issues one might encounter when liberating lives, I have done my best to provide explanations and answers in my book, *The Path: A Guide to Happiness*.[30] Everyone can consult this volume.

Someone who is truly soft and kind, in addition to doing what they can to liberate lives, will treat sentient beings in a generous and gentle manner in everyday life. This extends to those creatures that intrude into the places where we live, such as ants, cockroaches, and mice. While they sometimes do cause some trouble, we need to understand that our living space is also their living space. If you are simply unable to bear living with them, you can find ways of inviting them outdoors to live rather than giving rise to murderous intent and harming them. In the Buddha's time, monks walked barefoot in order to avoid accidentally stepping on insects when wearing shoes. In Tibet, when people walk or circumambulate maṇḍalas or stūpas, they always bow their heads and move slowly. The moment they see an insect on the path, they pick it up, hold it carefully in the palm of their hand, and place it in grass where people don't often walk. Besides abandoning intentional acts of harm to sentient beings, in everyday life one should always be careful not to inadvertently harm other creatures.

One's childhood education has a great influence on one's entire life; parents' words and actions, therefore, leave a deep imprint on their growing children's minds. When they are adults, their children will pass on the education they inherit from their parents to the next generation. Parents should pay attention to nurturing children's love by teaching them, first, how to care for small animals and, then, gradually how to care for all beings. If one does not learn respect for life from the time one is young, it is difficult to have compassion as an adult. This is an abominable situation: to say nothing of small animals, such persons will not have empathy toward humans.

These days, many video games are full of killing and fighting, and if children often play these games, they will develop the negative tendency of regarding killing as a game. Parents should guide their children correctly and instill in them the values of respect for life and equality of life.

9. The Future of Tibetan Women

Padma 'tsho (Baimacuo)

Introduction

LARUNG GAR is well known throughout the world as one of the largest Buddhist monastic institutions in Tibetan areas today. Larung Gar has been important for Tibetan women, especially nuns, since its founder Khenpo Jigme Phuntsok gave teachings to nuns in the 1980s and first bestowed the title of khenmo to nuns in 1990. Khenmo is a new role for Tibetan nuns in contemporary Buddhist monasteries, equivalent to female monastic professors. When Khenpo Jigme Phuntsok bestowed the first title of khenmo at the end of 1990, this began a new phase of history for Tibetan nuns.[1]

From that time forward, the new system of education for Tibetan women and nuns has continued to develop. Especially, the opportunity and education for nuns has been improved by khenmos who now teach the formal courses of the five major subjects of Buddhist philosophy.[2] Many nuns have studied diligently for more than ten years, and a select few have earned the khenmo degree after passing exams. In my research on khenmos and nuns at Larung Gar since 2010,[3] I have witnessed many changes and new developments. One of the exciting developments that I introduce in this chapter is the new journal founded in 2011 called *Gangkar Lhamo*, meaning *Goddess of the Snowy Range*, which features writings by Tibetan nuns.

Gangkar Lhamo: *A Journal for Tibetan Nuns*

Gangkar Lhamo is the first Tibetan journal for nuns. It is an important example of Tibetan women's awakening to their potential to engage in social action. Since its first edition in 2011, the journal has continued to be published and edited by a group of nuns annually. All articles are written by Tibetan women.[4]

The journal was founded by Khenmo Kusum Chodron in 2011; she worked on her own to edit and publish the first three issues. Initially, she called it the *Annual Journal for Tibetan Nuns* and did most of the work on her own from 2011 to 2013. Then Khenpos Sodargye and Tretsul Lodrub noticed the importance of her work and made the decision in 2014 to support her. They set up an association called the Small Editing Group of Gangkar Lhamo, which is part of the Larung school.[5] Khenpo Sodargye, alongside the school, gave thirty thousand yuan to the association to publish the journal.[6]

After 2014, the journal underwent several changes. Khenmo Kusum Chodron now collaborates with a group of eight khenmos and one khenpo to publish the journal, so she no longer needs to worry about all the details, such as finances and typing. Since 2014, the journal has become more open and includes laywomen authors alongside nuns.[7] At that point, they no longer put *The Annual Journal for Tibetan Nuns* on the cover.

From 2017 forward, the association started to give awards to nuns whose writing was the best in each year, and the award was decided by Metrul Tenzin Gyatso the following year.[8] Since its founding, the journal has always received support from Jetsun Ani Mumtso, the niece and lineage heir of Khenpo Jigme Phuntsok.[9] Her poetry can be found in volumes 2 and 5. Here is an example of a poem she composed about Dzogchen, or the Great Perfection, and published in the journal:

> The highest peak of the sūtras and tantras is the Great Perfection.
> With fierce effort and devotion toward its instructions
> for traversing the paths and bhūmis in an instant,
> rouse conviction and complete the practice, maintaining the
> essential meaning.[10]

With endorsements from such influential figures, each year the journal publishes anywhere from one to two thousand copies, giving many away to monastics and selling others.[11]

The Founder of Gangkar Lhamo

Khenmo Kusum Chodron comes from the village of Nangchen in Yushu. She learned Tibetan from her father when she was a child and helped with work in the pastures. She was ordained as a nun when she was fifteen years old and moved to Larung Gar in 1996. After she became a nun in her hometown monastery, she did a pilgrimage to Lhasa for more than a year. Then she returned home and went into a traditional three-year retreat. Because she wanted an education, she went to study with Khenpo Jigme Phuntsok at Larung Gar. She became a khenmo in 2010 after she had studied the five major subjects of Buddhist philosophy for fourteen years and passed the exams for Epistemology, Madhyamaka, and Abhidharma. The year after she became a khenmo, she founded *Gangkar Lhamo*.

When I interviewed Khenmo Kusum Chodron in 2018, I asked her why she published the journal. She stated:

> In general, there were not many journals for women's writing, and, in particular, this journal focuses on writings by [Tibetan] nuns. I used my own money to compile the articles; I typed them into a computer and completed the work myself from 2011 through 2013. I thought that if I do this work, it will improve nuns' writing, and that is one of three disciplines [in our monastic education system]: teaching, debate, and writing. By editing a journal each year, I felt that it would help nuns' writing, so that their writing could be published as books in the future.
>
> Even if my work does not provide benefit in this way, still, since the articles by nuns had never been published in the past, at least now there is one journal for Tibetan women in one Buddhist academy. No one else had done this for nuns. If I continue this work each year, collecting and printing their articles, it will encourage more nuns to write. If I can present their articles well in a journal, it will improve their level of writing and their knowledge in the future. This is why I did this work.

Clearly, we can see an awareness of feminism in her reply in terms of improving education for nuns and providing a unique platform for their writings to be published. This is one reason why the journal is significant for Tibetan women and nuns.

When we discussed women's equality, Khenmo Kusum Chodron told me that she noticed there were not many women who had high status and not many women's writings historically in the material she studied as a nun. That insight led her to think about women's status and writing. She told me if we as Tibetan women wish to elevate our status, we must have knowledge and engage in action. For that reason, establishing the journal *Gangkar Lhamo* shows the awakening of a feminist consciousness among Tibetan women and explicit engagement in recovering their voices through social action, in this case publishing a journal focused on writings by nuns.

A Nun Writing on Women's Rights

The article translated in this chapter is about women's rights and indicates an awareness of feminism at Larung Gar and possibly beyond that in local Tibetan areas and nunneries. The article is titled "The Way Forward for You and Me," and it is found in the second volume of *Gangkar Lhamo*, published in 2012. The author, Khenmo Rigzin Chodron, was born in 1978 at Ningtri Drepa Yultso in Kongpo.[12] At the age of six, she started to study Tibetan at the local school and finished six years of elementary school before she became a nun.[13] At the age of fourteen, she ordained at the nunnery of Gangri Thokar Shugseb.[14] At Shugseb, she learned some rituals, finished the tantric preliminary practices, and memorized the liturgy for Longchen Nyingtik practices. For two years, she served as an assistant to the khenpo at Shugseb.

At that point, Khenmo Rigzin Chodron wanted to learn more Dharma, and she knew that Khenpo Jigme Phuntsok educated nuns and had a strong devotion to him. In 1996, she went to Larung Gar and studied diligently for a year. Soon thereafter, she received the title of khenmo from Khenpo Jigme Phuntshok in November 1997. After she was awarded the title of khenmo, she continued to study Dharma intensively, especially the five major subjects of Buddhist philosophy with several khenpos and, also, with Khenmo Yangkyi. For about ten years, Khenmo Rigzin Chodron gave teachings as an assistant.[15] After that, she started teaching formal classes in Buddhist philosophy in 2007 and has been training a dozen khenmos since 2017.

When I interviewed Khenmo Rigzin Chodron in 2013, she introduced me to the *Gangkar Lhamo* journal and gave me copies of several issues. I had a chance to follow up with her and discuss her article in June 2018, and she was very open and warm. She told me that in general women are very important for any family or nationality, so they need to become educated in order to gain confidence and courage. Women should have the same opportunities that men do, and men and women should be equal, as she discusses in her article.

Generally speaking, women are held in high esteem in Tibetan culture and Vajrayāna Buddhist doctrine yet traditionally have little voice and are routinely undervalued in the public sphere.[16] Today Tibetan women, both in monasteries and the secular sphere, have begun to recognize their status and seek equality as women's education is developing. Over the past ten years, different kinds of women's publications in the form of collections and magazines have appeared and appeal to the public.[17] The article I have translated below specifically concerns Tibetan women's rights and equality.

During my interview with Khenmo Rigzin Chodron, she stated that her article focuses on three main topics. First, it describes the general situation and reasons why and how people think about Tibetan women and nuns. This includes negative stereotypes about women not having knowledge, ability, or courage, and social conditions such as the lack of equal rights in society or monasteries. Second, the khenmo emphasizes that Tibetan women and nuns need to build their capabilities for the future. They must find the courage to take action and work diligently to gain an education to accomplish their work and to benefit Tibetans as a whole. They must strive to eliminate cultural bias regarding "male superiority and female inferiority"[18] through a demonstration of their own abilities and skills. Third, she asserts that equal rights do not result from arguments and words; rather, they come through individual action and effort.[19] While the khenmo's emphasis on individual action may seem to place the burden on women to improve their situation, it is also an empowering call to seek knowledge and reclaim their own confidence on the basis of newly found opportunities and capacities.

Conclusion

We can see that a feminist awareness has been blooming in the past ten years in Tibetan culture through the founding of *Gangkar Lhamo* and specifically in Khenmo Rigzin Chodron's article "The Way Forward for You and Me."[20] In the past, Tibetan women have had less of a voice and fewer rights in the public sphere because many Tibetans treat women as inferior. They think women do not have the capacity for serious work, especially education, and until recently, Tibetan women have accepted this treatment and settled for a traditional life as mother, wife, housekeeper, and domestic servant. However, gender equality has a special and important meaning today for Tibetan nuns and women. While Khenmo Rigzin Chodron recognizes the importance of equal opportunities for women, she emphasizes that a key aspect of that is women gaining confidence, knowledge, skill, and courage. Redefining equal rights in Buddhist terms, she asserts that the most authentic form of equal rights is the ability to benefit one's own nationality, meaning here Tibetans as a people, and to accomplish the Dharma for sentient beings.

Acknowledgments

For this chapter, I would like to thank Khenmo Kusum Chodron and Khenmo Rigzin Chodron whom I interviewed as well as Michael Smith and Holly Gayley for their help with editing and translation.

The Way Forward for You and Me

KHENMO RIGZIN CHODRON (2012)

To begin this article on "The Way Forward for You and Me," I would like to speak about women's rights. From a woman's perspective, if we articulate a reasonable opinion about our status with honesty: our rights should be equal to men. In my view, "equality" means that whatever activities men are able to do, women should also be allowed to do them and thereby have the same opportunities as men.

More than sixty years ago, the United Nations propagated and implemented a declaration of equality between men and women of all ethnicities and cultures. Today, equality continues to evolve in many countries, both East and West. For example, women have become the political leaders of Thailand in Asia, Germany in Europe, and Australia in Oceania. Because these are democratic countries, women achieved equal status and rights through their own bravery, strength, knowledge, and capacities.

If we want to move in that direction, then we won't gain anything by advocating out of uninformed confusion and anger. "We want rights. Men and women should be equal"—these are just empty words. Regarding Tibetans, since the three great Buddhist kings ruled Tibet until now, for more than one thousand years, basically, we Tibetan women have not suffered to the same degree from oppression, violence, and discrimination as women of other ethnicities or countries. On this general point, there is no need for debate.

Since arguing with empty words brings no benefit, I would like to express my own perspective honestly and publicly. If we advocate for rights but lack confidence, others will say to us, "From the beginning, you have already been given the opportunity to be great people who benefit the Dharma and beings, patrons who make merit for our nationality, and scholars with keen discernment. Your status is in your own hands according to your own capacity." When others shame us in that way, we either laugh it off or feel silenced.

Currently, people—ourselves and others—have the mindset that women are inferior. Where does this come from? Half the Tibetan population are women, yet only a few possessing wisdom and good character are able to enjoy high status and bring benefit to all nationalities and to the Buddhist teachings. Due to this problem, it is no wonder that people have this mind-set. Where does the problem originate? Who do we blame for the situation? As Śāntideva says, "If my mind is weak, it lacks diligence." It is like this.

So, we can evaluate the various issues related to our differences [in status] and then make an effort to catch up in any areas where there is a discrepancy. If we continue to be diligent, at some point, we definitely can change previous opinions and the mindsets of all people. We will definitely become stronger and more valued. However, if we debate with empty words and wait with empty wishes, it will never be possible to be liberated from our former conditions, and it won't be possible to accomplish our hopes and goals.

In particular, in this article, I want to point out that many Tibetans think that our women generally don't have knowledge and understanding. If a child is a girl, when she is young, [her parents] not only won't support her to study but they will even forbid her from getting an education. Instead, they consider her to be a servant of their own or another family[21] and make her do the housework and engage in masonry, the agricultural work of tilling, plowing, and harvesting, and the production of butter and cheese. The girl accepts this as the value of her life and feels content. When they send their children to study in school, parents create a distinction and prevent girls from studying. This is done by beating and intimidation or using gentle words and rewards in order to mislead girls into feeling good [about this path]. In that way, they are impaired with respect to education.

Likewise, lamas and leaders of some monasteries are first and foremost concerned with improving the finances and education at the monastery—but only for monks; they do not include nuns in the meetings to discuss and consult on these matters. Nuns are brushed aside and not invited to participate [with the attitude], "If they have something to say, let them chant or talk among themselves. If there's work to do, let the nuns do the work." As a result, nuns feel incapable—without responsibility for anything—so they don't pursue any public or private endeavors. I think this is why nuns are currently left behind in many respects.

Moreover, Tibetan laywomen are often bound by marriage ties against their own will. There are many young women given away as brides for the price of property or made to marry enemies in order to settle quarrels.

Specifically, attitudes toward monks and nuns are different. For monks, everyone respects them and holds them in high esteem. Yet, even if a nun is knowledgeable, has superior aspirations, and endeavors to benefit beings, people don't focus on her good qualities, but instead think that she shaved her hair [and became a nun] because she was desperate—with no means to support herself in everyday society. These erroneous ideas are a big problem that I really want to discuss with respect to our nationality. The reason is that nuns don't receive an education to instill knowledge, bravery, and superior aspiration. Without that, people look down on them for no reason, and the nuns cannot turn their mindset toward future goals. In that way, they become intimidated, lose their self-confidence, and cannot enjoy the happiness and fulfillment that comes from a human life.

Similarly, as discussed above, if laywomen don't have independence, their state of mind cannot be free from anxiety and sorrow for even a moment. The root of all well-being comes from a joyful mind, and that depends on women knowing what we really want, rather than parents and relatives burdening us with a life that we didn't choose. The minds and hearts of women are directed toward household life rather than thinking about benefiting our nationality and studying our culture with diligence. Without choice or resources, women just hope the family will not make them suffer more and will remain gentle and cheerful with them. They go through their whole life thinking, "I don't want to fight or quarrel; I will do the basic housework for the family," and so they don't have any other hopes or dreams.

With roughly half of the Tibetan population being women, it seems to me that if most of our women are in the situation above, then half of the capacity for the development of our nationality's economy and culture declines. This is a problem for both Buddhism and secular life. So, I request everyone to be concerned about this and to consider helping as much as possible.

In addition, we women, both laywomen and nuns, need to realize and always maintain our intention. The purpose and direction of equal rights is not just for our own narrow self-interest, nor is it only for the purpose of being equal with men in terms of opportunities and circumstances. Rather, equality is most important so that we can benefit our nationality and accomplish the Dharma for sentient beings. This is equal rights in its most authentic and lasting sense. In essence, each of us must have knowledge, bravery, capability, and pure intention within our own being.

To increase these, we must rouse effort and devote ourselves one hundred percent. We need to prove our own equality to others via a path of skillful means. If we demonstrate knowledge, who can belittle us? But if we don't, even if we have some rights, what's the use? As the omniscient Mipham Rinpoche has said, "If one lacks wisdom and goes to an enemy for wealth and sustenance, power is held by another. It's like an elephant put to service by the hook. However, gaining knowledge, one can transform problems and enjoy the fruit of happiness in this life—like green shoots in spring." In that vein, let us have abundant confidence in our way forward in accord with the changing times today around the world. With that in mind, I encourage you to make a concerted effort.

We are all sisters, close relatives of the same flesh and bone. So please don't be timid or discouraged. Even if it takes our whole life, if we make effort and direct our minds toward moving forward, then whatever we are able to accomplish will be meaningful. Mipham Rinpoche said,

> If one makes a big effort
> to reach as high as the mountain peak
> or as low as the ocean depths—
> if one has that kind of bravery,
> even the deities will be afraid.
> There's no question about such a person.

Since we all have wisdom as our nature—women of the past and women alive now—we share the same potential with women around the world who display bravery and intelligence. It is certain that we can accomplish whatever we set out to do—if we make plans and act bravely without weakness.

In conclusion, once again, my hope is that all women of the Snow Mountains (Tibet) leave an indelible footprint that benefits the entire world and our nationality in particular. No matter how difficult it is to speak about our aspirations, without a doubt, we must continuously work toward equality and respect. In order for our noble traditions not to decline, I make this request again and again. Please keep it in mind.

When someone like me with immature intellect and partial vision writes, there are numerous errors and shortcomings in many respects. So, maybe I shouldn't have composed this. However, from another perspective, since I know how to write our script, I put that knowledge to use and have shared my own thoughts honestly. In that way, there's no problem. Thus, in order to show my respect for our nationality and fulfill our heartfelt wishes, Larung Kongpo Rigzin Chodron, whose pen name is Sarasvatī Amṛta, wrote this and asks all readers to keep our traditions in mind.

10. Lessons from Buddhist Foremothers

Padma 'Tsho and Sarah H. Jacoby

Introduction

Never before have Tibetans collected such an expansive anthology of Buddhist writings by and about women as the fifty-three-volume *Ḍākinīs' Great Dharma Treasury* published in 2017 by the Larung Ārya Tāre Book Association Editorial Office.[1] In fact, before this group of Larung Gar nuns began their editorial work with the 2013 publication of a sixteen-volume version of this anthology, titled *Garland of White Lotuses: The Biographies of the Great Female Masters of India and Tibet*, never before had Tibetans created an anthology of Buddhist writings by and about women at all.[2] Anthologies of Tibetan Buddhist works built around sectarian identities, doxographical categories, and textual genres abound, but the concept of anthologizing Tibetan Buddhist works based on a shared female identity is a distinctively modern concept emerging out of the ethos of twenty-first-century Larung Gar.

Both the magnitude and the modernity of this undertaking, not to mention the considerable challenges Larung Gar nuns endured to find, type, and compile these hundreds of works by and about Buddhist women, raise the following questions. First, how do the nuns in the Larung Ārya Tāre Book Association understand and express their goals and motivations for this massive publication project? Second, what influenced them to take on this endeavor and what benefits do they envision? This chapter presents perspectives on these questions from members of the Ārya Tāre Book Association, based on interviews conducted with the nuns from 2016–18 at Larung Gar. In addition, it features our translation of the preface to the *Ḍākinīs' Great Dharma Treasury*, provided here in full along with a general outline of the fifty-three-volume collection.

Members of the Ārya Tāre Book Association told us that they began this project in 2011 with seven Larung Gar nuns, all classmates, and now the association has expanded to more than ten nuns, including some who have completed the khenmo degree. The original idea to anthologize Buddhist women's writings came from these nuns. They then consulted with their teacher Jetsun Ani Mumtso, the spiritual heir and niece of Larung's founder, who granted permission for the project. Nuns we spoke to reiterated that their aim in forming this association had nothing to do with earning money, but rather focused on disseminating the Dharma and making remarkable Buddhist women's life stories and religious teachings available for women to read.

The process of collecting manuscripts for inclusion was slow going because they did this work on the side between their demanding classes. Members of the association traveled around eastern Tibet—Nyarong, Pelyul, Dzongsar, Katok, and Dzachuka—as well as to central Tibet to Drepung and Sera Monasteries, Tibet University, and libraries in Lhasa, among other places. After collecting writings by and about over two hundred different remarkable Buddhist women, they typed them into the computer, which was a laborious process since prior to beginning this work they had to teach themselves how to type. Then, after many rounds of editing and correcting, they compiled the works into volumes, first sixteen and then most recently fifty-three.

Initially, funding for their project came entirely from the nun's own resources; nuns bought the initial three computers they used to type in all the texts with money from their families. After they had published the first volumes, Larung Gar khenpos as well as nunneries associated with Larung Gar offered additional financial support. Association members we spoke with clarified that none of their funding came from Chinese sponsors or from the Chinese government. When the nuns formed the association it was not an official part of Larung Gar, but was rather its own entity called the Ārya Tāre Book Association, the name one can still see in the publication insignia on the cover of the sixteen-volume series. By 2016, the association had been formally incorporated into Larung Gar as part of its education division.[3] This incorporation is reflected in the new insignia imprinted in the hardcover of each of the fifty-three volumes published in 2017 with the association name "Larung Ārya Tāre Book Association Editorial Office" listed in Tibetan, Chinese, and English.

The authors of the preface to this landmark collection highlight the scope of the *Ḍākinīs' Great Dharma Treasury* by opening their piece with a respectful expression of gratitude toward the "vast multitude of mothers." By the honorific term they chose for "mother" (*ma yum*), they mean not only flesh-and-blood mothers who have literally birthed and nurtured countless generations but also foremothers in a metaphoric sense. Among these foremothers worthy of veneration, we find an expansive list including both notable secular and religious figures—not only do they celebrate ḍākinīs, *yoginīs*, female arhats, and female *vidyādharas* (accomplished female tantric masters), but they also honor extraordinarily beautiful women, Tibetan empresses, and even "clever"[4] Tibetan women such as Milarepa's mother Nyangtsa Kargyen, who is more often portrayed as a demoness than a respectable foremother.[5] Not only does the scope of the foremothers honored in the opening of the preface include both secular and religious women, but it is also global, including not only extraordinary Tibetan women but also those from world history.

This expansive scope is reflected in the contents of the *Ḍākinīs' Great Dharma Treasury* as well, though the remarkable women included therein are exclusively female religious figures from Indian, Tibetan, and Chinese Buddhist lineages. Notably, these remarkable Buddhist female figures span human and divine, including a broad range of historical women as well as female bodhisattvas and wisdom ḍākinīs. The preface lists four main parts of the *Treasury* including a collection of biographies titled "Garland of White Lotuses," a collection of advice and writings titled "Heart Treasury of the Trikāya Ḍākinīs," a collection of praise for the ḍākinīs called "Jewel Treasure Chest," and a collection of advice for women called "Lantern Illuminating the Path of Liberation." At the end of this chapter, we break this down by volumes in the *Ḍākinīs' Great Dharma Treasury*.

Just as the contents of this collection are a veritable herstory of Buddhist women, the Larung Ārya Tāre editors have a specific readership in mind for this cornucopia that is equally explicit about its female orientation—their intended beneficiaries are "future generations of Tibetan mothers and daughters." The editors assert that the responsibility falls on their shoulders to improve the conditions that future generations of Tibetan women will inherit, and they aspire to accomplish this by providing them with powerful models of moral virtue and courage applicable to both their religious and secular lives. More broadly, they intend their volumes to have a "general global readership." One khenmo we spoke with who is an editor of the *Ḍākinīs' Great Dharma Treasury* clarified orally that the volumes are not just for Tibetan women of the future, "but they are for all women in the world."[6] She reiterated that this collection "is not just for Tibetan women; it is also for Chinese and Indian women." From these oral and written statements, the Ārya Tāre editors make clear that an important part of their work is that it is by women, about women, and for women. In the khenmo's words, "In general we think about the situation of women as a whole through the present context in the world." Thus, womanhood for her is a social category that is locally grounded in Tibet as well as global and multiethnic.

The Ārya Tāre editors express two central objectives for their publication project in the preface, which we discussed further with them. The first aim is straightforward: to compile and preserve Buddhist women's writings in order to safeguard them for future generations. The khenmo explains,

> The reason we are gathering these writings is because if we don't do this, they will disappear after some years. In general, there are many Buddhist texts, but, in particular, there aren't many by women. Gathering these writings is very important so they don't disappear. That is our main work and our main goal.

Their second objective laid out in the preface is for

> our Tibetan girls in particular not to think "we are women" and consider ourselves inferior on account of differences between men and women that are based on a few biased outdated customs of male superiority and female inferiority, which have been tossed aside as merely bygone history, or based on a few differences in physical strength.

This powerful statement appears to reject common explanations of gender difference that denigrate women as inferior and elevate men as superior. Even the etymology of the word for *women* used by the nuns in the statement "we are women" serves to underscore their point about longstanding cultural biases that position women as inferior, for one interpretation of the word for *women* they used is "undeveloped."[7]

That said, their word choice is less denigrating than other common words for *woman* they could have chosen, such as "low-birth"[8] or "faulty one."[9] They address their intended audience as "our Tibetan girls in particular," casting a personal and affectionate tone toward the future generations of Tibetan women they hope their efforts will benefit. When we asked the khenmo about this second objective, she addressed the subject of "male superiority and female inferiority" carefully, mitigating some of the force of the written statement. In person, the khenmo did not deride the view of male superiority and female inferiority as "merely bygone history" but more like a fact of life in Tibetan nomadic and farming life, which she knows about firsthand from growing up in a rural nomadic community in eastern Tibet prior to becoming a nun as a teenager.

Another primary objective of the Ārya Tāre Book Association in producing the *Ḍākinīs' Great Dharma Treasury* is, according to the preface, to provide future generations of Tibetan women "examples of what types of undertakings one should accomplish in both this life and future lives." This emphasis on providing role models for Tibetan women resonates with what Caroline Humphrey has termed the "morality of exemplars" in reference to Mongolian culture. Instead of presenting fixed and uniform codes of behavior, this "exemplar-focused way of thinking about morality" provides a highly variable set of potential models for how to live a good life, some more or less applicable to individual women.[10] Drawing on Humphrey, Hildegard Diemberger has underscored the importance of reenacting historical exemplars in present-day Tibet, suggesting that they can serve as bridges between historical and contemporary Tibetan social and religious contexts.[11] We can see an instantiation of this in the khenmo's oral description to us of her motivations for anthologizing Buddhist women's works:

> So, whatever we do, we need to know what to accept and reject. So, where should we learn what to accept and reject? The main thing is that first we need to learn about the lineage of remarkable women from the past, and then we need to carry their actions forward.

In the khenmo's view, if the view of men's superiority and women's inferiority is to change, it will do so by providing future generations of Tibetan girls with role models for how to act with confidence in the world. She says,

> Taking historical women as examples, we can continue learning about and studying them. Or we can understand them through the teachings of a good teacher. If there is an example, we can

learn from the example. If we see the example, we know their actions, motivations, and the results they have accomplished. Status comes from taking action. Action comes from thinking and from self-confidence. And thinking is developed by knowledge.

According to the preface, cultivating knowledge requires access to historical role models to "reinforce how externally one should conduct oneself virtuously in accordance with present conditions and how internally one should have courage and strength, along with intelligence." The khenmo points out that collections of men's writings have long since been compiled for the benefit of new generations, but the same support for women and girls has not been available. Because, in her view, the status of future women cannot improve without evidence of women's remarkable contributions to Tibetan history, politics, religion, and society, she and her fellow members of the Ārya Tāre Book Association have taken definitive action to redress this omission.

From our conversations with members of the Ārya Tāre Book Association and from the preface, we can best understand the particular form of action taken by these nuns as part of a larger Buddhist modernism on the Tibetan plateau whose epicenter is twenty-first-century Larung Gar. Characteristics of this modernity-inflected Tibetan Buddhism include a focus on the compatibility of Buddhism and science, participation of laypeople in religious practice, philanthropic outreach into local Tibetan communities, charismatic (male) leadership with large followings of Han Chinese devotees and satellite communities of disciples throughout Chinese-speaking Asian countries, and modernized education curricula.[12] The latter includes enhanced educational opportunities for nuns at Larung Gar.

Crucial for the genesis of the *Ḍākinīs' Great Dharma Treasury* is the enhanced educational opportunities for nuns, in particular the khenmo degree, which Larung Gar has been at the forefront of conferring since the 1990s. The founding of the Larung Ārya Tāre Book Association Editorial Office in 2011 reflects the strong education its members received at Larung Gar, and can be seen as a result of its expansion of higher learning opportunities for nuns.[13] Tibetan women as well as Buddhist women around the world will benefit from this positive result for generations to come in the form of access to the long history of remarkable Buddhist women provided by the *Ḍākinīs' Great Dharma Treasury*. And, we have more to look forward to from the Larung Ārya Tāre Book Association Editorial Office, for as of

2018 they have already embarked on a new project to publish Dharma text-books for use in Larung Gar classes.

Let us now turn to the direct words of the editors who compiled the *Ḍākinīs' Great Dharma Treasury* coming from the preface that opens the *Treasury's* fifty-third volume, titled the *Precious Golden Key: Ḍākinīs' Great Dharma Treasury Table of Contents.*[14] The closing lines of the preface state that it was authored by "the editor(s) of the Ārya Tāre Book Series." An earlier version of this preface opened each of the sixteen volumes of the *Garland of White Lotuses* anthology of Buddhist women's writings first published in 2013 by the Ārya Tāre Book Association.

Acknowledgments

This research could not have been accomplished without the support of the American Academy of Religion's Collaborative International Research Grant that was awarded to both of the authors in 2016 for our project titled "The Formation of Female Religious Exemplars in Tibet," out of which this chapter is one part. A preliminary version of this research was presented by Sarah H. Jacoby at the 2016 International Association of Tibetan Studies Meeting in Bergen, Norway in the form of a paper titled "A Garland of White Lotuses: Oral History and Women's History in Contemporary Tibet." The authors sincerely thank Holly Gayley for including our work in this volume. The translation included herein was augmented by reading it in a Tibetan language graduate course with Northwestern University PhD students Nisheeta Jagtiani, Rachel Levy, Darcie Price-Wallace, and Sherab Wangmo.

Preface to Ḍākinīs' Great Dharma Treasury

THE EDITORS OF THE ĀRYA TĀRE BOOK SERIES (2017)

In general, it goes without saying that the ones who bestow the precious vitality of life to the people of the world, who rear them lovingly and give them the sweet glow of nourishment, are the vast multitude of mothers.

In particular, in world history, among mothers there have been many suitable models for people in general, such as intelligent and learned women with expansive views of both worldly and religious affairs, ḍākinīs who've attained accomplishment, female arhats, and beautiful women who instantly steal the hearts of all. Likewise, in our Tibet also, in past history there have been inexpressible multitudes of women who were descendants of the red-faced demoness.[15] To give a few examples, there have been female political leaders such as the Empress Lady of Tro named Tri Malo,[16] as well as female vidyādharas who have attained accomplishment such as the Lady of Karchen, Yeshe Tsogyal. There have been yoginīs such as Machik Lapdronma and excellent women with strong female character and cleverness such as Nyangtsa Kargyen.[17] That there have been inexpressible numbers of such women can be proven by means of authentic history.

Moreover, the group of Tibetan mother yoginīs were highly intelligent and attained mastery in learning, contemplating, and meditating on the scriptural traditions of Buddhist tenet systems. One can see proof of this by means of the biographies in these volumes detailing how each of them reached a high stage of accomplishment in one lifetime. Also, one can see proof of this by means of their many written commentaries, from which the warm breath of blessings wafts, that serve as an authentic validating support infusing faith in future generations of disciples.

Therefore, once our future generations of Tibetan women have gained stability in learning and contemplating the biographies of our foremothers and the cycles of their profound teachings and advice that are like wish-fulfilling jewels, the virtue of these excellent ones, their surpassing courage, and their positive qualities of realization and conduct will serve as powerful models. So that future generations of Tibetan mothers and daughters will know about the outstanding tradition of excellent mothers of the Snow Land of Tibet, and so that they will not contradict the essence of holy divine

Dharma and secular ethics as appropriate for their era, we think that it is extremely important to recognize that the responsibility falls on our shoulders to take steps to improve their circumstances.

The principle lady of the assembly of mother ḍākinīs, the supreme Yangchen Yeshe Tsogyal, was the lady master of all the heart treasures of the great supreme knowledge holder Padmasambhava, whose kindness toward us Tibetans surpasses all others. This great woman arose again here in this domain of the Snow Land during this degenerate age in the form of a female spiritual friend who is the general leader of the Greatly Secret Lotus Ḍākinīs' Nunnery. She is the venerable lady of unfathomable kindness, Mume Yeshe Tsomo.[18] Touching the dust from her supreme feet as their crown jewel and bearing the aforementioned responsibility to future generations of Tibetan women in mind, a group of nuns from the central monastery Trikāya Lotus Ḍākinīs' Nunnery made use of the intervals between their studies to earnestly apply themselves to searching for, collecting, compiling, typing, and proofreading the fifty-two[19] volumes of this *Ḍākinīs' Great Dharma Treasury* series. The series includes the Garland of White Lotuses cycle of outer, inner, and secret biographies of the deeds of the great Tibetan women of the past, without sectarian bias; the Heart Treasury of the Trikāya Ḍākinīs cycle containing their unfathomably precious advice and writings; the Jewel Treasure Chest cycle of praise for the ḍākinīs; and the Lantern Illuminating the Path of Liberation cycle containing their advice for women. With the permission of the sole refuge on whom the flower of the Buddha family fell, the supreme venerable lady Mume Yeshe Tsomo, and under the advice of the great scholar Chime Rigzin, the scholar Wangchuk Tsegyal, and others who are great heart sons [of Khenpo Jigme Phuntsok], the Dharma master Wish-Fulfilling Jewel, who is the supreme guide and leader of all the worlds' scholar-adepts, the Larung Ārya Tāre Book Association Subcommittee published, distributed, and promoted this series.

Our main objectives are first and foremost to protect and promote the writings of the female scholar-adepts who have come before in India and Tibet, which are like the principle wealth of the world. Second, our objective is for the global readership in general and for our Tibetan girls in particular not to think "we are women" and consider ourselves inferior on account of differences between men and women that are based on a few biased outdated customs of male superiority and female inferiority, which have been tossed aside as merely bygone history or based on a few differences in physical strength. Additionally, as examples of what types of undertakings one should accomplish in both this life and future lives, our main objective is to provide learning materials that reinforce ways of correctly knowing which endeavors to accept and reject, as well as to reinforce how externally one should conduct oneself virtuously in accordance with the present conditions and how internally one should have courage and strength along with intelligence. We have published, distributed, and promoted this priceless collection as medicine to nourish the well-being and happiness of the world in general, and, in particular, as a gift for female Dharma practitioners of the Snow Land, who are its great stewards.

Nevertheless, aside from just our great devotional aspiration to protect and promote these cycles of biographies and writings, in general, because our editorial subcommittee has a limited degree of knowledge and inadequate experience, it goes without saying that the compilation of this book series contains many errors and deficiencies.

We did not include some sections of teachings that contained secret profound pith instructions or some biographies. Otherwise, even though we mustered as much intelligence and effort as possible to search for and collect these types of texts for several years, still there are probably many teachings and biographies of great women who have come before from various places that we have overlooked. Among those we found, the original manuscripts were few, and they contained archaic terms that were difficult to decipher in many instances. Given the unclear words, incomplete texts, archaic orthography, and frequency of abbreviations, let alone the regional dialects, we mainly left the original manuscripts as they were, not correcting the grammar and spelling. For whatever errors exist, we earnestly ask forgiveness to the assembly of mother ḍākinīs residing in the pure expanse and to learned readers and wise ones. To those who have shown concern and support toward mother women, we offer our sincere heartfelt thanks.

Respectfully offered by the editors of the Larung Ārya Tāre Book Series on the first day of the eleventh month of the fire bird year in the seventeenth Tibetan calendrical cycle [December 19, 2017].

Overview of the Contents of the *Ḍākinīs' Great Dharma Treasury*

1. Garland of White Lotuses: A Collection of Biographies of Remarkable Indian, Chinese, and Tibetan Women, Ḍākinīs, and Female Bodhisattvas

- Vols. 1–3 Biographies of Female Religious Practitioners Compiled from the Vinaya Piṭaka
- Vols. 3–5 Biographies of Female Bodhisattvas Compiled from the Sūtra Piṭaka
- Vol. 6 Biographies of Goddesses and Indian Ḍākinīs
  - This includes Tārā, Vasudhārā, Parṇaśabarī, Sarasvatī, Vajrayoginī, Gelongma Palmo, Niguma, and others.
- Vol. 7 Biographies of Nepalese Ḍākinīs
  - These are mostly about Mandāravā, but also Kālasiddhi, Tashi Kheudren, Śākyadevī, and Emperor Songtsen Gampo's Nepalese Queen Tritsun.
- Vol. 8 Mother Tantra Protectors and Chinese Ḍākinīs
  - Protectors include Ekajaṭī, Palden Lhamo, and others. Chinese ḍākinīs include Emperor Songtsen Gampo's Chinese Queen Kongjo and seventeen life stories of Chinese women translated into Tibetan by Khenmo Dawa Drolma with names such as "The Girl Who Recited the Diamond Sūtra" and "The Four Ladies who Attained Mastery over Birth and Death."
- Vol. 9 *Biography of the Ocean of Ḍākinīs*[20]
  - This is a treasure text revealed by Khandroma Wangdron.[21]
- Vols. 10–11 Multiple versions of Yeshe Tsogyal's biography
- Vol. 12 Biographies of the Snow Land's Knowledge Women (Female Vidyādharas) (A)
  - This includes biographies of King Tri Songdetsen's daughter Lhacham Pemasel, Nangsa Obum, Drowa Zangmo, and several versions of Machik Lapdron's biography.
- Vol. 13 Biographies of the Snow Land's Knowledge Women (B)
  - another Machik Lapdron biography, biographies of treasure revealers Jomo Menmo and Kunga Buma, biographies of Mana Ongjo, Trinchen Rema, Trulku Jobum, Jojo Bong Lhajema, Lechen Bumo Metok Seldronma, Ache Riktong

Gyalmo, and finally that last six chapters are the biography of Sonam Peldren

- Vol. 14 Biographies of the Snow Land's Knowledge Women (C)
  - This includes biographies of Sakya Dungrab Jetsun Tamdrin Wangmo, Lhadzin Yangchen Drolma, Jo Dronma, Trinle Wangmo, and Drupchen Orgyen Butri; Incarnation history of Samding Dorje Pakmo and the Gungru wisdom ḍākinīs; biographies of Kyodrak Khandro Chodzom, Jetsun Mingyur Pelkyi Dron, Kunsang Chokyi Dronma, Sringchung Dechen Wangmo
- Vol. 15 Biographies of the Snow Land's Knowledge Women (D)
  - This includes biographies of Yumchen Kuntu Zangmo and Shuksepma Ani Lochen Rigzin Chonyi Zangmo.
- Vol. 16 Biographies of the Snow Land's Knowledge Women (E)
  - This includes biographies of Gongtang Semo Rinchen Tso, Jetsunma Kunsang Chodron, Uza Khandro (Sera Khandro), Ḍākki Tamdrin Lhamo; women from Do Khyentse Yeshe Dorje's lineage including Semo Khaying Drolma, Do Tsedzin Wangmo, and Ḍākki Losel Drolma; biographies of Rigzin Kundrol Huṃchen Lingpa's daughter Ḍākki Khacho Wangmo, Khandro Tāre Lhamo, Ling Drungkhen Yumen, Jetsunma Mume Yeshe Tsomo
- Vol. 17 Several Remarkable Tibetan Women's Pure Visions and Revenant Accounts
  - This includes pure visions of Jomo Drolma, Sherab Chokyi Dronma and revenant accounts, or accounts of returning from the dead, of Lingza Chokyi, Karma Wangdzin, and Sangye Chodzom.
- Vol. 18 Several Remarkable Tibetan Women's Revenant Accounts
  - This includes revenant accounts of Khandro Nangsa Obum, Kunsang Chokyi Drolma, Tsunma Tsultrim Chotso, Kelsang Drolma

2. Heart Treasury of the Trikāya Ḍākinīs: A Cycle Containing Collected Works of Remarkable Indian and Tibetan Women
  - Vol. 19 Pilgrimage Guides to the Ḍākinīs' Land of Oḍḍiyāna and Tārā Tantras

- Vol. 20 Ḍākinī Tantras
- Vol. 21 Secret Treasury of Biographies of the Ocean of Ḍākinīs and Symbolic Hymns
- Vol. 22 Religious Teachings and Questions and Responses about the Inconceivably Secret Fierce Activities of Queen Ḍākinīs
- Vol. 23 Goddesses and Indian Ḍākinīs' Religious Teachings
  - This is a collection of sādhanās and ritual texts, including the collected works of Gelongma Palmo and the collected works and cycle of advice from Khandroma Niguma.
- Vol. 24 Khandro Yeshe Tsogyal and Machik Lapdron's Religious Teachings
- Vol. 25–27 Machik Lapdron's Collected Works
  - This is two volumes titled "Machik Lapdronma's Teachings and Several Related Ones" and the third is Machik's "Complete Explanation of Casting the Body out as Food."
- Vol. 28 Jomo Menmo's Treasure Dharma and Khandroma Kunga Bum's Treasure Dharma
- Vol. 29 Jetsunma Mingyur Peldronma's Religious Teachings
- Vol. 30 Several Ḍākinīs' Religious Teachings, including those of Jetsunma Trinle Chodron
  - This includes writings by Jetsunma Trinle Chodron, Jetsunma Mume Yeshe Tsomo, Achi Chokyi Drolma, Choying Dechen Tsomo, Khaying Tenzin Wangmo, Sangyum Kuntu Zangmo, Tsunma Orgyen, Dudjom Semo Dharma, Gyarong Khandro Dechen Wangmo, Kunsang Chodron, Khandroma Wangdron
- Vols. 31–38 Uza Khandro Kunzang Dekyong Wangmo's[22] Treasure Dharma
- Vols. 39–40 Khandro Tāre Lhamo's Treasure Dharma
- Vol. 41 Do Dasel Wangmo's[23] Religious Teachings Collected Works
- Vols. 42–49 Thupten Rigje Lhamo's[24] Religious Teachings
  - This consists of scholastic commentaries on the Three Vows including *prātimokṣa*, bodhisattva, and mantra; Epistemology (Pramāṇa); Abhidharma; Middle Way Philosophy (Madhyamaka); and Perfection of Wisdom (Prajñāpāramitā).

3. Jewel Treasure Chest: A Collection of Praise for the Ḍākinīs
  - Vol. 50

- This includes praise texts for an array of ḍākinīs including Tārā, Vajravārāhī, Vajrayoginī, Sarasvatī, Machik Lapdron, Jetsunma Mume Yeshe Tsomo, and others.

4. Lantern Illuminating the Path of Liberation: A Collection of Advice for Women.
   - Vol. 51
     - This includes advice texts for nuns as well as questions and answer texts.
   - Vol. 52
     - This includes advice texts for various women drawn from Indian tantric texts, the *Maṇi Kabum*, *Sanglingm*a, Milarepa's *Hundred Thousand Songs*, Tangtong Gyalpo's biography, and works by Tāranātha, Dudjom Lingpa, Shabkar Tsokdruk Rangdrol, Andzom Gyalse Gyurme Dorje, and Jamyang Chokyi Lodro
   - Vol. 53 *Precious Golden Key: The Ḍākinīs' Great Dharma Treasury* Table of Contents
     - This contains the preface translated here and a 253-page table of contents.

NOTES

EPIGRAPH

1. This is a supplication for the longevity of Khenpo Jigme Phuntsok, understood to be the emanation of the great treasure revealer Lerab Lingpa (1856–1926), who traced his past lives to Dorje Dudjom among Padmasambhava's disciples in the eighth century. It is titled "The Nectar to Attain Immortality: A Longevity Supplication" (Zhabs brtan gsol 'debs 'chi med grub pa'i bdud rtsi), composed by Karma Chopel Zangpo. It can be found in the chant book produced by Larung Gar, titled *Chanting Prayers Before and After Dharma Teachings* (*Slob khrid sngon dang mjug gi zhal 'don*). The chant book is available in Tibetan and English on Khenpo Sodargye's website (khenposodargye.org/teachings/larung-daily-prayers/). The translation for the dedication of this book was adapted by Holly Gayley.

INTRODUCTION

1. On his importance in the revitalization of Buddhism in Tibetan areas during the 1980s and '90s, see Germano 1998. For a biography of Khenpo Jigme Phuntsok, see Antonio Terrone's contribution to *Treasury of Lives* (treasuryoflives.org/biographies/view/Khenpo-Jigme-Puntsok/10457).
2. Its official name is Larung Buddhist Academy of the Five Sciences (Bla rung lnga rig nang bstan slob gling).
3. See Gaerrang 2015 for a cogent argument along these lines. However, there are also important ways that Khenpo Jigme Phuntsok and his successors resist global capitalism and refashion state discourse in order to champion Buddhist values and civilizational inheritance.
4. Jigme Phuntsok 1995: 3–4. Note that I have inverted the structure of this paragraph. In the Tibetan, the last two lines come just prior to the rest of the paragraph, but for rhetorical effect in this excerpt, I decided to move them to the end.
5. Surveys of Buddhist modernism, to the extent that they include Tibetans, tend to focus on figures in the Tibetan diaspora, particularly lamas who have played a significant role in transmitting Buddhist teachings in the West, such as His Holiness

the Dalai Lama or Chögyam Trungpa Rinpoche. For example, see Lopez 2002, McMahan 2008, and chapter 1 of Gleig 2019. When a Tibetan from the plateau is mentioned in such studies, it is usually the iconic Gendun Chopel (1903–1951). An important exception to this is Jacoby and Terrone 2012.

6. For example, Goldstein and Kapstein 1998 and Kolås and Thowsen 2005.

7. By focusing on specific and localized articulations of modernist elements in this anthology, we recognize that there are multiple expressions of Buddhist modernism at different times and places in Asia and beyond—as others like Natalie Quli and Scott Mitchell (2015), David McMahan (2015), and Mark Teeuwen (2017) have emphasized. Indeed, this anthology follows in the spirit of Teeuwen's remark regarding "the great variety of ways in which different 'Buddhisms' have reacted to the many variants of modernity that they have faced in the recent past or are facing today," especially that "Buddhist responses to their local brands of modernity display many similarities but are always conditioned by local circumstances" (2017: 4). On modernity in Tibet, see Tuttle 2005 and 2011

8. These terms are, respectively, *jelu* (*rjes lus*) and *mongde* (*rmongs dad*) in Tibetan and *luohou* and *mixin* in Chinese.

9. See Teeuwen 2017 for a discussion of Heinz Bechert's conception of Buddhist modernism in relation to more recent variations and a plurality of postmodern expressions of Buddhism emerging around the world. See Gleig 2019 regarding postmodern elements of Buddhism in American as the result of generational shifts in demographics.

10. See Hansen 2007, Braun 2013, and Turner 2017. Over the twentieth century, there have also been various movements of engaged Buddhism with monastics and laity alike harnessing the Buddhist teachings to address social and environmental issues and engage development work.

11. It is important to emphasize the variety of expressions of Buddhist modernisms in different times and places, both in Asia historically and as a global phenomenon today; see McMahan 2015 and Quli and Mitchell 2015. On the emergence of mass meditation in colonial Burma, see Braun 2013. On the humanistic vision of establishing a pure land on earth, by Taixu and later reformers, see Pittmann 2001 and Jones 2003. On psychologization as a factor of Buddhist modernism, especially in the transmission of Buddhism to Europe and North America, see McMahan 2008. For case studies involving engaged Buddhism in Asia, see Queen and King 1996. For examples, see Queen and King 1996.

12. See van der Veer 2011.

13. On the discourse of superstition in relation to religion in China, see Goossaert and Palmer 2010.

14. See Kolås and Thowsen 2005 for an overview of revitalization efforts.

15. Gene Smith (2001, chapter 17) was the first to do foundational research on the ecumenical trends among nineteenth-century masters in Kham. More recently, a link between the writings of nineteenth-century ecumenical masters and early modernity was made by Adam Krug in a paper titled, "*Ris med* as an Early 'Alter-

native Modernity' in Eastern Tibet: Evidence from Karma Tashi Chopel's Contents (*dkar chag*) to *The Indian Mahāmudrā Works* (*Phyag chen rgya gzhung*)," presented at the fifteenth seminar of the International Association of Tibetan Studies in Paris, France in July 2019.

16. See McMahan 2008 whose categories of psychologization, demythologization, and detraditionalization are more salient to Buddhism in North America and Europe than the contemporary Tibetan context within China.

17. Large-scale ritual gatherings include Accomplishing the Pure Land of Great Bliss typically held in the fall and the Dharma Assembly of the Awareness Holders held during the new year.

18. These five subjects are: Epistemology (*Tshad ma; Pramāṇa*), Madhyamaka (*Dbu ma*), Prajñāpāramitā (*Phar phyin*), Abhidharma (*Mngon pa*), and the Vinaya or monastic code (*'Dul ba*).

19. Due to their importance, we decided to include chapters on two founding figures: Khenpo Jigme Phuntsok himself and the Tenth Panchen Lama who helped him turn his encampment (*sgar*) in the Larung Valley into an officially sanctioned Buddhist academy in 1987.

20. While this is the first time my translation of the preamble from *Heart Advice to Tibetans for the Twenty-First Century* has appeared in print, the introductory essay is an abridged and revised version of a chapter originally published in *Mapping the Modern in Tibet* (2011), edited by Gray Tuttle.

21. On these debates, see Hartley 2002. On the so-called "New Thinkers," see Wu Qi 2013.

22. On the long and circuitous genealogy of the discourse on Buddhism and science, see Lopez 2008.

23. This work is an example of the longstanding genre of questions and answers (*dris lan*) usually in the form of didactic dialogues between master and disciple.

24. On the new ten virtues (*dge bcu*) promulgated by Larung Gar, see Gayley 2013.

25. These reform efforts have met with criticism from secular intellectuals. See Buffetrille 2014 and Gayley 2016.

26. On the amulet for peace (*zhi bde rtags ma*), see Gayley and Padma 'tsho 2016.

27. Khenpo Tsultrim Lodro describes some of these alternative methods in later speeches. See Gayley 2017.

1. The Serta Speech

1. See Panchen Rinpoche 1985.

2. See Welch 1968; Zhe Ji 2013.

3. See Zhe Ji 2013; interview with Arjia Rinpoche Lobsang Tubten Jigme Gyatso. Tibetan Mongolian Buddhist Cultural Center, Bloomington, IN, July 15, 2016.

4. His monastery was Dobi Dratsang (Rdo sbis grwa tshang). Tuttle 2005.

5. Jagou 2011.

6. Sangdup Topla 2012: 168.

7. Barnett 2009: 31–32.
8. Liu Zaifu (1941–) and Li Zehou (1930–) were initiators of this trend in the early 1980s and their works became highly influential in intellectual and political circles. Wang 1996: 199–206; Kelly 2003: 435–37.
9. Wang 1996: 47–56.
10. Panchen Rinpoche 1985: 4.
11. Panchen Rinpoche 1985: 12.
12. Panchen Rinpoche 1985: 12–13.
13. Panchen Rinpoche 1985: 10.
14. Panchen Rinpoche 1985: 16.
15. Panchen Rinpoche 1985: 17.

2. HEART ADVICE FOR THE TWENTY-FIRST CENTURY

1. Jigme Phuntsok 1995.
2. As an indicator of its importance to framing the khenpo's discussion in *Heart Advice*, the term *mi rigs* (Ch: *minzu*)—which can be translated as "ethnicity," "nationality," or "people"—occurs more than twenty times in the first dozen pages of *Heart Advice*, not including contractions based on this term, such as *Bod rigs* (*Bod kyi mi rigs*) or *rang rigs* (*rang gi mi rigs*). Indeed, throughout *Heart Advice* Khenpo Jigme Phuntsok uses "Tibetan nationality" (*Bod kyi mi rigs*) more frequently than poetic epithets for Tibetans like that found in the title, "Those of the Snow Land" (*Gangs can pa*). I read this as an indication of his engagement with the state discourse of nationalities, even as he endeavors to refashion its terms.
3. On the founding of Larung Gar, see Germano 1998.
4. For example, see chapter 1 in this volume for Antonio Terrone's discussion of the important role that the Panchen Lama played in the founding of Larung Gar as a Buddhist academy.
5. See Hartley 2002.
6. Here, I argue against a suggestion made in Kolås and Thowsen 2005: 178.
7. In Khenpo Jigme Phuntsok's discussions of progress in *Heart Advice*, the key term is *mdun lam*. According to the *Great Tibetan-Chinese Dictionary*, *mdun lam* can mean either "the path going forward" (*mdun phyogs kyi 'gro lam*) in a spatial sense or "the conditions of the future" (*ma 'ongs ba'i gnas tshul*) in a temporal sense (Drang Yisun 1985: 1380). Goldstein gives the definition of *mdun lam* as "future prospects" (2001: 569). I choose to translate this term literally since the khenpo's usage can be understood primarily as a course of action—"the path forward" into the future—in which Tibetans should exert themselves through a unified outlook (*blo sems chig sgril gyis ma 'ongs pa'i mdun lam la 'bad rtsol*, 1995: 5). But, he also uses the term to refer to the future prospects of the Tibetan people toward which Tibetans should not remain indifferent (*ma 'ongs pa'i bod mi rigs kyi mdun lam gyi don du ji mi snyam du mi 'jog*, 12).
8. The Nyingma (*Rnying ma*) is the "Old School," which traces its lineages of teach-

ings to the advent of Buddhism on the Tibetan plateau (seventh to ninth century) when the Tibetan empire was at its height.

9. The term for "knowledge" here is *rig gzhung*, which can also be translated as "erudition" or "civilization." The *Great Tibetan-Chinese Dictionary* glosses this term as *rig gnas kyi gzhung* (Drang Yisun 1985: 2686), combining the terms *rig gnas* (culture or science) and *gzhung* (scripture or text). This gloss suggests that *rig gzhung* refers to the literary aspect of Tibet's cultural inheritance, which agrees with the khenpo's usage in *Heart Advice*.

10. On the civilizing project of the state and its representations of minorities, see Harrell 1995 and Gladney 2004. In Harrell's terms, such a project goes beyond economic markers like poverty to assert the cultural and moral superiority of the "civilizing center" which acts paternally as a modernizer upon peripheral peoples.

11. Harrell 1995: 6.

12. Jigme Phuntsok 1995: 97.

13. I borrow the term *internal orientalism* from Louisa Schein (1997).

14. Jigme Puntshok 1995: 11. Here, the khenpo emphasizes that the survival of a culture depends mainly on the attitude of its constituent members, i.e., whether or not people have esteem (*brtsi 'jog*) and high regard (*mthong chen*) for their own cultures.

15. Jigme Puntshok 1995: 99.

16. The official criteria used by the Nationalities Commission to determine ethnic groups or nationalities beginning in the 1950s was based on Stalin's formulation of four commons (common language, common territory, common economic life, and common psychology as expressed in culture), although in practice establishing a shared history and ancestry was an important means to resolve problematic cases, and religion was also an operative category for early Chinese anthropologists who worked to classify nationalities. On the emergence of the category of *minzu* (from the Japanese *minzoku*) and the process of ethnic identification after the founding of the People's Republic of China (PRC), see Heberer 1989, Harrell 1995, and Gladney 2004.

17. *bsam blo'i 'khyer so.*

18. As interesting as they are, the khenpo's discussion of these points must await a future project. Here, I am mainly concerned with the opening and closing sections of the text, in which he proposes a set of values as a unified approach among Tibetans and details specific points of action based on these values.

19. *Rang tshugs ma shor gzhan sems ma dkrugs.* Based on the khenpo's definition of Tibetan identity in both cultural and ethical terms, the slogan contains a clever parallelism whereby to remain steadfast or not lose one's determination has (1) a moral valence, namely, to maintain one's values in the midst of change, and (2) a cultural one, namely, to remain true to one's cultural roots.

20. In one song dedicated to Khenpo Jigme Phuntsok called "Elegy (*Dran gdung*)," specific reference is made to his well-known slogan (though its lines are reversed) while the music video shows images of the khenpo and Larung Gar. This song (lyrics by Lungtok Tenzin and vocals by Sherten) can be found on a VCD pro-

duced by Yuthok Namgyal Gon titled *Rigs zhen gyi 'bod pa*, translated on the jacket cover as *New Spring Melody* (ISRC CN-H09-07-302-00/V.J6).

21. Rigzin Dargye 2004: 5.

22. Rigzin Dargye 2004: 5.

23. In *Heart Advice*, while the khenpo promotes universal compassion toward all nationalities, he also advocates special affection toward Tibetans.

24. In this regard, he follows the rhetoric emanating from Dharamsala, and it is no coincidence that this work was composed in the wake of his visit to India in 1990.

25. Interview in June 2006 with Khenpo Tsultrim Lodro.

26. On the discourse on religion (Ch: *zongjiao*) and superstition (Ch: *mixin*) in modern China, see Goossaert and Palmer 2010.

27. Lawrence defines modernism as "the search for individual autonomy driven by a set of socially encoded values emphasizing change over continuity; quantity over quality; efficient production, power, and profit over sympathy for traditional values or vocations, in both the public and private spheres" (1995: 27). For a brief analysis of Lawrence alongside other writers on religious modernism, such as Joseph Kitagawa, see Jones 2003.

28. Prasenjit Duara suggests this tack in his discussion of campaigns against religion in China since the May 4 movement (1995: 90) as do anthropologists investigating alternative modernities, such as Bruce Knauft, who states that "modernity emerges as a discursive space within which notions of what it means to be traditional or modern are contested and negotiated" (2002: 33).

29. Germano's assessment of Khenpo Jigme Phuntsok that "the modern other may simply be too foreign for the traditional Terton to digest in Buddhist format" (1998: 94) refers to the content of his revelations of treasures (*gter ma*) and seems to predate if not the publication of *Heart Advice*, at least the author's knowledge of it.

30. Regarding the social vision of Ariyaratne and the aniconism of Buddhadāsa Bhikkhu, see Bond 1996 and Swearer 2003.

31. Hartley 2002: 5.

32. My thanks to Jann Ronis for calling my attention to *An Analysis of the Connection between Mind and Brain* by Metrul Tenzin Gyatso. See also Tsultrim Lodro 2007d.

33. Avalokiteśvara is the bodhisattva of compassion who plays a key role in Tibetan identity as the progenitor of the Tibetan people in the form of a monkey who mated with a local demoness. In addition, the Tibetan emperor Songtsen Gampo was retrospectively identified with him, and the Dalai Lamas and Karmapas are understood to be his emanations.

34. I chose to translate the Tibetan phrase *chos ldan bod kyi rgyal khams* as the "Buddhist kingdom of Tibet" based on an article by Ishihama Yumiko 2004 about the Tibetan term *chos srid*.

35. The verse comes from Tsongkhapa's poem titled "A Literary Gem of Poetry." See Thupten Jinpa 2014.

36. The term I am translating "good heart" (*bsam pa bzang po*) could also mean "noble intent." The term *bzang po* can mean good, descent, noble, or wholesome, while *bsam pa* can mean attitude, mind, intent, or heart.

37. We say "flesh and blood" in English whereas Tibetans use "flesh and bone" (*sha rus*).

38. *Bodhicaryāvatāra* 5:15. See Shantideva 2006: 63.

39. The Tibetan is rendered *wos pa'i ku*. It may refer to the Ubykh language, which went extinct after the death of its one remaining fluent speaker in the early 1990s. Thanks to Gerald Roche for the suggestion.

40. I have not been able to find a plausible equivalent for Pālu'u. In terms of phonetic resonances, there are two endangered languages (Sonsorol and Tobian) in the Pacific island country of Palau, while Palu'e is considered a threatened language on an island of the same name in Indonesia. See the Endangered Language Project (endangeredlanguages.com).

41. My translation is based on Khenpo Jigme Phuntsok's rendering of the verse in Tibetan. It differs from the Tibetan version of Āryadeva's *Catuḥśataka* 7.23 in several ways, using "the tathāgata" (*de bzhin gshegs pa nyid*) rather than "the tathāgatas" (*de bzhin gshegs pa rnams*) in the second stanza and "dharmatā" or "true nature" (*chos nyid*) rather than "emptiness" (*stong nyid*) in the third stanza. Karma Phuntsho has translated the Tibetan as follows: "The tathāgatas have taught that / Dharma, in brief, is nonharming / [and the] emptiness qua nirvāṇa. / [In this tradition,] these are the only two." Phuntsho 2005: 36.

42. This may be a description of nuclear weapons and the long rate of decay for radioactive materials.

43. In an interview in June 2006, Khenpo Tsultrim Lodro elaborated on this point by mentioning the high rates of suicide in developed countries. Along similar lines, one can also think of high rates of depression and addiction.

44. I have taken the liberty to interpret the Tibetan *thams med* as a typographic error for *thabs med* to make sense of this line.

45. The six realms of Buddhist cosmology include the realms of gods, demigods, humans, animals, hungry ghosts, and hell beings. These realms are depicted in the well-known wheel of existence or *bhāvacakra* (*srid pa'i 'khor lo*).

46. The reason rebirth is so important to Khenpo Jigme Phuntsok is that, in traditional terms, Buddhist ethics depends on the belief in karma in which all of the results of one's own actions are understood to bear fruit in this or future lives.

3. A Spontaneous Song of Victory

1. These treatises include Dolpopa's commentary on the *Uttaratantra Śāstra*, Lama Tsongkhapa's *Three Principal Aspects of the Path* and *In Praise of Dependent Origination*, Sakya Paṇḍita's *Treasure of Logic on Valid Cognition*, and Thokme Zangpo's *Ocean of Good Explanation*, a commentary on *The Way of the Bodhisattva*. .

2. Khenpo Sodargye's oral commentaries in Chinese on these works remain

unpublished. *Song of Victory: The Wondrous Sound of the Celestial Drum* (*Rnam par rgyal ba'i dus gtam lha'i rnga sgra*) is found in Jigme Phuntsok 2002, vol. 3: 345–46, and *Wangdu, Great Clouds of Blessings: The Prayer That Magnetizes All That Appears and All That Exists* (*Snang srid dbang du sdud pa'i gsol 'debs byin rlabs sprin chen*) is found in Mipham Gyatso 1998.

3. These are Indian commentaries on the classic topics of Buddhist philosophy, including the *Abhisamayālaṃkāra*, one of the five great texts attributed to Maitreya, *Madhyamakāvatāra* by Candrakīrti, *Pramāṇavārttika* by Dharmakirti, *Abhidharmakośa* by Vasubandhu, and *Vinayasūtra* by Guṇaprabha.

4. *Yeshe Lama* (*Ye shes bla ma*) is a revelation by Jigme Lingpa, while the *Trilogy of Finding Comfort and Ease* (*Ngal gso skor gsum*) and *Trilogy of Natural Freedom* (*Rang grol skor gsum*) are among the great works of Lonchenpa.

5. Chinese: *Fo Jiao Ke Xue Lun*, English: *A Treatise on Buddhism and Science* (unpublished).

6. The translation and outline for this text comes from Khenpo Sodargye's Chinese version. His commentary is available online at: khenposodargye.org/teachings/khenpos-classical-teachings/song-of-victory/.

7. The dohā is a song style associated by Tibetans with the expression of spontaneous realization; it harkens back to the vernacular styles employed the great tantric siddhas or "accomplished ones" in India. For a discussion of Tibetan song genres inherited from India, see Jackson 1996.

8. The translation and outline for this text comes Khenpo Sodargye's Chinese version. His commentary is available online at: khenposodargye.org/teachings/khenpos-classical-teachings/wang-du-great-cloud-blessings.

9. These four are explained in the commentary below.

10. This is an alternative name for Jigme Phuntsok Rinpoche.

11. See note 3 above.

12. This is one of Atiśa's famed disciples. See his biography by Alexander Gardner on Treasury of Lives (treasuryoflives.org/biographies/view/Dromton-Gyelwa-Jungne/4267).

13. This was one of Jigme Phuntsok Rinpoche's root teachers.

14. Mount Wutai, or Wutai Shan, is the sacred abode of Mañjuśrī in central China.

15. The origin of this story is the *Mañjuśrīvikrīḍita Sūtra*. Its translation, "The Miraculous Play of Mañjuśrī" by Jens Erland Braarvig, is available online through 84000: Translating the Words of the Buddha (read.84000.co/translation/toh96.html).

16. This buddha's name in Chinese is De Guang Yao Pu Sa.

17. This buddha's name in Chinese is Guang Ru Lai

18. More details can be found in the *Mañjuśrīvikrīḍita Sūtra*.

19. This translation is by the Padmakara Translation Committee, quoted in a commentary on the *Thirty-Seven Verses on the Practice of a Bodhisattva* by Dilgo Khyentse. See Dilgo Khyentse 2007: 189.

20. This translation is by the Padmakara Translation Committee. Shantideva 2006: 127.

21. On this figure, see Cuevas 2015.
22. Shantideva 2006: 127.
23. This translation comes from an earlier edition of *The Way of the Bodhisattva*, translated by the Padmakara Translation Committee. Shantideva 1997: 35.
24. See Buswell and Lopez 2016: 40–41.
25. Shantideva 2006: 35.
26. Shantideva 1997: 34.
27. This translation is based largely on *The Lamrim Prayers*, an e-book published by the Foundation for the Preservation of the Mahayana (2019), available for donation at shop.fpmt.org/Lamrim-Prayers-eBook-PDF_p_2486.html.
28. This translation is by the Padmakara Translation Committee, with one adjustment, as quoted in a commentary on Nāgārjuna's *Letter to a Friend* by Kangyur Rinpoche. See Nagarjuna 2006: 29.
29. Dilgo Khyentse 2007: 33–34.
30. The first two lines follow the translation by the Padmakara Translation Committee in Ngawang Pelzang 2004: 133.
31. These sixteen guidelines are referred to as "human values" (*mi chos*) in contrast to the Buddhist ethics with its code of ten virtues (*dge bcu*).
32. This is the place where Larung Valley is located.

4. The Unity of Religion and Tibetan Culture

1. See Lauran Hartley 2002 in which she introduces Shokdung, who even in recent scholarship on the New Thinkers such as Wu Qi 2013 is still identified as their main figure.
2. This 1998 essay can be found in Metrul Tenzin Gyatso 2013.
3. Hartley 2002: 5.
4. Shokdung 2008.
5. Wu Qi 2013: 242.
6. Metrul Tenzin Gyatso 2002.
7. See Metrul Tenzin Gyatso and Tsultrim Lodro 2003.
8. *chos kyi grong khyer.*
9. *chos srid zung 'brel.* For an overview of how this concept has functioned in Tibetan history and especially in the contemporary context, see the introductory essay by Holly Gayley and Nicole Willock (2016) for a special journal issue of *Himalaya* on "The Secular in Tibetan Cultural Worlds."
10. This is a play on words about the trio of refuting the opponent, presenting one's own system, and responding to objections (*gzhan lugs dgag pa, rang lugs bzhag pa,* and *rtod pa spong ba*). I find Tenzin Gyatso's usage of this to be an allusion to a line by Pema Karpo that uses the same metaphor and language.
11. In his book, *Buddhism and Science: A Guide for the Perplexed,* Donald Lopez debunks the idea that Einstein endorsed Buddhism in this way (2008: 1–2).
12. This is a Tibetan saying that means to keep up one's reputation and honor.
13. See note 11 above.

5. A Case for Animal Compassion

1. *tshe thar.* For a general discussion of this practice, see Holler 2002.

2. When I observed these life-ransoming events, care was taken to make sure that the species of fish was appropriate for the lake it was being introduced into and that the fish were distributed around various parts of the lake. That said, it seems reasonable to assume that releasing this many fish into an ecosystem will impact it profoundly.

3. For more on Khenpo Tsultrim Lodrö's ethical vision and its roots in the work of his teacher Khenpo Jigme Phuntsok, see chapter 2 of this volume and Gayley 2013.

4. *slob don khang gi gtso 'gan pa.*

5. For an analysis of responses to Khenpo Tsultrim Lodrö's animal welfare advocacy, see Buffetrille 2014 and Gayley 2016.

6. This comes from oral communication with a member of the Tibetan intellectual elite who wishes to remain anonymous in Chengdu in 2011.

7. *Words to Increase Virtue* is found in several collections of Khenpo Tsultrim Lodrö's writing, and I have also seen it posted to monastery walls as a stand-alone broadside. For this translation, I have relied primarily on the version in Tsultrim Lodro 2004b. At times, I consulted the version published in Tsultrim Lodro 2016.

8. *sa ga zla ba.* This is the annual holiday commemorating the Buddha's birth, enlightenment, and death, all of which are said to have occurred on the fifteenth day of the fourth lunar month according to the Tibetan calendar

9. That Khenpo Tsultrim Lodrö is well-versed in these particular texts is demonstrated in his *Clear Mirror of Advice*, a comprehensive anti-meat text aimed at a monastic audience and translated in Hardie 2019.

10. This refers to a type of slaughtering practice where an animal's muzzle is bound so that it cannot breathe, causing it to suffocate. First, the feet are tied together, and the animal is laid on its side. For yaks, the horns are inserted into the ground to immobilize the head, after which the muzzle is tied tightly closed until the animal suffocates. Meat slaughtered in this manner is generally held to be richer and tastier than other types of meat.

11. Perhaps the most important work suggesting that Buddhism denies a kinship between humans and animals is Waldau 2001. For some more recent and more nuanced discussion, see Ohnuma 2017, Stewart 2015, and Finnigan 2017.

12. For a further discussion of this issue from the Tibetan perspective, see Barstow 2019a.

13. For a full translation of the relevant passage, see Johnson 2019: 134–35.

14. Perhaps the most famous figure to advance this position is Shabkar Tsokdruk Rangdrol, but others have made similar arguments as well, including Norchen Kunga Zangpo, Gorampa Sonam Senge, Karma Chakme, Jigme Lingpa, Nyala Pema Dundul, and Shardza Tashi Gyeltsen. For Shabkar's writings on vegetarianism, see Shabkar Tsokdruk Rangdrol 2004. For excerpts from writings by some of these other figures, see Barstow 2019b.

15. For a discussion of meat eating in the *Laṅkāvatāra Sūtra* as well as a full translation of the relevant chapter of that text, see the first chapter of Barstow 2019a.
16. For a detailed discussion of Jamyang Kyi's critique of Khenpo Tsultrim Lodrö's animal advocacy, see Buffetrille 2014.
17. This is based on oral communication with several Tibetans who wish to remain anonymous, primarily in Sichuan and Qinghai between 2011 and 2012, but also during the summer of 2017. I have not been able to collect systematic data about contemporary Tibetans' views of Khenpo Tsultrim Lodrö, and these stories remain anecdotal. It is my experience, however, that there are a good number of Tibetans, particularly in urban areas, who find Khenpo Tsultrim Lodrö's promotion of vegetarianism deeply troubling. One went so far as to tell me that the khenpo's opposition to animal slaughter is "destroying Tibetan culture."
18. For some striking examples of extreme rhetoric on this issue, see Buffetrille 2014: 117. For more on the debates over clerical authority and the gap between the khenpo's views and their implementation by others, see Gayley 2016.
19. It is unclear to me if this is referring to Khenpo Tsultrim Lodrö's own appeals, or if he is referring to Khenpo Jigme Phuntsok, who began asking people to stop slaughtering their animals in the mid to late 1990s. See Gayley 2016.
20. "Misconceptions" here presumably refers to the idea that slaughtering animals is not a sin.
21. This text was originally presented orally to a crowd and later transcribed and published as a written text.
22. In discussions with me, Khenpo Tsultrim Lodrö has emphasized several times that vegetarianism was more difficult in the past, when vegetables were harder to come by and modern manufactured foods did not exist.
23. The Tibetan term *yak* (*gyag*) refers only to the male of the species. The word used here is *dri* (*'bri*), referring to the female. The term I use, *female yak*, is thus technically incorrect, but hopefully more recognizable to a contemporary English language audience than the term *dri*. Hybrids (*dzo* and *dzomo*, masculine and feminine, respectively) are yaks bred with cattle, the females of which produce a rich milk.
24. This refers to a type of slaughtering practice where an animal's muzzle is bound so that it cannot breathe, causing it to suffocate.
25. This is a classic Buddhist argument: given that we have all had an infinite number of lives over an infinite timespan, simple math suggests that at one point or another we have all been related to each other. The implication is that since all beings were our mother at one time or another, we should treat them with the same respect we would give our mother in this present life.
26. A human birth is said to be both valuable and perilous because we have the intellectual ability to control our actions rather than being primarily driven by instinct. This means that the karmic repercussions of actions committed as a human—both positive and negative—are particularly strong.
27. As Khenpo Tsultrim Lodrö states, such passages appear in many different classical Buddhist texts, including both sūtras and tantras. On the sūtra side, two of

the most famous are the *Laṅkāvatāra Sūtra* and *Mahāparinirvāṇa Sūtra*, whose relevant passages have been translated in chapter 1 of Barstow 2019b. On the tantra side, perhaps the most famous anti-meat passages come from the *Kālacakra Tantra*, the relevant portions of which have been translated in Newman 1987: 265–68. In addition, many anti-meat quotations from other sūtras and tantras can be found quoted by the various Tibetan authors included in Barstow 2019b. In particular, the texts by Ngorchen Kunga Zangpo (chapter 3) and Karma Chakme (chapter 7) are particularly rich veins for those wishing to mine the Indian Buddhist canon for anti-meat passages.

6. Buddhism and the New Science of Rebirth

1. Jinpa 2003: 71–75. For a translation of Gendun Chopel's letter, see Jinpa and Lopez 2014: 403–7.
2. Lopez 2008: 106.
3. *tshan rig.*
4. Tsultrim Lodro 2007b.
5. Metrul Tenzin Gyatso 2011.
6. Jinpa 2003: 80.
7. Chukye Gendun Samten 1996: 28–38 and 2000: 434–41.
8. Cabezon 2003: 56–61.
9. For a discussion of this method, see Jinpa 2010 and Lopez 2010. For discussion of this method in the ongoing dialogue, and a case of the Buddhism and science dialogue without the use of bracketing, see Presti 2018: xvi–xxi.
10. Lopez 2010: 891 and 893.
11. Duckworth 2015.
12. Tsultrim Lodro 2013: 48–69.
13. Tsultrim Lodro 2013: 69–112. For a summary of this work, see Duckworth 2015: 268–70.
14. Duckworth 2015: 271. See also Tsawa Danyuk 2011: 126–37.
15. Tsultrim Lodro 2017b: 6–7.
16. *rtog dpyod kyi blo.* The Tibetan term translated as both "cerebrum" and "brain" is *lechen* (*klad chen*, Ch: *dà nǎo*).
17. Tsultrim Lodro 2017b: 11.
18. In addition to the books by Moody, both *Life After Life* and *The Light Beyond*, it appears as though the khenpo had access to Stevenson's *Twenty Cases Suggestive of Reincarnation*. Moody 1975 and 1988, Stevenson 1974.
19. Moody 1975: 173.
20. Moody 1975: 115 and 113–16. Michael Grosso also references *The Tibetan Book of the Dead* in Moody 1988: 116.
21. Moody 1975: 105.
22. *lta ba log pa.*

23. For a Tibetan language transcript of a talk that exemplifies this, see Tsultrim Lodro 2012. This is a lecture by Khenpo Tsultrim Lodro spoken at the Sichuan Provincial Tibetan School on September 23, 2012, where he gives a talk titled, "The Philosophy of Tibetan Buddhism." In this lecture to Tibetan students, the khenpo historically situates Euro-American science with early naturalists including René Descartes (1596–1650) and Sir Isaac Newton (1643–1727), discusses epistemological grounds for Buddhism and science, references Carl Gustav Jung's (1875–1961) psychological commentary on the *Tibetan Book of the Dead*, argues for the paranormal based on Ian Stevenson's (1918–2007) reincarnation research, and raises doubts about the modern scientific project. See also Duckworth 2015: 268.

24. Kunga Sherab 2014: 8.

25. Kunga Sherab 2014: 47.

26. *The Mirror* was first published in 2003.

27. This was the Mind & Life Dialogue I in Dharamsala, India.

28. This was the Mind & Life Dialogue II in Newport Beach, California.

29. Moody 1975: 5.

30. Moody 1988: 154 reads, "In the absence of firm scientific proof, people frequently ask me what I believe: Are NDEs evidence of life after life? My answer is 'Yes.'"

31. This is a reference to researchers who have conducted near-death studies, including Melvin Morse, Michael Sabom, Michael Grosso, Kenneth Ring, Robert Sullivan, and so forth. See Moody 1988: 101–31 and his introduction.

32. The khenpo cites cases of children being born who lived without a cerebrum part of their brain (Tsultrim Lodro 2006: 8). See also Baskervill 1989 and Kunga Sherab 2014: 20.

33. This is a reference to the Buddhist all-ground consciousness (*kun gzhi rnam shes, ālayavijñāna*).

34. Moody 1988: 134–35.

35. The khenpo references the cardiologist Sabom (*hra min*). Tsultrim Lodro, 2017b: 11 and 98.

36. Moody 1988: 109–13.

37. On reporting near-death experiences, see Moody 1975: 80–84.

38. The vajra seat is the place of the Buddha's enlightenment, Bodhgaya in India.

39. Moody 1975: 42.

40. Moody 1975: 42–43 and a similar account is provided in Moody 1988: 7.

41. Moody 1975: 43.

42. Moody 1975: 44.

43. Moody 1975: 49–50.

44. This is a reference to the six types of rebirth in Buddhist cosmology: gods, jealous demigods, humans, hungry ghosts, animals, and denizens of hell.

45. Moody 1975: 52–55.

46. Moody 1975: 70–71.

7. Answers to Questions on Madhyamaka

1. Tsultrim Lodro 2007c.
2. Heshang was Kamalaśila's opponent in the legendary Samye debate. He is represented as advocating the rejection of all mental engagement and reasoning. In Tibetan histories, he was the loser of the debate.
3. The three vows are: the vows for individual liberation, the bodhisattva vows, and the tantric vows.
4. Tsultrim Lodro 2007c: 308–36.
5. Tsultrim Lodro 2007a: 309. Jamyang Mipham Gyatso is elsewhere referred to in this book as Jamgon Mipham Rinpoche.
6. Mipham 1990.
7. Tsultrim Lodro 2007a: 310. Mipham 1990: 502. See also Mipham's statement that: "In the perspective of authentic vision—a perspective like the sight of the absence of floating hairs for which nothing at all is found—there are no commonly appearing objects; and due to that essential point, an operator [e.g., *ultimately*] does not need to be applied to the object of negation." Mipham 1990: 503.
8. See Tsultrim Lodro 2007b: 82.
9. Mipham 1993a.
10. Tsultrim Lodro 2007a: 309–10. Mipham 1993a: 472.
11. Tsultrim Lodro 2007a: 310. Mipham 1993a: 472.
12. Tsultrim Lodro 2007a: 315.
13. Tsultrim Lodro 2007a: 315.
14. Tsultrim Lodro 2007a: 315.
15. Tsultrim Lodro 2007a: 316.
16. For a discussion of these criteria, see note 43 below.
17. Tsultrim Lodro 2007a: 316.
18. Tsultrim Lodro 2007a: 320.
19. Tsultrim Lodro 2007a: 320–21.
20. In *A Beginners Guide to the Reformulation of a Reductio* (Tsultrim Lodro 2007b: 66), Tsultrim Lodro cites Jayānanda's definition of a reductio: "Here the defining character of a reductio is that which points out what is undesirable to another through taking up the assertion of another." See Jayānanda's *Commentary on "Introduction to the Middle Way"*: 120a. Later, on p. 67, the Khenpo cites Jayānanda's claim that "expressing a reductio results in only a negation of the claim of another; thus, it is not connected with the meaning of the contraposition of the reductio." See Jayānanda: 123a.
21. Tsultrim Lodro 2007a: 321.
22. Tsultrim Lodro 2007a: 321–23.
23. Tsultrim Lodro 2007a: 328.
24. Tsultrim Lodro 2007a: 329.
25. Tsultrim Lodro 2007b: 95.
26. Mipham says, "The unique way that Prāsaṅgikas present the conventional is as

dependently arisen appearances that do not withstand [ontological] analysis—
the appearances that accord with all the world, oneself, and others—through
engaging in accord with the world of mere appearances without [ontological]
analysis." Mipham 1993a: 408; for an English translation see Padmakara Translation Group, *The Wisdom Chapter*, 208.

27. Tsultrim Lodro 2007a: 330.

28. Tsultrim Lodro 2007a: 330–31. Mipham did not use this language; rather, he said
that the common object was "mere appearance," that is, appearance not separate
from emptiness. See Mipham 1997: 32. For an English translation, see Pettit 1999:
220.

29. Tsultrim Lodro 2007a: 331.

30. Tsultrim Lodro 2007a: 331.

31. Tsultrim Lodro 2007a: 331–32.

32. See also Tsultrim Lodro 2007b: 59.

33. See also Tsultrim Lodro 2007b: 46.

34. The categorized ultimate is the conceptual and expressible ultimate, as opposed
to the uncategorized ultimate, which is inexpressible and nonconceptual.

35. Nāgārjuna, *Dispelling Disputes* (*Vigrahavyāvartanī, Rtsod pa bzlog pa'i tshig le'ur
byas pa*, D. 3828): v. 30.

36. Mipham 1993a: 472.

37. Mipham 1993a: 472.

38. Mipham 1990: 502.

39. This comes from Mipham Rinpoche's famous work, *The Beacon of Certainty* (*Nges
shes sgron me*). Mipham 1997: 6; English translation in Pettit 1999: 197.

40. The *Raplen Rejoinder* is Mipham's response to Lozang Pari Rapsel, called *Shedding Light on Thusness*.

41. Mipham 1993b: 300.

42. Mipham 1990: 503. I took the liberty to translate the *des* in Tsultrim Lodro's text
as *dpe*, which is found in Mipham's text, as this was apparently a typo. Without
this change, the citation would read, "The argument, and the process of negation
by it, is described by Candrakīrti . . . ," but this would not make sense.

43. In Buddhist formal logic systematized by Dignāga, the presence of these three
features of an argument—reason, entailment, and contrapositive—establishes
the argument's validity.

44. The mind is referred to as "unimpaired" here in order to distinguish between the
valid perception of a white conch and a jaundiced vision of a yellow one.

45. Candrakīrti, *Introduction to the Middle Way* (*Madhyamakāvatāra, Dbu ma la 'jug
pa*, (D. 3861): 6.81c.

46. Mipham 1993b: 312.

47. Candrakīrti, 6.25ab.

48. Mipham 1997: 32; English translation in Pettit 1996: 220–21.

49. Maitreya, *Sublime Continuum* (*Uttaratantra, Theg pa chen po rgyud bla ma'i bstan
bcos*, D. 4024): 1.55–57.

8. Liberating Lives

1. *tshethar, soklu*; Ch: *fangsheng*
2. The origins of life liberation in China have been traced to roughly the latter part of the third century ce. Rituals for the release of life first gained popularity among rulers and officials for ceremonial purposes in the fifth and sixth centuries and later, beginning in the Song dynasty, among lay Buddhists. Some Confucians and Daoists also performed life release, so it was an ethical practice that was shared more widely, and not exclusively Buddhist. In Tibet, the custom of ritually saving animals appears to have taken hold widely during the second dissemination of Buddhism (tenth to twelfth centuries). Despite the commonality of life liberation as a theme and practice across the Sino-Tibetan world, the life liberation cultures of China and Tibet are by no means identical. For one thing, there exists a wide variation in traditional styles and formats of releasing lives and/or consecrating animals. For more on the history and development of life liberation in Tibet, see Holler 2007. For more on life liberation in pre-communist China, see Pu 2014; Brook 1994; Handlin 1999; Yu 1981; Welch 1967; and Tarocco 2007.
3. The reform era (also referred to as the post-Mao era) refers to the period of political and economic reform and opening up in mainland China that commenced in 1978, lasting until midway through the 2010s. A widespread revival of religious life burgeoned forth in the reform era's more open ideological environment. Han Chinese participation in Tibetan Buddhism, a phenomenon with long historical antecedents, has grown particularly rapidly since the turn of the new millennium.
4. Lay life-liberation societies established a vibrant presence in urban Chinese religious life in the Ming period that endured throughout the Qing and Republican eras. While the Maoist decades saw the disappearance of life liberation rituals and groups dedicated to the practice in the mainland, the tradition continued in overseas Chinese communities, including Taiwan, Hong Kong, Malaysia, and Singapore. The popular spread of life liberation in mainland China throughout the reform era is thus not so much a novel phenomenon but the revival of a pre-existing tradition under new historical circumstances.
5. It should be emphasized that while the focus here is on the practice of life liberation among Han Chinese Tibetan Buddhist networks, the revival of Buddhism generally in mainland China has also seen life liberation rituals become popular throughout the Chinese Buddhist milieu. The practice of life liberation by Tibetans in Tibetan areas, independent of Chinese networks, has also energetically revived. While, for present purposes, it is analytically useful to distinguish these different Buddhist milieus, it should be noted that there is cross-pollination and interconnection in life liberation practice among the three.
6. This chapter features examples of life liberation advocacy by Khenpo Sodargye and Khenpo Sherab Zangpo. Khenpo Yeshe Phuntsok and Khenpo Tsultrim Lodro, two other notable Larung second-generation Dharmic intermediaries with the Sinophone world, have also propagated life liberation through their

teachings and activities among Han Chinese Buddhist audiences. So, too, have many other Chinese-networked Tibetan lamas associated with the Larung school.

7. For more on the Larung school's vegetarianism advocacy, see Khenpo Tsultrim Lodro's essay translated by Geoff Barstow in this anthology. See also Gaerrang 2016, Gayley 2017, Barstow 2017, and Hardie 2019. For more on the Larung school's campaigns of opposition to the practice of selling livestock into slaughter, see Gayley 2013 and Gaerrang 2015.

8. The Larung school has promoted life liberation and refraining from killing in both Tibetan and Chinese language teachings. Han Chinese areas, however, have received special attention in its leaders' life-liberation advocacy efforts. When Khenpo Jigme Phuntsok first launched a nationwide life liberation movement in 1997, it was to Han regions that he immediately dispatched his principle disciples. In a teaching given in 2000, he described the negative karma of killing (Ch: *shaye*) in Han Chinese cities as excessively heavy and advocated life liberation as a necessary antidote. See "Don't kill anymore!" in Khenpo Sodargye's *Life Salvation*. Life liberation was also seen as a skilful means of engaging newcomers in the Buddhadharma and, from the outset, connected to the Larung school's religious outreach in Han Chinese regions.

9. There are long traditions of life liberation advocacy by Buddhist leaders in both the Chinese and Tibetan Buddhist traditions. In Tibetan Buddhism, the nonsectarian (*ris med*) period in Kham from the middle of the eighteenth century to the early twentieth was a time when animal-focused practices of compassion, including ransoming lives and vegetarianism, gained a particular salience. In Chinese Buddhism, eminent figures from the Tiantai and Pure Land traditions were especially active in life liberation advocacy. Notably, during the Ming dynasty, widely disseminated essays encouraging the release of life by the charismatic evangelical trailblazer, Zhuhai, are credited as a major inspiration for the lay trend in organizing societies for its practice. For more on the advocacy of animal-focused practices of compassion in Tibetan Buddhism, see Barstow 2017. For life liberation advocacy in Chinese Buddhism, see Yu 1981 and Shiu and Stokes 2008.

10. Animated debates about life liberation have not only taken place on Chinese language digital platforms but also in the Tibetan language blogosphere, where criticisms have primarily targeted the practice of life liberation by Tibetans in Tibetan areas. In the last five years, controversies have blown up on Tibetan social media following documented incidences of irresponsible but well-intentioned life liberation.

11. Social criticism of life liberation, at least in the Chinese world, seems to have existed as long as the practice itself. Novel aspects of contemporary criticisms include the amplifying effect of the internet and social media, and the prominence of science-based objections that prioritize the ecosystem as a living entity worthy of protection. Modern animal-protection discourse has also influenced contemporary criticisms, heightening the importance of attending to the

well-being and survival of the animals released. Over the last three decades, irresponsible life liberation has also come under fire in other Asian societies as well as in the West. In some countries, the practice has become subject to tight government regulation. See Shiu and Stokes (2008).

12. Sodargye 2009c.

13. Convened on an almost annual basis since 2010, the World Youth Buddhist Symposium (Ch: *Shijie Qingnian Foxue Yantaohui*) is a multiday ecumenical Buddhist conference and dialogue for Sinophone youth. The symposium involves an annually changing lineup of invited religious leaders from Buddhist and non-Buddhist traditions and academic scholars from within China and overseas. Simultaneous English interpreting is provided for non-Chinese-speaking participants.

14. This epithet in Tibetan is Lama Yishin Norbu (Bla ma yid bzhin nor bu); in Chinese, it is Fawang Ruyibao.

15. While the Larung school upholds the Nyingma tradition and nonsectarian (*ris med*) lineage, Ester Bianchi has insightfully described how the notion of the ecumenical has been extended in its khenpos' teachings to Sinophone audiences "in order to embrace not only all Tibetan Buddhist schools and movements, but also Chinese ones." See Bianchi (2018: 110).

16. Sherab Zangpo 2013.

17. *Cidi Kaihua* (Hainan Chubanshe, 2011); *Jijing Zhi Dao* (Shijie Chuban Gongsi Beijing Gongsi, 2012); *Shengming Zhe Chuxi* (Huawen Chubanshe, 2013); and *Touguo Fofa Kan Shijie* (Zhongxin Chubanshe, 2014).

18. He is referring here to the round of death and suffering in saṃsāra.

19. The five turbidities (Skt: *pañcakaṣāya*; Ch: *wu zhuo*) refer to the five features of a kalpa in decay: the decrease in lifespan, the turbidity of views, the turbidity of afflictions, the turbidity of sentient beings, and the turbidity of the eon.

20. Ch: "Fangsheng Gongde Ganlumiaoyu"

21. Ch: "Zui kegui shi shenme?"

22. Ch: "Quangao Fangshengshu"

23. Lakla Sonam Chodrup, *Chags med bde smon dang de'i 'grel pa*. Translated into Chinese by Khenpo Sodargye and officially published as *Lala Quzhi Renboqie* [Suodaji Kanbu, trans.] 2012. *Zangchuan Jingtulun* [Treatise of Pure Land from the Tibetan Lineage] Zangwen Guji Chubanshe.

24. Unlike a traditional monastery or nunnery, Larung Gar was explicitly founded as a seat for the fourfold saṅgha (constituted by male and female monastics as well as non-celibate practitioners of both genders). Here, Khenpo Sodargye addresses a fourfold Sinophone audience of monastic and lay Buddhist students.

25. This is a shorter title for *Liberation through Hearing During the Intermediate State* (*Bar do thos grol*) revealed by Karma Lingpa.

26. This is referring to the *Single Son of the Buddha Tantra* (*Sangs rgyas sras gcig gi rgyud*), which is often produced in pocket-sized format and worn as an amulet that carries the power to "liberate-on-wearing or holding" (*btags grol*)

27. Jamyang Loter Wangpo, *Commentary on the Treasury of Abhidharma* (*Mngon pa mdzod kyi rtsa 'grel*. Translated by Khenpo Sodargye into Chinese and published as Jiangyang Luode Wangbo Zunzhe [Suodaji Kanbu, trans.] 2019. *Jushelunyi* [*Commentary on the Treasury of the Abhidharma*], Zangwen Guji Chubanshe.
28. Vasubandhu, *Treasury of Abhidharma and Its Autocommentary* (*Abhidharma-kośabhāṣya*).
29. Guṇaprabha, *Vinayasūtra* (*'Dul ba'i mdo rtsa ba*).
30. Xi'a Rongbo Kanbu (2011).

9. The Future of Tibetan Women

1. There is more information and analysis in my article in progress, "The New Role of Khenmo for Tibetan Nuns in Larung Gar." There are also Han Chinese khenmos and nuns at Larung Gar who study together in a separate system from the Tibetan nuns. Since 2011, Khenpo Sodargye has given khenpo and khenmo titles to his Han students twice, totally more than fifty monastics.
2. See Baimacuo 2015.
3. My first visit to Larung Gar was in 2003 when I went to study Buddhist philosophy. For many years after that, I conducted research on Yachen and other nunneries and since 2010 have done numerous questionnaires and interviews on nuns' education and their life in Larung Gar.
4. In 2013, the journal had fifty-three contributors, and in 2016, there were just sixteen contributing nuns. There were thirty-one articles in 2011, twenty-two in 2012, forty-two in 2014, thirty in 2015, and twenty-nine articles in 2017.
5. This association belongs to the education sector of Larung Gar. The Tibetan for its name is Gangs dkar lha mo'i rtsom sgrig tshan chung.
6. Khenmo Kusum Chodron told me that the cost of each printed copy of the magazine went up from 5 yuan in 2014 to 5.5 yuan in 2017, but they still sell each of magazine for 4 yuan, lower than the actual cost.
7. Khenmo Kusum Chodron told me the authors were all nuns in 2011. There was one laywomen author in 2012, and a few of authors were laywomen in 2013. When I interviewed Tsunma Norbu Lhamo who began doing the layout and design of the journal in 2014, she told me that, at that time, there were about ten authors who were lay Tibetan women.
8. The association usually posts announcements for submissions to the journal online or through WeChat from April to September. Then, every afternoon the group of khenmos volunteer their time to work together even though they do not have a designated office. They read and select articles, then ask Tulku Tenzin Gyatso for his suggestions, and then reread and edit several times. The journal usually comes out in November or December depending on when the work of the association is completed.
9. Her full name is Jetsunma Mume Yeshe Tsomo.

10. The poem in Tibetan reads: *mdo sngags rgya mtsho'i yang rtse rdzogs pa che/ sa lam gcig char 'grod pa'i gdams pa la/ dad 'dun btson pa drag pos stobs bskyed nas/ snying po'i don la gzhol ba'i nyams len mdzod.*

11. Khenmo Kusum Chodron told me that she and the association printed the journal in Chengdu. When she published the journal by herself, she printed two thousand copies each year and gave some away and sold others to monks, nuns, and literate lay Tibetans. Past issues are out of print and no longer available. The association printed one thousand copies of the journal in 2016 and 2017.

12. *Ning khri 'bras pa yul tsho.*

13. Khenmo Rigzin Chodron told me that she studied at the village's school for three years and at the county's elementary school for three years. Her main classes were Tibetan, math, and some Chinese.

14. *Gangs ri thod dkar shug gseb.*

15. She said that she received the title of khenmo from Jigme Phuntsok Rinpoche in 1997. After one year, there were five or six nuns from same area, and she became an assistant to help them learn Madhyamaka, Vinaya, and Lojong (*Blo sbyong*).

16. See Baimacuo 2014.

17. Chapter 10 in this anthology, which I coauthored with Sarah Jacoby, offers an important example.

18. *pho mchog mo dman.*

19. The term she uses for equal rights throughout the article is *thob thang 'dra mnyam.* It is important not to confuse the concepts of equality and respect. Equality for women does not mean disrespect for men.

20. Rigzin Chodron 2012.

21. The reference to another family likely has to do with life after a woman is married.

10. Lessons from Buddhist Foremothers

1. Larung Ārya Tāre Book Association Editorial Office 2017. The English translation published on the cover of each *Treasury* volume reads "Larung Tara Literatures Editorial Institute," but our translation "Larung Ārya Tāre Book Association Editorial Office" accords more closely with how the Larung Gar nuns refer to themselves as an association (*tshogs pa*) and how they explained the meaning of their association name to us.

2. One exception to this could be seen as the compilation of biographies of Bon women revealed as a treasure in 1918 by the female Bon treasure revealer (*gter ston*) Dechen Chokyi Wangmo (b. 1868), although this collection is narrower in scope. See Khandro Dechen Wangmo 1985, also published in volume nine of *Ḍākinīs' Great Dharma Treasury*. The Larung Gar nuns' first anthology in sixteen volumes is titled *Garland of White Lotuses*; see Larung Ārya Tāre Book Association Editorial Office 2013a. A spin off of the Larung Gar nuns' *Garland of White Lotuses* publication project titled *Women of the Snow Land Book Series* was published shortly thereafter in Chengdu including only a selection of the

Tibetan women featured in the *Garland of White Lotuses*, without the Indian Buddhist figures featured in the *Garland*; see Sichuan Tibetan Manuscript Editorial Office 2015. Tibetan women featured in this Chengdu collection include Khandro Yeshe Tsogyal, Machik Labkyi Dronma, Jetsunma Migyur Paldron, Tromge Dawa Dronma, Shugseb Jetsunma, Khandro Sonam Paldren, and Sera Khandro Dechen Dewe Dorje.

3. *slob ston khang.*

4. *zhe ru can.*

5. For a well-known portrayal of Nyangtsa Kargyen's murderous revenge, see Tsangnyon Heruka 2010: 34–35.

6. All quotes not otherwise attributed from here forward come from interviews with one prominent member of the Ārya Tāre Book Association conducted by Padma 'tsho and her Southwest Nationalities master's student, also a Tibetan woman, in Larung Gar in July 2016. The interview was recorded by Padma 'tsho and translated in a collaborative process by Padma 'tsho and Sarah Jacoby.

7. The word for *woman* we are referring to here is *bud med*. For more on its etymology, see Tsering Chotsho 1997: 60.

8. *skye dman.*

9. *nag mo.*

10. See Humphrey 1997.

11. See Diemberger 2010.

12. This characterization of Tibetan Buddhist modernity comes from Antonio Terrone's talk titled "'Striving to Do Virtuous Deeds:' The Tenth Panchen Lama and Larung Gar in the Making of Modern Buddhism in Tibet" presented at the American Academy of Religion panel "Voices from Larung Gar" in November 2017. See chapter 1 in this volume.

13. Padma 'tsho has been conducting a separate and extensive research project on nuns' education curricula at Larung Gar. For more of her research, see Padma 'tsho 2004 and Baimacuo 2015.

14. See Larung Ārya Tāre Book Association Editorial Office 2017b: 1–5.

15. The "red-faced demoness" (*gdong dmar srin mo*) refers to the myth that the Tibetan people are the descendants of a female demoness in the form of a rock ogress and a male bodhisattva in the form of a monkey. For an English version of this myth, see Sonam Gyaltsen 1996: 75–79. Additionally, for an analysis of the myth that the Tibetan land itself is a supine demoness pinned down by the taming and civilizing force of strategically placed Buddhist temples, see Janet Gyatso 1987.

16. The Empress Lady of Tro named Tri Malo (Btsan mo 'Bro bza' khri ma lod) was a powerful empress of Tibet who died in 712–713 and whose grandson Tri Detsuktsen (Khri lde gtsug brtsan) inherited the throne from her. See Beckwith 1987: 78.

17. Nyangtsa Kargyen was Milarepa's mother.

18. Mume Yeshe Tsomo (Mu me ye shes mtsho mo, 1966–) is the niece of the founder

of Larung Gar, Khenpo Jigme Phuntsok. An incarnation of Yeshe Tsogyal and Mingyur Peldron, she has been the leader of Larung Gar since 2004 following the passing of her uncle. For a trilingual biography of her, see Larung Ārya Tāre Book Association Editorial Office 2013b. For Tibetan biographies of her, see volume sixteen of *Garland of White Lotuses* and volumes sixteen and fifty of *Ḍākinīs' Great Dharma Treasury*.

19. The volumes number fifty-two without the table of contents, which comprises the fifty-third volume.

20. Khandro Dechen Wangmo 1985.

21. Khandroma Wangdron is another name for the female Bon treasure revealer Dechen Chokyi Wangmo.

22. Uza Khandro means "The Ḍākinī from Central Tibet" and is the popular name in eastern Tibet for Sera Khandro (1892-1940). Kunzang Dekyong Wangmo is Sera Khandro's treasure name (*gter ming*). For a study of her auto/biographical writings, see Jacoby 2014.

23. Do Dasel Wangmo (Mdo zla gsal dbang mo, 1928–) is the great-granddaughter of Do Khyentse Yeshe Dorje (1800–1866). She is a Tibetan medical doctor and Buddhist nun.

24. Thupten Rigje Lhamo (Thub bstan rig byed lha mo) is a contemporary khenmo at Larung Gar who also goes by the name Khenmo Yonten (Mkhan mo Yon tan). She is the only Larung Gar nun whose writings are included in this series.

Bibliography

Tibetan Sources

Chukye Gendun Samten (Chus skyes dge 'dun bsam gtan). 1996. *Tshad ma rnam 'grel gyi dgongs don legs par bshad pa blo gsal 'jug bde'i lam bu* [An Easy Road for the Intelligent: An Elucidation of the Intended Meaning of the Commentary on Valid Cognition]. Lanzhou: Gansu Nationalities Press.

————. 2000. *Bod brgyud nang bstan shes rig chen po'i gzhi rtsa'i rnam bshad dus rabs nyer gcig pa'i blo gros pad mo'i kha 'byed* [Opening the Lotus of Intelligence for the Twenty-First Century: An Explanation of the Fundamentals of the Great Civilization of Tibetan Buddhism]. Lanzhou: Gansu Nationalities Press.

Drang Yisun (Krang dbyi sun), ed. 1985. *Bod rgya tshig mdzod chen mo* [Great Tibetan-Chinese Dictionary]. Beijing: Mi rigs dpe skrun khang.

Jayānanda. *Commentary on "Introduction to the Middle Way" (Madhyamakā-vatāraṭīkā, Dbu ma la 'jug pa'i 'grel bshad)*, D. 3870.

Jigme Phuntsok, Khenpo ('Jigs med phun tshogs, Mkhan po). Composed 1995. *Dus rabs nyer gcig pa'i gangs can pa rnams la phul ba'i snying gtam sprin gyi rol mo* [Heart Advice to Tibetans for the Twenty-First Century: Music in the Clouds]. N.p. BDRC W25144.

————. 2002. *Chos rje dam pa yid bzhin nor bu 'Jigs med phun tshogs 'byung gnas dpal bzang po'i gsung 'bum* [The Collected Works of the Sublime Dharma Master, the Wish-Fulfilling Jewel, Jigme Phuntsok Jungne Palzangpo]. 3 vols. Hong Kong: Xianggang xinzhi chubanshe.

Khandro Dechen Wangmo (Mkha' 'gro bde chen dbang mo). 1985. *Mkha' 'gro rgya mtsho'i rnam thar* [Biography of the Ocean of Ḍākinīs]. Dolanji: Tibetan Bonpo Monastic Community.

Kusum Chodron, Khenmo (Sku gsum chos sgron, Mhkan mo), ed. 2012–2017. *Gangs dkar lha mo: Bod kyi btsun mo'i lo deb* [Goddess of the Snowy Range: Annual Journal for Tibetan Nuns], vol. 2–7.

Larung Ārya Tāre Book Association Editorial Office (Bla rung ārya tāre'i pe tshogs rtsom sgrig khang), ed. 2013a. *'Phags bod kyi skyes chen ma dag gi rnam par thar ba pad ma dkar po'i phreng ba* [Garland of White Lotuses: The Biographies of the Great Female Masters of India and Tibet]. 16 vols. Lhasa: Bod ljong bod yi dpe rnying dpe skrun khang. BDRC W1KG16649.

————. 2013b. "Mi 'gyur dpal gyi sgron ma'i rnam rol rje btsun ma mu med ye shes mtsho mo'i rnam thar dad pa'i shing rta" [Chariot of the Faithful: Biography of the Emanation of Mingyur Pelkyi Dronma, Jetsunma Mume Yeshe Tsomo]. In *'Phags bod kyi skyes chen ma dag gi rnam par thar ba pad ma dkar po'i phreng ba* [Garland of White Lotuses: The Biographies of the Great Female Masters of India and Tibet]. 12: 167–96. Lhasa: Bod ljongs bod yig dpe rnying dpe skrun khang. BDRC W1KG16649.

————. 2017a. *Mkha' 'gro'i chos mdzod chen mo* [Ḍākinīs' Great Dharma Treasury]. 53 vols. Lhasa: Bod ljongs bod yig dpe rnying dpe skrun khang. BDRC W3CN2459.

————. 2017b. "Sngon 'gro'i gtam" [Preface]. In *Mkha' 'gro'i chos mdzod chen mo'i dkar chag rin chen gser gyi lde mig* [Precious Golden Key: Ḍākinīs' Great Dharma Treasury Table of Contents], 1–5. Vol. 53 of *Mkha' 'gro'i chos mdzod chen mo* [Ḍākinīs' Great Dharma Treasury]. Lhasa: Bod ljongs bod yig dpe rnying dpe skrun khang. BDRC W3CN2459.

Lobsang Dorje (Blo bzang rdo rje), Lobsang Tashi (Blo bzang bkra shis), Sangdup Tobla (Gtsang phrug sthobs lags), and Yelhun (Ye lhun), eds. 2009. *Paṇ chen sku 'phreng bcu pa'i mdzad rnam* [The Life and Works of the Tenth Panchen Lama]. Dharamsala: Central Association for H.H. the Panchen Lama. BDRC W1KG6196.

Metrul Tenzin Gyatso (Rme sprul Bstan 'dzin rgya mtsho). 2002. "Gsar rtsom dpyod shes rgyang 'bod la che long du brtag pa" [A Rough Analysis of the New Era Essay: A Call from Afar for Scrutiny]. *Sngags mang zhib 'jug* 4, 75–123.

————. 2011. *Klad chen dang sems kyi 'brel ba la dpyad pa* [An Analysis of the Connection between Mind and Brain]. Dharamsala: Library of Tibetan Works and Archives. BDRC W1KG14139.

————. 2013. "Chos srid zung 'brel dang bod rig pa'i 'phel phyogs la dpyad pa" [An Analysis of the Development of Tibetan Culture when Religion Is Influential]. In *Rme sprul bstan 'dzin rgya mtsho'i gsung rtsom* [Collected Writings of Metrul Tenzin Gyatso], vol. 2: 211–50. Lanzhou, Gansu: Kan su'u mi rigs dpe skrun khang.

Metrul Tenzin Gyatso (Rme sprul Bstan 'dzin rgya mtsho), and Khenpo Tsultrim Lodro (Mkhan po Tshul khrims blo gros), eds. 2003. *Gangs ri dkar po'i srog mkhar 'dzin pa 'phrog byed dar ma'i nga ro* [The Lion's Roar Guarding the Citadel of the Life Force of the Snow Mountains]. Serta, Sichuan: Bla rung theg gsum chos gling. BDRC W24590.

Mipham Gyatso (Mi pham rgya mtsho). 1990. "Dam chos dogs sel" [Eliminating Doubts]. In *Dbu ma rgyan rtsa 'grel* [Root Text and Commentary of Madhyamakālaṃkāra]. Sichuan: Nationalities Press.

————. 1993a. "Brgal lan nyin byed snang ba" [Light of the Sun]. In *Spyod 'jug sher 'grel ke ta ka* [Ketaka Jewel: Commentary on the "Wisdom Chapter" of the *Bodhicaryāvatāra*]. Sichuan: Nationalities Press.

————. 1993b. "Gzhan gyis brtsad pa'i lan mdor bsdus pa rigs lam rab gsal de nyid snang byed" [Shedding Light on Thusness]. In *Spyod 'jug sher 'grel ke ta ka* [Ketaka Jewel: Commentary on the "Wisdom Chapter" of the *Bodhicaryāvatāra*]. Sichuan: Nationalities Press.

———. 1997. "Nges shes sgron me" [Beacon of Certainty]. In *Nges shes sgron me rtsa 'grel* [Root Text and Commentary of the Beacon of Certainty], 1–54. Sichuan: Nationalities Press. Translated by John Pettit as *Mipham's Beacon of Certainty* (Boston: Wisdom Publications, 1999).

———. 1998. "Dbang sdud gsol 'debs." In *Gsang chen snga 'gyur ba'i bka' gter zhal 'don phyogs bsgrigs*, 107–8. Xining: Mtsho sngon zhing chen mtsho lho dge 'os slob grwa'i par khang. BDRC W25186.

Panchen Rinpoche (Paṇ chen rin po che). 1985. *Kun gzigs paṇ chen rin po che mchog kis gser thar mchod rten thog tu gnang ba'i gsung bshad* [The Omniscient Panchen Lama's Speech at the Serta Chorten]. Serta, Sichuan: Rdzong chos lugs cus.

Rigzin Chodron, Khenmo (Rig 'dzin chos sgron, Mkhan mo). 2012. "Nga dang khyed kyi mdun lam" [The Way Forward for You and Me]. *Gangs dkar lha mo: Bod kyi btsun mo'i lo deb* [Goddess of the Snowy Range: Annual Journal for Tibetan Nuns] 2: 13–18.

Rigzin Dargye, Khenpo (Rig 'dzin dar rgyas, Mkhan po). *Chos rje dam pa 'Jigs med phun tshogs 'byung gnas dpal bzang po mchog gi mjug mtha'i zhal gdams rang tshugs ma shor gzhan sems ma dkrugs zhes pa'i 'grel ba lugs gnyis blang dor gsal ba'i sgron me* [The Torch to Illumnate the Two Systems: A Commentary on the Slogan "Don't Lose Self-Determination; Don't Agitate the Minds of Others," Parting Advice of the Sublime Dharma Master, the Supreme Jigme Phuntsok Jungne Palzangpo]. Serta, Sichuan: Bla rung lnga rig slob gling, 2004.

Sangdup Tobla (Gtsang phrug stobs lags). 2012. *Paṇ chen er te ni zhib 'jug* [A Study of Panchen Erteni]. Dharamsala, India: Bod kyi mtho rim slob gnyer khang. BDRC W1KG13818.

Shokdung (Zhogs dung). 2008. *Dpyod shes rgyang 'bod* [A Call from Afar for Scrutiny]. Lanzhou, Gansu: Kan su'u mi rigs dpe skrun khang.

Sichuan Tibetan Manuscript Editorial Office (Si khron bod yig dpe rnying bsdu sgrig khang), eds. 2015. *Gangs can skyes ma'i dpe tshogs* [Women of the Snow Land Book Series]. Chengdu: Si khron mi rigs dpe skrun khang.

Tsawa Danyuk (Tsha ba mda' smyug). 2011. *Rtog ge pa'i mig nang gi chos lugs kyi 'jig rten* [An Intellectual's Eye on the Buddhist World]. Lanzhou: Gansu Nationalities Press.

Tsultrim Lodro, Khenpo (Tshul khrims blo gros, Mkhan po). 2003–2004. *Yang dag lam gyi 'jug sgo blo gsar yid kyi dga' ston* [Festival for the Novice Mind: An Entrance into the Authentic Path]. 2 vols. Hong Kong: Fojiao cihui fuwu zhongxin.

———. 2004. *Skye ba snga phyi'i rnam gzhag dang lugs gnyis gsal ba'i me long* [A Presentation of Past and Future Lives and A Mirror That Illuminates the Two Systems]. Hong Kong: Fojiao cihui fuwu zhongxin.

———. 2004. "Dge bskul shu yig" [Words to Increase Virtue]. In *Sha chang tha ma kha sogs kyi nyes dmigs phyogs bsdus* [A Collection of Texts on the Faults of Meat, Alcohol, and Tobacco]. Serta, Sichuan: Bla rung lnga rig slob gling.

———. 2007a. "Dbu ma'i dris lan" [Answers to Questions on Madhyamaka]. In *Dpal bla rung gi mkhan po tshul khrims blo gros kyi gsung 'bum blo gsar yid kyi dga' ston* [The Collected Works of Larung Gar Khenpo Tsultrim Lodro: Festival for the Novice Mind], vol. 3: 308–36. Beijing: Nationalities Press.

———. 2007b. "Thal bzlog gi 'grel ba lo gsar 'jug sgo" [A Beginner's Guide to the Reformulation of a Reductio]. In *Dpal bla rung gi mkhan po tshul khrims blo gros kyi gsung 'bum blo gsar yid kyi dga' ston* [The Collected Works of Larung Gar Khenpo Tsultrim Lodro: Festival for the Novice Mind], vol. 3: 1–106. Beijing: Nationalities Press.

———. 2007c. "Lta ba'i dpyad pa drang srong rgan po dgyas pa'i mchod sprin" [Contemplations on the View: An Offering Cloud that Delights the Old Sage]. In *Dpal bla rung gi mkhan po tshul khrims blo gros kyi gsung 'bum blo gsar yid kyi dga' ston* [The Collected Works of Larung Gar Khenpo Tsultrim Lodro: Festival for the Novice Mind], vol. 3: 256–78. Beijing: Nationalities Press.

———. 2007d. "Skye ba snga phyi'i rnam gzhag srid pa gsal ba'i me long" [The Mirror That Illuminates Existence: An Analysis of Past and Future Lives]. In *Dpal bla rung gi mkhan po tshul khrims blo gros kyi gsung 'bum*: Festival for the Novice Mind [The Collected Works of Larung Gar Khenpo Tsultrim Lodro], 1–146. Beijing: Nationalities Press.

———. 2012. "Bod brgyud nang bstan gyi mtshan nyid rig pa" [The Philosophy of Tibetan Buddhism]. In *Mtha' gnyis rab sel* [Illuminating the Two Extremes], edited by Pad ma dbang grangs and Tshul khrims blo gros, 99–188. Chengdu: Si khron zhing chen bod yig slob grwa.

———. 2013. "'Dzam gling shar nub kyi gna' deng rig pa'i rnam gzhag mdo tsam brjod pa blo gsar yid kyi bdud rtsi" [A Brief Presentation of Ancient and Modern Thought from the Eastern and Western World]. In *'Dzam gling shar nub kyi gna' deng rig pa'i rnam gzhag dang 'dzam gling skad yig gi skye 'chi'i lo rgyus* [A Brief Presentation of Ancient and Modern Thought from the Eastern and Western World], 1–343. Lanzhou: Gansu Nationalities Press.

———. 2016. "Dge bskul shu yig" [Words to Increase Virtue]. In *Bod kyi dkar zas ring lugs* [The Vegetarian Tradition in Tibet], edited by Bstan 'dzin dbang phyug, 340–43. Serta, Sichuan: Bla rung lnga rig slob gling, 2004.

Chinese Sources

Baimacuo (Padma 'tsho). 2015. "Dang dai zang zu ni zhong jiao yu ti xi de diao cha yan jiu" [An Investigation of a New Educational System for Contemporary Tibetan Nuns]. *Zong Jiao Xue Ayan Jiu* [Religious Studies], *CSSCI Journal of Religious Studies in Sichuan* (October): 158–63.

Jigme Phunstok, Khenpo [Fawang Ruyibao Jimei Pengcuo]. 2009. "Bu yao zai xia sheng!" [Don't Kill Anymore!]. In *Shengsi Jidu* [Life Salvation], edited by Khenpo Sodargye, 1–7. Eslite Pty Ltd.

Sherab Zangpo, Khenpo [Xi'a Rongbo Kanbu]. 2011. *Cidi Kaihua* [The Path]. Hainan, Hainan Chubanshe [Hainan Publishing House].

———. 2012. *Jijing Zhi Dao* [The Silent Way]. Beijing, Shijie Tushu Chuban Gongsi [World Publishing Corporation].

———. 2013. "Shengming de pingdeng" [The Equality of Life]. In *Shengming Zhe Chuxi* [Life Is Play], edited by Sherab Zangpo, 39–58. Beijing, Huawen Publishing House.

———. 2013b. *Shengming Zhe Chuxi* [Life Is Play]. Beijing, Huawen Chubanshe [Sino-Culture Press].

———. 2014. *Touguo Fofa Kan Shijie* [Seeing the World through the Buddhadharma]. Beijijng, Zhongxin Chubanshe [CITIC Press].

Sodargye, Khenpo [Suodaji Kanbu]. 2009. "Fangsheng Gongde Ganlumiaoyu" [The Beneficial Qualities of Life Liberation: Marvelous Ambrosia Rain]. In *Shengsi Jiudu* [Life Salvation], edited by Khenpo Sodargye, 16–49. Xinyitang Youxian Gongsi [Eslite Pty Ltd].

———. 2009b. "Quangao Fangshengshu" [Letter Urging Friends to Release Lives]. In *Shengsi Jiudu* [Life Salvation], edited by Khenpo Sodargye,10–15. Xinyitang Youxian Gongsi [Eslite Pty Ltd].

———. 2009c. "Zai tan fangsheng: jiuzheng fangsheng zhong bu rufa de xianxiang" [Discussing Life Liberation Again: Remedying Things That Do Not Accord with the Dharma in the Practice of Life Liberation]. In *Shengsi Jiudu* [Life Salvation], edited by Khenpo Sodargye, 52–71. Xinyitang Youxian Gongsi [Eslite Pty Ltd].

———. 2009d. "Zui kegui shi shenme?" [What Is the Most Precious Thing?]. In *Shengsi Jiudu* [Life Salvation], edited by Khenpo Sodargye, 8–9. Xinyitang Youxian Gongsi [Eslite Pty Ltd].

Wang, Yunfeng. "Shishi Banchan dashihe liushi Gongtangcang dashi de youyi" [Friendship between the Tenth Panchen Lama and the Sixth Gungthang Rinpoche]. Accessed August 10, 2018. tibetcul.com/people/mrzf/23089.html.

Wang, Zhen. 1991. *Shi shi Banchan* [The Tenth Panchen Lama]. Shenzhen, Haitian chubanshe.

Zhao, Puchu. 1990. "Wo he Banchan dashi" [The Panchen Lama and I]. *Zhongguo minzu* [Chinese Nation] 3: 22–23.

ENGLISH SOURCES

Arjia Rinpoche, Lobsang Tubten Jigme Gyatso. 2010. *Surviving the Dragon: A Tibetan Lama's Account of 40 Years under Chinese Rule*. New York: Rodale.

Baimacuo (Padma 'tsho). 2014. "Courage as Eminence: Tibetan Nuns at Yachen Monastery in Kham." In *Eminent Buddhist Women*, edited by Karma Lekshe Tsomo, 185–94. Albany: State University of New York Press.

Barnett, Robert. 2009. "Beyond the Collaborator-Martyr Model: Strategies of

Compliance, Opportunism, and Opposition within Tibet." In *Contemporary Tibet: Politics, Development, and Society in a Disputed Region*, edited by Barry Sautman and June Teufel Dreyer, 25–66. London: Routledge.

Barstow, Geoffrey. 2018. *Food of Sinful Demons: Meat, Vegetarianism, and the Limits of Buddhism in Tibet*. New York: Columbia University Press.

———. 2019a. "On the Moral Standing of Animals in Tibetan Buddhism." *Études Mongoles et Sibériennes, Centrasiatiques et Tibétaines* 50. doi.org/10.4000/emscat.3865.

———, ed. 2019b. *The Faults of Meat: Tibetan Buddhist Writing on Vegetarianism*. Boston: Wisdom Publications.

Baskervill, Bill. July 13, 1989. "Boy without a Brain 'Just Glows,' Mom Says." *New Philadelphia Times Reporter*.

Beckwith, Christopher. 1987. *The Tibetan Empire in Central Asia: A History of the Struggle for Great Power among Tibetans, Turks, Arabs, and Chinese during the Early Middle Ages*. Princeton, NJ: Princeton University Press.

Bianchi, Ester. 2017. "*Yi jie wei shi*: Theory and Practice of Monastic Discipline in Modern and Contemporary Chinese Buddhism." *Studies in Chinese Religions* 3/2: 111–41.

———. 2018. "Teaching Tibetan Buddhism in Chinese on Behalf of Mañjuśrī 'Great Perfection' (Dzokchen/Dayuanman) and Related Tantric Practices among Han Chinese and Taiwanese Believers in Sertar and Beyond." In *The Hybridity of Buddhism: Contemporary Encounters between Tibetan and Chinese Traditions in Taiwan and the Mainland*, edited by Fabienne Jagou, 109–31. Paris: EFEO.

Birnbaum, Raoul. 2003. "Buddhist China at the Century's Turn." *The China Quarterly* 174: 428–50.

Bond, George. 1996. "A.T. Ariyaratne and the Sarvodaya Shramadana Movement in Sri Lanka." In *Engaged Buddhism: Buddhist Liberation Movements in Asia*, edited by Christopher Queen and Sallie King, 121–46. Albany: State University of New York Press.

Braun, Erik. 2013. *The Birth of Insight: Meditation, Modern Buddhism, and the Burmese Monk Ledi Sayadaw*. Chicago: University of Chicago Press.

Brook, Timothy. 1994. *Praying for Power: Buddhism and the Formation of Gentry Society in Late-Ming China*. Cambridge, MA: Harvard University Press.

Buffetrille, Katia. 2014. "A Controversy on Vegetarianism." In *Trails of the Tibetan Tradition: Papers for Elliot Sperling*, edited by Roberto Vitali, 113–27. Dharamsala: Amye Machen Institute.

Buswell, Robert, and Donald Lopez. 2016. *The Princeton Dictionary of Buddhism*. Princeton, NJ: Princeton University Press.

Cabezón, José. 2003. "Buddhism and Science: On the Nature of the Dialogue." In *Buddhism and Science: Breaking New Ground*, edited by B. Alan Wallace, 35–68. New York: Columbia University Press.

Chotso, Tsering. 1997. "A Drop from an Ocean: The Status of Women in Tibetan Society." *The Tibet Journal* 22, no. 2: 59–68.

Cuevas, Bryan. *The All-Pervading Melodious Drumbeat: The Life of Ra Lotsawa*. New York: Penguin Classics, 2015.

Department of Information and International Relations (DIIR). 2003. *From the Heart of the Panchen Lama: Major Speeches and a Petition (1962–1989)*. Dharamsala, India: Central Tibetan Administration.

Diemberger, Hildegard. 2010. "Life Histories of Forgotten Heroes? Transgression of Boundaries and the Reconstruction of Tibet in the Post-Mao Era." *Inner Asia* 12, no. 1: 113–25.

Dilgo Khyentse. 2007. *The Heart of Compassion: The Thirty-Seven Verses on the Practice of a Bodhisattva*. Translated by Padmakara Translation Group. Boston: Shambhala Publications.

Duara, Prasenjit. 1995. *Rescuing History from the Nation: Questioning Narratives of Modern China*. Chicago: University of Chicago Press.

Duckworth, Douglas. 2015. "Echoes of Tsultrim Lodro: An Indigenous Voice from Contemporary Tibet on the 'Buddhism and Science Dialogue.'" *Journal of Contemporary Buddhism* 16, no. 2: 267–77.

Finnigan, Bronwyn. 2017. "Buddhism and Animal Ethics." *Philosophy Compass* 12, no. 7: 1–12.

Gaerrang (Kabzung). 2015. "Development as Entangled Knot: The Case of the Slaughter Renunciation Movement in Tibet, China." *The Journal of Asian Studies* 74, no. 14: 927–51.

———. 2016. "Tibetan Identity and Tibetan Buddhism in Trans-Regional Connection: The Contemporary Vegetarian Movement in Pastoral Areas of Tibet (China)." *Études Mongoles et Sibériennes, Centrasiatiques et Tibétaines* 47: doi.org/10.4000/emscat.2755

Gardner, Alexander. "Dromton Gyelwa Jungne," *Treasury of Lives*, accessed June 01, 2020, treasuryoflives.org/biographies/view/Dromton-Gyelwa-Jungne/4267.

Gayley, Holly. 2011. "The Ethics of Cultural Survival: A Buddhist Vision of Progress in Mkhan po 'Jigs phun's *Heart Advice to Tibetans for the 21st Century*." In *Mapping the Modern in Tibet*, edited by Gray Tuttle, 435–502. Andiast: International Institute for Tibetan and Buddhist Studies GmbH.

———. 2013. "Reimagining Buddhist Ethics on the Tibetan Plateau." *Journal of Buddhist Ethics* 20): 247–86.

———. 2016. "Controversy over Buddhist Ethical Reform: A Secular Critique of Clerical Authority in the Tibetan Blogosphere." *Himalaya, the Journal of the Association for Nepal and Himalayan Studies* 36, no. 1: 22–43.

———. 2017. "The Compassionate Treatment of Animals." *Journal of Religious Ethics* 45, no. 1: 29–57.

Gayley, Holly, and Nicole Willock. 2016. "Theorizing the Secular in Tibetan Cultural Worlds." *Himalaya* 36, no. 1: 12–21.

Gayley, Holly, and Padma 'tsho. 2016. "Non-Violence as a Shifting Signifier on the Tibetan Plateau." *Contemporary Buddhism* 17, no. 1: 62–80.

Germano, David. 1998. "Re-membering the Dismembered Body of Tibet: Contemporary Tibetan Visionary Movements in the People's Republic of China." In *Buddhism in Contemporary Tibet: Religious Revival and Cultural Identity*, edited by Melvyn Goldstein and Matthew Kapstein, 53–94. Berkeley: University of California Press.

Gladney, Dru. 2004. *Dislocating China: Reflections on Muslims, Minorities, and Other Subaltern Subjects*. London: Hurst and Company.

Gleig, Ann. 2019. *American Dharma: Buddhism beyond Modernity*. New Haven, CT: Yale University Press.

Goldstein, Melvyn and Matthew Kapstein, eds. 1998. *Buddhism in Contemporary Tibet: Religious Revival and Cultural Identity*. Berkeley: University of California Press.

———, ed. 2001. *The New Tibetan-English Dictionary of Modern Tibetan*. Berkeley: University of California Press.

Goossaert, Vincent, and David Palmer. 2010. *The Religious Question in Modern China*. Chicago: University of Chicago Press.

Gyatso, Janet. 1987. "Down with the Demoness." In *Feminine Ground: Essays on Women and Tibet*, edited by Janice Willis, 33–51. Ithaca, NY: Snow Lion Publications.

Handlin-Smith, Joanna F. 1999. "Liberating Animals in Ming-Qing China: Buddhist Inspiration and Elite Imagination." *Journal of Asian Studies* 58, no. 1: 51–84.

Hansen, Anne. 2007. *How to Behave: Buddhism and Modernity in Colonial Cambodia: 1860–1930*. Honolulu: University of Hawai'i Press.

Hardie, Catherine. 2019. "Khenpo Tsultrim Lodrö's Appeal to Contemporary Tibetan Religious Practitioners to Abandon Meat and Practice Non-Killing." In *The Faults of Meat: Tibetan Buddhist Writing on Vegetarianism*, edited by Geoffrey Barstow, 259–309. Boston: Wisdom Publications.

Harrell, Stevan. 1995. "Introduction." In *Cultural Encounters on China's Ethnic Frontiers*, edited by Stevan Harrell, 3–36. Seattle: University of Washington Press.

———. 1995b. "The History of the History of the Yi." In *Cultural Encounters on China's Ethnic Frontiers*, edited by Stevan Harrell, 63–91. Seattle: University of Washington Press.

Hartley, Lauran. 2002. "'Inventing Modernity' in A mdo: Views on the Role of Traditional Tibetan Culture in a Developing Society." In *Amdo Tibetans in Transition: Society and Culture in the Post-Mao Era*, edited by Toni Huber, 1–25. Leiden: Brill.

Herberer, Thomas. 1989. *China and Its National Minorities: Autonomy or Assimilation?* London: M. E. Sharpe, Inc.

Holler, David. 2002. "The Ritual of Freeing Lives." In *Tibet, Past and Present: Religion and Secular Culture in Tibet*, edited by John Ardussi, 207–26. Leiden: Brill.

Humphrey, Caroline. 1997. "Exemplars and Rules: Aspects of the Discourse of Moralities in Mongolia." In *The Ethnography of Moralities*, edited by Signe Howell, 25–47. London: Routledge.

Ishihama Yumiko. 2004. "The Notion of 'Buddhist Government' (*chos srid*) Shared by Tibet, Mongol, and Manchu in the Early 17th Century." In *The Relationship* between Religion and State (*Chos srid zung 'brel*) in Traditional Tibet, edited by Christoph Cuppers, 15– 31. Lumbini, Nepal: Lumbini International Research Institute.

Jackson, Roger. 1996. "'Poetry' in Tibet: *Glu, mGur, sNyan ngag* and 'Songs of Experience.'" In *Tibetan Literature: Studies in Genre*, edited by José Cabezón and Roger Jackson, 368–92. Ithaca, NY: Snow Lion Publications.

Jacoby, Sarah. 2014. *Love and Liberation: The Autobiographical Writings of the Tibetan Buddhist Visionary Sera Khandro*. New York: Columbia University Press.

Jacoby, Sarah, and Antonio Terrone. 2012. "Tibetan and Himalayan Buddhism." In *Buddhism in the Modern World*, edited by David McMahan, 89–111. New York: Routledge.

Jagou, Fabienne. 2011. *The Ninth Panchen Lama (1883–1937): A Life at the Crossroads of Sino-Tibetan Relations*. Chiang Mai, Thailand: Silkworm Books.

Jinpa, Thupten. 2003. "Science as an Ally or a Rival Philosophy? Tibetan Buddhist Thinkers' Engagement with Modern Science." In *Buddhism and Science: Breaking New Ground*, B. Alan Wallace, 71–85. New York: Columbia University Press.

———. 2010. "Buddhism and Science: How Far Can the Dialogue Proceed?" *Zygon*, 45, no. 4: 871–82.

Jinpa, Thupten, and Jaś Elsner, trans. 2014. *Songs of Spiritual Experience: Tibetan Buddhist Poems of Insight and Awakening*. Boston: Shambhala Publications.

Jinpa, Thupten and Donald S. Lopez, trans. 2014. *Grains of Gold: Tales of a Cosmopolitan Traveler*. Chicago: University of Chicago.

Johnson, Anna Wolcott. 2019. "Khedrup Je on Meat in the Monastery." In *The Faults of Meat: Tibetan Buddhist Writing on Vegetarianism*, edited by Geoffrey Barstow, 119–58. Boston: Wisdom Publications.

Jones, Charles. 2003. "Transitions in the Practice and Defense of Chinese Pure Land Buddhism." In *Buddhism in the Modern World: Adaptations of an Ancient Tradition*, edited by Steven Heine and Charles Prebish, 125–42. Oxford: Oxford University Press.

Karma Phuntso. 2005. *Mipham's Dialectics and the Debates on Emptiness*. New York: Routledge.

Kelly, David. 2003. "Marxism in China." In *Encyclopedia of Chinese Philosophy*, edited by Antonio S. Cua, 431–38. London: Routledge.

Kieschnick, John. 2005. "Buddhist Vegetarianism in China." In *Of Tripod and Palate: Food, Politics, and Religion in Traditional China*, edited by Roel Sterckx, 186–212. New York: Palgrave Macmillan.

Knauft, Bruce. 2002. "Introduction." In *Critically Modern: Alternatives, Alterities, Anthropologies*, edited by Bruce Knauft, 1–54. Bloomington: Indiana University Press.

Kolås, Åshild, and Monika P. Thowsen. 2005. *On the Margins of Tibet: Cultural Revival on the Sino-Tibetan Frontier*. Seattle: University of Washington Press.

Lawrence, Bruce. 1995. *Defenders of God: The Fundamentalist Revolt against the Modern Age*. Columbia: University of South Carolina Press.

Lopez, Donald. 1999. *Prisoners of Shangri-La: Tibetan Buddhism and the West*. Chicago: University of Chicago Press.

———. 2002. *A Modern Buddhist Bible: Essential Readings from East and West*. Boston: Beacon Press.

———. 2008. *Buddhism and Science: A Guide for the Perplexed*. Chicago: University of Chicago Press.

———. 2010. "The Future of the Buddhist Past: A Response to Readers." *Zygon* 45, no. 4: 883–96.

McMahan, David. 2008. *The Making of Buddhist Modernism*. Oxford: Oxford University Press.

———. 2015. "Buddhism and Multiple Modernities." In *Buddhism Beyond Borders: New Perspectives on Buddhism in the United States*, edited by Scott Mitchell and Natalie Quli, 181–95. Albany: State University of New York Press.

Mipham, Ju. 2005. *Introduction to the Middle Way: Chandrakirti's Madhyamakāvatāra with Commentary by Ju Mipham*. Translated by Padmakara Translation Group. Boston: Shambhala Publications.

———. 2017. *The Wisdom Chapter: Jamgön Mipham's Commentary on the Ninth Chapter of The Way of the Bodhisattva*. Boston: Shambhala Publications.

Moody, Raymond A. 1975. *Life After Life: The Investigation of a Phenomenon—Survival of Bodily Death*. New York: Bantam/Mockingbird Books.

———. 1977. *Reflections on Life After Life*. New York: Bantam/Mockingbird Books.

———. 1988. *The Light Beyond*. New York: Bantam Books.

Nagarjuna. 2006. *Letter to a Friend: With Commentary by Kangyur Rinpoche*. Translated by Padmakara Translation Group. Ithaca, NY: Snow Lion Publications.

Newman, John R. 1987. "The Outer Wheel of Time: Vajrayāna Buddhist Cosmology in the Kālacakra Tantra." PhD diss., University of Wisconsin.

Ngawang Pelzang. *A Guide to The Words of My Perfect Teacher*. Translated by the Padmakara Translation Committee. Boston: Shambhala Publications, 2004.

Ohnuma, Reiko. 2017. *Unfortunate Destiny: Animals in the Indian Buddhist Imagination*. New York: Oxford University Press.

Padma 'tsho. 2014. "Courage as Eminence: Tibetan Nuns at Yachen Monastery in Kham." *Eminent Buddhist Women*, edited by Karma Lekshe Tsomo, 185–94. Albany: State University of New York Press.

Patrul Rinpoche. 2010. *Words of My Perfect Teacher*. Translated by Padmakara Translation Group. New Haven, CT: Yale University Press.

Pettit, John. 1999. *Mipham's Beacon of Certainty: Illuminating the View of Dzogchen, the Great Perfection*. Boston: Wisdom Publications.

Phuntsho, Karma. 2005. *Mipham's Dialectics and the Debates on Emptiness*. New York: Routledge.

Pittmann, Don. 2001. *Toward a Modern Chinese Buddhism: Taixu's Reforms*. Honolulu: University of Hawai'i Press.

Presti, David E. 2018. *Mind Beyond Brain: Buddhism, Science, and the Paranormal*. New York: Columbia University Press.

Pu, Chengzhong. 2014. *The Ethical Treatment of Animals in Early Chinese Buddhism*. Newcastle upon Tyne: Cambridge Scholars Publishing.

Queen, Christopher and Sallie King, eds. 1996. *Engaged Buddhism: Buddhist Liberation Movements in Asia*. Albany: State University of New York Press.

Quli, Natalie, and Scott Mitchell. 2015. "Buddhist Modernism as Narrative: A Comparative Study of Jodo Shinshu and Zen." In *Buddhism Beyond Borders: New Perspectives on Buddhism in the United States*, edited by Scott Mitchell and Natalie Quli, 197–215. Albany, NY: State University of New York Press.

Ricard, Matthieu. 2016. *A Plea for the Animals: The Moral, Philosophical, and Evolutionary Imperative to Treat All Beings with Compassion*. Boston: Shambhala Publications.

Ritzinger, Justin R. 1999. "Taixu: To Renew Buddhism and Save the Modern World." Undergraduate thesis, Lawrence University.

Safran, William. 1998. "Introduction." In *Nationalism and Ethnoregional Identities in China*, edited by William Safran, 1–8. London: Frank Cass Publishers.

Schein, Louisa. 1997. "Gender and Internal Orientalism in China." *Modern China* 23, no. 1: 69–98.

Shabkar Tsokdruk Rangdrol. 2001. *The Life of Shabkar: The Autobiography of a Tibetan Yogin*. Translated by Matthieu Ricard. Ithaca, NY: Snow Lion.

———. 2004. *Food of Bodhisattvas: Buddhist Teachings on Abstaining from Meat*. Translated by Padmakara Translation Group. Boston: Shambhala Publications.

Shantideva. 2006 (1997). *The Way of the Bodhisattva*. Translated by Padmakara Translation Group. Boston: Shambhala Publications.

Sherab, Kunga. 2014. "The Interpretation of Scientific 'Proofs' for Past and Future Lives amongst Contemporary Tibetan Buddhist Scholars in the PRC." Master's thesis, University of Toronto.

Shiu, Henry, and Leah Stoke. 2008. "Buddhist Animal Release Practices: Historic, Environmental, Public Health and Economic Concerns." *Contemporary Buddhism* 9, no. 2: 181–96.

Shushan, Gregory. 2018. *Near-Death Experience in Indigenous Religions*. Oxford: Oxford University Press.

Slobodník, Martin. 2004. "Destruction and Revival: The Fate of the Tibetan Buddhist Monastery Labrang in the People's Republic of China." *Religion, State, and Society* 32, no. 1: 7–19.

Smith, Gene. 2001. *Among Tibetan Texts: History and Literature of the Himalayan Plateau*. Boston: Wisdom Publications.

Sonam Gyaltsen. 1996. *The Clear Mirror: A Traditional Account of Tibet's Golden Age*. Translated by McComas Taylor and Lama Choedak Yuthok. Ithaca, NY: Snow Lion.

Stevenson, Ian. 1974. *Twenty Cases Suggestive of Reincarnation*. Charlottesville: University of Virginia Press.

Stewart, James. 2015. *Vegetarianism and Animal Ethics in Contemporary Buddhism*. London: Routledge.

———. 2017. "Dharma Dogs: Can Animals Understand the Dharma? Textual and Ethnographic Considerations." *Journal of Buddhist Ethics* 24: 39–62.

Stoddard, Heather. 1988. "The Long Life of rDo-sbis dGe-bses Ses-rab rGya-mcho (1884–1968)." In *Tibetan Studies: Proceedings of the 4th Seminar of the International Association for Tibetan Studies Schloss Hohenkammer (Munich 1985)*, edited by Helga Uebach and Jampa L. Panglung, 465–71. Munchen: Komm. für Zentralasiat. Studien, Bayerische Akademie der Wissenschaften.

Swearer, Donald. 2003. "Aniconism versus Iconism in Thai Buddhism." In *Buddhism in the Modern World: Adaptations of an Ancient Tradition*, edited by Steven Heine and Charles Prebish, 9–25. Oxford: Oxford University Press.

Tarocco, Francesca. 2007. *The Cultural Practices of Modern Chinese Buddhism: Attuning the Dharma*. London: Routledge.

Teeuwen, Mark. 2017. "Buddhist Modernities: Modernism and Its Limits." In *Buddhist Modernities: Re-Inventing Tradition in the Globalizing Modern World*, edited by Hannah Havnevik, Ute Hüsken, Mark Teeuwen, and Koen Wellens, 1–12. New York: Routledge.

Terrone, Antonio. 2008. "Tibetan Buddhism Beyond the Monastery: Revelation and Identity in rNying ma Communities of Present-day Kham." *Images of Tibet in the 19th and 20th Centuries*, edited by Monica Esposito, 746-779. *Études Thématiques* 22, no. 2.

———. 2013. "Khenpo Jigme Puntsok," *Treasury of Lives*, accessed June 01, 2020, treasuryoflives.org/biographies/view/Khenpo-Jigme-Puntsok/10457.

Tsangnyon Heruka. 2010. *The Life of Milarepa*. Translated by Andrew Quintman. New York: Penguin Books.

Tsongkhapa. 2010. *Three Principal Aspects of the Path*. Translated by Lama Zopa. Portland, OR: FPMT Inc.

Turner, Alicia. 2017. *Saving Buddhism: The Impermanence of Religion in Colonial Burma*. Honolulu: University of Hawai'i Press.

Tuttle, Gray. 2005. *Tibetan Buddhists in the Making of Modern China*. New York: Columbia University Press.

———, ed. 2011. *Mapping the Modern in Tibet*. Andiast: International Institute for Tibetan and Buddhist Studies GmbH.

van der Veer, Peter. 2011 "Smash Temples, Burn Books: Comparing Secularists Projects in India and China." In *Rethinking Secularism*, edited by Craig Calhoon, Mark Juergensmeyer, and Jonathan VanAntwerpen, 270–81. New York: Oxford University Press.

Waldau, Paul. 2001. *The Specter of Speciesism: Buddhist and Christian Views of Animals*. New York: Oxford.

Wang, Jing. 1996. *High Culture Fever: Politics, Aesthetics, and Ideology in Deng's China*. Berkeley: University of California Press.

Welch, Holmes. 1967. *The Practice of Chinese Buddhism, 1900–1950*. Cambridge, MA: Harvard University Press.

———. 1968. *The Buddhist Revival in China*. Cambridge, MA: Harvard University Press.

———. 1972. *Buddhism under Mao*. Cambridge, MA: Harvard University Press.

Wu Qi. 2013. "Tradition and Modernity: Cultural Continuum and Transition among Tibetans in Amdo." PhD diss., University of Helsinki.

Yu, Chunfang. 1981. *The Renewal of Buddhism in China: Chu-hung and the Late Ming Synthesis*. New York: Columbia University Press.

Zhe Ji. 2013. "Zhao Puchu and His Renjian Buddhism." *The Eastern Buddhist* 44: 35–48.

LIST OF CONTRIBUTORS

Geoffrey Barstow is Assistant Professor of Religious Studies at Oregon State University. His research focuses on the history and practice of vegetarianism in Tibetan religion and culture. He is the author of *Food of Sinful Demons: Meat, Vegetarianism, and the Limits of Buddhism in Tibet* (Columbia University Press, 2018) and the editor of *The Faults of Meat: Tibetan Buddhist Writings on Vegetarianism* (Wisdom, 2019).

Douglas Duckworth is Professor and Director of Graduate Studies in the Department of Religion at Temple University. He is the author of *Mipam on Buddha-Nature: The Ground of the Nyingma Tradition* (2008), *Jamgön Mipam: His Life and Teachings* (2011), and *Tibetan Buddhist Philosophy of Mind and Nature* (2019). He also introduced and translated *Distinguishing the Views and Philosophies: Illuminating Emptiness in a Twentieth-Century Tibetan Buddhist Classic* by Bötrül (2011). His latest works include *Tibetan Buddhist Philosophy of Mind and Nature* (Oxford University Press, 2019) and a translation of an overview of the "Wisdom Chapter" of *The Way of the Bodhisattva* by Künzang Sönam, a direct disciple of the famed Patrul Rinpoche, titled *The Profound Reality of Interdependence* (Oxford University Press, 2019). He also is the coeditor, with Jonathan Gold, of *Readings of Śāntideva's Guide to Bodhisattva Practice (Bodhicaryāvatāra)* (Columbia University Press, 2019).

Holly Gayley, Associate Professor of Buddhist Studies at the University of Colorado–Boulder, is a scholar and translator of contemporary Buddhist literature in Tibet. Her research areas include gender and sexuality in Buddhist tantra, ethical reform in contemporary Tibet, and theorizing translation, both literary and cultural, in the transmission of Buddhist teachings to North America. Gayley is author of *Love Letters from Golok: A Tantric*

Couple in Modern Tibet (Columbia University Press, 2016), coeditor of *A Gathering of Brilliant Moons: Practice Advice from the Rimé Masters of Tibet* (Wisdom, 2017), and translator of *Inseparable across Lifetimes: The Lives and Love Letters of the Buddhist Visionaries Namtrul Rinpoche and Khandro Tāre Lhamo* (Snow Lion, 2019). Her articles on an ethical reform movement spearheaded by cleric-scholars at Larung Buddhist Academy in Serta have appeared in the *Journal of Buddhist Ethics, Contemporary Buddhism, Journal of Religious Ethics*, and *Himalaya Journal.*

Catherine Hardie is currently a Research Assistant Professor in the Department of Translation, Interpreting, and Intercultural Studies at Hong Kong Baptist University. She holds a PhD from the Institute of Social and Cultural Anthropology at the University of Oxford. Her research investigates the contemporary grassroots Sino-Tibetan Buddhist milieu in mainland China. In addition to her contribution to this volume, she has recently published a translation of another impactful essay from Larung Gar: "Khenpo Tsultrim Lodrö's Appeal to Contemporary Tibetans to Abandon Meat and Practice Non-Killing" in *The Faults of Meat: Tibetan Buddhist Writings on Vegetarianism* (Wisdom, 2019) edited by Geoffrey Barstow.

Sarah H. Jacoby is an Associate Professor in the Religious Studies Department at Northwestern University in Evanston, Illinois. She specializes in Tibetan Buddhist Studies, with research interests in gender and sexuality, the history of emotions, Tibetan literature, religious auto/biography, Buddhist revelation (*gter ma*), and the history of eastern Tibet. She is the author of *Love and Liberation: Autobiographical Writings of the Tibetan Buddhist Visionary Sera Khandro* (Columbia University Press, 2014), coauthor of *Buddhism: Introducing the Buddhist Experience* (Oxford University Press, 2014), and coeditor of *Buddhism Beyond the Monastery: Tantric Practices and Their Performers in Tibet and the Himalayas* (Brill, 2009).

Padma 'tsho (Baimacuo) is a Professor in the Tibetan Studies Department of Southwest University for Nationalities in Chengdu, China. She holds a PhD from Sichuan University in Chengdu and an MA from Central Nationalities University in Beijing. Her areas of research and teaching include Tibetan Buddhism, ritual studies, gender issues, and Tibetan monasteries, as well as the education of Buddhist nuns in Tibetan areas. Her articles have appeared in edited volumes such as *Eminent Buddhist*

Women, edited by Karma Lekshe Tsomo, and numerous journals including *Contemporary Buddhism, China Tibetology, Journal of Ethnology, Sichuan Tibetan Studies,* and *Asian Highlands Perspective.* In the last decade, Professor Padma 'tsho has spent time at several North American universities as a Visiting Research Scholar, including Harvard, Columbia, University of Virginia, and University of Colorado–Boulder, researching Tibetan Buddhism in the West. She is a frequent presenter at conferences, such as the American Academy of Religions (AAR) and International Association of Tibetan Studies (IATS).

Pema Jamyang is an ordained Tibetan Buddhist nun. She completed her PhD and postdoctoral studies in Chemical Engineering in the United States. In 2007, Pema Jamyang took refuge and has since delved systematically into a thorough study of Buddhist teachings as a disciple of Khenpo Sodargye. In 2011, Pema Jamyang received her ordination as a Buddhist nun from Khenpo Sodargye and has since continued her immersion in the study of sūtras, śāstras, and tantras. Having completed her studies in the Five Great Treatises, Pema Jamyang has been mainly working on the translation of Khenpo Sodargye's teaching from Chinese into English.

Jann Ronis is a scholar of Tibetan Buddhism and completed his PhD at the University of Virginia in 2009. His dissertation was about the history of a large monastery and Buddhist academy in eastern Tibet, located on one of the major trading routes linking Tibet to China. More recently, his research has explored contemporary Tibetan literature. After completing his PhD, he held postdoctoral positions in Paris and University of California–Berkeley. He taught at UC Berkeley for seven years until becoming the Executive Director of the Buddhist Digital Resource Center (BDRC) in 2018.

Michael R. Sheehy is Director of Scholarship at the Contemplative Sciences Center, Research Assistant Professor in Tibetan and Buddhist Studies, and affiliated faculty with the Tibet Center at the University of Virginia. He was formerly the Director of Programs at the Mind & Life Institute where he directed interdisciplinary contemplative research programs, including Mind & Life Dialogues XXXII and XXXIII. Michael has conducted extensive fieldwork inside Tibet, including three years training in a monastery in the Golok region of far eastern Tibet. His work gives attention to literary and philosophical histories of Buddhism in Tibet and contributions of Tibetan contemplative traditions to discourses in the humanities, cognitive science, and cultural psychology. He is coeditor of *The Other Emptiness: Rethinking the Zhentong Buddhist Discourse in Tibet* (SUNY Press, 2019), and coeditor of the *Contemplative Sciences* and *Traditions and Transformations in Tibetan Buddhism* book series published by the University of Virginia Press.

Antonio Terrone is an Assistant Professor of Instruction in the Department of Asian Languages and Cultures at Northwestern University where he specializes in religion, politics, and ethnic policies in East Asia, especially China (Tibet and Xinjiang). His recent publications include "Burning for a Cause: Self-Immolations, Human Security, and the Violence of Nonviolence in Tibet" (*Journal of Buddhist Ethics*, 2018), "Nationalism Matters: Among Monks and Mystics in Tibet" (*Religion and Nationalism in Chinese Societies*, 2017), "Propaganda in the Public Square: Communicating State Directives on Religion and Ethnicity to Uyghurs and Tibetans in Western China" (*Ethnic Conflict and Protest in Tibet and Xinjiang: Unrest in China's West*, 2016), and "The Earth as a Treasure in Tibetan Buddhism: Visionary Revelation and Its Interactions with the Environment" (*Journal for the Study of Religion, Nature, and Culture*, 2014). He is currently writing a monograph on the Tenth Panchen Lama.

INDEX